Praise for *Publicize Y...*

P9-DYP-696

CHICAGO PUBLIC LIBRARY

R03000 02330

DISCARD

"Want to see the title of your book in the ... to help you sell copies? Read this book. W... using a publicist or working directly with the press, you'll learn how to pitch the right angle at the right time ... and why that is essential. The media is hun... *Publicize Your Book!* covers all the publicity ...

 —Ellen ... *sekeeping magazine*

"Here is ev... ver tell you but you ne... ese pages— either it's ...

 —N...

"For au... ook highly. Successf... everything authors ... ...e—appearances."

 —Sh... ...yton

"Valuabl... ...asoned pro. I loved t... ...le packing in tons of v... ...before his or her book is p...

 —Do...

 Bu...

"Getting ... ...dertaking than ever before, and ... ...get. This book gives them a head... ...resent themselves to the media a... ...or, I highly recommend this bo... ...ce."

 —Nancy ... ...azin...

"A treasur... ...hor seeking to publicize their work ... ...spir...guide, inv...ng the reader to creative ... ...mp...ely grounded in the real world of ... ...exc...g vision and hands-on experience ... t. ...sourc..."

 —Shar... be... *Trusting ...Own Deepest Experience* and

 Lovi... ...Revolutionary... Happiness

Praise for *Reckless Appetites: A Culinary Romance*

"If you like to read, eat, laugh and make love all at the same time, the adventures of this picaresque heroine in her *education sentimentale et culinaire* are for you."
—Betty Fussell

"What a sweet education is this! Neither fiction, nor yet fact, but whimsy overlaid with longing. Romance with recipes! What could be better!"
—Marq de Villiers

"Food, passion and literature converge in Jacqueline Deval's delectable debut novel, *Reckless Appetites*. Although bursting with recipes and anecdotes about the literary history of food, the book is also a witty morality fable about appetite, indulgence and regret, as well as an investigation into the nature of passion and creativity—in food, in love, in art and in life."
—Lisa Jensen, *San Francisco Chronicle*

". . . Charming debut novel. . ."
—Louisa Ermalino, *People*

"The recipes are delightful, and Ms. Deval's food-oriented reading of the greats is far more succulent than deconstruction."
—*The New York Times Book Review*

Most Perigee Books are available at special quantity discounts for bulk purchases for sales promotions, premiums, fund-raising, or educational use. Special books, or book excerpts, can also be created to fit specific needs.

For details, write: Special Markets, The Berkley Publishing Group, 375 Hudson Street, New York, New York 10014.

Publicize Your Book!

AN INSIDER'S GUIDE TO GETTING YOUR BOOK THE ATTENTION IT DESERVES

Jacqueline Deval

A Perigee Book

A Perigee Book
Published by The Berkley Publishing Group
A division of Penguin Putnam Inc.
375 Hudson Street
New York, New York 10014

Copyright © 2003 by Jacqueline Deval
Text design by Tiffany Kukec
Cover design by Dorothy Wachtenheim

All rights reserved. This book, or parts thereof,
may not be reproduced in any form without permission. The scanning,
uploading, and distribution of this book via the internet or via any other means
without the permission of the publisher is illegal and punishable by law.
Please purchase only authorized electronic editions, and do not participate in
or encourage electronic piracy of copyrighted materials.
Your support of the author's rights is appreciated.

First edition: April 2003

Visit our website at www.penguinputnam.com

Library of Congress Cataloging-in-Publication Data

Deval, Jacqueline.
Publicize your book! : an insider's guide to getting your book the attention it deserves /
Jacqueline Deval.— 1st Perigee ed.
p.   cm.
Includes index.
ISBN 0-399-52863-6 (pbk.)
1. Authorship—Marketing. 2. Books—Marketing.   I. Title.

PN161 .D46   2003
070.5'2—dc21
2002035544

Printed in the United States of America

10 9 8 7 6 5 4 3 2

R0300002330

CONTENTS

DISCARD

Oriole Park Branch
7454 W. Balmoral Ave.
Chicago, IL 60656

ACKNOWLEDGMENTS

Thank you to everyone who assisted me during the research and writing of this book: James Barron, Nelvia Brady, Beth Bruno, Fauzia Burke, Caitlin Connelly, Charles Cook, Tami DePalma, Carol Fass, Carol Fitzgerald, Mark Gebbie, Tracey George, Lynn Goldberg, Katherine Wyse Goldman, Jane Heller, Lucine Kasbarian, Paul Krupin, David Lida, Justin Loeber, Diane Mancher, Brad Meltzer, Meryl Moss, Steve O'Keefe, Linda Palladino, Bill Parkhurst, Liz Perle, Kristen Powers, Diane Roback, M. J. Rose, Sharyn Rosenblum, Marly Rusoff, Michael Schrage, Andrew Sobel, Judy Spagnola, Joan Stewart, Mariah Stewart, Laura Van Wormer, Lois Wyse, Kim Yorio, and Karyn Zoldan.

I would like to extend special thanks to Stuart Applebaum, a master of publicity strategy, who took me under his wing when I was a novice.

To Alberto Vitale, who once told me to think not like a publicist, but like a publisher. This was an important remark.

To Loretta Barrett, for her unswerving support.

To Jeanne Krier, for her flair as a publicist and insights as first reader.

To Kelvin Christopher James, for being a publicist's dream to work with and for thoughtful editorial comments.

To Jean and Bill Deval, for their very helpful comments on the manuscript.

And to Jorden, who, when I was struggling to come up with an appropriate title for the book, helpfully suggested *The Mysteries of Science*, or else, *The Brain*. Which suggests that book marketing is a science, or that I have not properly explained to my child exactly what I do for a living.

INTRODUCTION

THE reality of book publishing is that there are too few resources to support every book. This means that some books will get publicity campaigns and budgets while others will go without. Additionally, most publishing houses are not staffed with enough publicists to mount a full-fledged campaign for every book. Because of this, editors must compete with one another to lobby the publisher, and the marketing and publicity departments, for the funds and staff attention to promote their books.

Some aspects of publishing boggle the minds of first-time writers. (That's OK. It boggles the minds of many veterans in publishing, too.) For example, you might wonder why the big-name authors get tons of money spent on their campaigns when their bestseller status would seem to be a foregone conclusion. Meanwhile, a new author could use some of those marketing funds to begin to build a reputation. The bald fact is that publishers need to protect their interest in the big authors and spending marketing dollars is one way to keep the author and agent happy. The harsher reality is that this dynamic is unlikely to change anytime soon.

The good news is that authors who know how to properly represent themselves to their publishers *can* find discretionary dollars for book promotion. Do not count on your agent to make this happen. Your agent may be terrific, but is truly unable to fight every battle on your behalf. You will need to become your own advocate with the right efforts at the right time. Too many authors simply wake up too late to the problem of under promotion. An author who can get involved creatively and make allies of the publishing staff can have the most impact on the marketing and publicity program and the best possible chance of reaching a readership.

It's never too soon to get started. These days, many proposals submitted to publishing houses are accompanied by a marketing plan written by the author in cooperation with his or her agent. This is particularly true of nonfiction in categories like self-help and how-to, which require a promotable author to publicize the book. In the absence of a marketing plan, which demonstrates the author's willingness to participate energetically in the book's successful publication, the publishing house has fewer reasons to publish the book. Therefore, you may find yourself writing a marketing plan before a publisher has signed up your book.

You may have heard from other writers, or your agent, or your editor that writing the book is only half of your job and that the other half is marketing it. That statement is not entirely valid because the marketing of your book *never* has to end. The campaign can last as long as you like after your publicist has finished his or her job. You are limited only by the effort you put out. Even with successful books, the publisher eventually steps back to focus on bringing its other titles to market. By paying attention to the market and learning a few marketing and publicity tricks and techniques, you can keep the marketing effort for your book moving forward indefinitely.

While marketing at first may seem like drudge work—and there are tedious aspects like assembling mailing lists—you may instead find that marketing delivers an enormous amount of fun and pleasure, and brings you rewarding new relationships and into closer contact with your readers. Marketing is particularly thrilling when you come up with a bright idea, carry it through, and, as a result, enjoy a boost in your book's sales.

If your publisher intends to put some muscle behind your book, you will nevertheless need to get involved in shaping your book's campaign. The promotional opportunities that are available to your book might require some research—a task your in-house publicist might not be able to accomplish in the hours available to her. (Throughout this book I will refer to book publicists as female because most are women.) Nor is your role limited to providing viable leads for promotion. You are a valuable resource in many other ways when it comes to determining how to market your book.

While you may never have had a book published before, or been involved with the marketing or publicity surrounding any kind of product, you might view yourself as an adventurer. You are embarking on an unusual enterprise. You will face risk and excitement in your chance to reach fortune. My role is a guide of sorts: a companion with sound advice on how to make it through what can be rough going.

I finally decided to write this book because a friend needed my help. With his novel on the verge of publication, he found himself bereft of publishing support, his editor departed for another house, and his publicist reluctant to meet him. I realized that our conversations were identical to many I'd had before with writers who felt either abandoned or unsure when their books were on the verge of publication, who wanted to promote their books, and yet lacked the deep pockets to afford a freelance publicist. Despite the ominous signs, my friend set about to create some publicity for his book and even managed to garner some resources from his publisher to do so. I wrote this book to help other writers like my friend.

Because I've been a publicity director, an author, and a publisher, my perspective encompasses the desires of the author (who wants to see the book sell and to reach a readership) and the reality of the publisher (who is constrained by budgets, time, and other books competing for attention that may have more obvious opportunities in the marketplace). Those two sometimes competing interests can be reconciled, with some up-front management of expectations for both parties.

While I talk about all aspects of marketing a book, I've concentrated most on publicity opportunities—the realm in which an author has the greatest chance to make a significant difference. Because one size does not fit all in book publicity, not all of the advice here will be appropriate to your book. For example, fiction and nonfiction have different opportunities. So do children's books and books intended for adults. While you read this book, keep a notebook of the ideas that seem appropriate to your book's promotion.

This book will explain what you might reasonably expect from your publisher during the course of publication and how to get involved with the planning. It answers those nagging questions that might seem too petty to trouble your editor with and provides creative solutions to many issues that will arise. Most important, this book will show how you might work effectively with your publishing team to create marketing and publicity opportunities that can drive book sales.

By getting involved in publicizing your book early and armed with the right information, you can get your book the publicity and promotion it deserves.

Jacqueline Deval
New York City
jdeval@yahoo.com

PROLOGUE

A COMMON MIDLIST SCENARIO TO AVOID AT ALL COSTS

W HAT follows is a scenario familiar to many published authors. What seemed like a promising start evaporates for no discernable reason and without warning. If you recognize your own situation in this scenario, the good news is that if you act in a timely fashion, you can fix it.

The publicist: Newly promoted to her position after one year in the business, Kate is bright and enthusiastic but untrained. Most of what she does she's figured out by the seat of her pants and from chatting with the other publicists. Kate is working actively on five to eight books at any one time—other books will be added to her list next month—and she has no assistant to help with mailings and other clerical work. She's relieved when she's assigned to authors who live outside New York City because they can't drop by the office to talk about their publicity campaigns. She's careful to avoid telling authors that they're getting a limited campaign. If she says the wrong thing, the authors might complain to their agents or editors and then she will get in trouble.

One of the books assigned to Kate is a debut literary novel by a writer named Jeremy. She enjoyed the novel, but is having trouble figuring out how to promote it because she hasn't publicized a novel before. The book's editor, Frank, is somewhat condescending to the younger publicists. She could tell he was unhappy she'd been assigned to the book, so she's intimidated to ask if he has any ideas about the book's campaign. Kate also knows that if the publicity director thought the book was important, then she wouldn't have assigned the book to her. So, she's mailed copies of the book to reviewers, none of whom she's ever met because the publicity director is the one who meets with the key media. Jeremy calls almost daily, wanting to know where his book will be reviewed. Kate's getting anxious about what to say to him. She works from nine until at least seven every evening and is paid $28,000 a year.

The editor: Frank's been in the business for ten years and has a large list of midlist authors—authors whose books have achieved only modest sales. He desperately needs a big breakout bestseller to get his career back on track. No longer the wonder boy he once seemed, he's impatient for that big winner. He's had some near hits—books that hovered frustratingly close to the *New York Times* bestseller list but never quite made it. Frank has a lot of enthusiasm and each acquisition, in his mind, has the potential to be the next big winner. When Frank presented Jeremy's novel at the launch meeting for the next season's new titles, he was disappointed by the group's reaction. Granted, Frank presented the title at 4:00 P.M. after the sales and marketing folks had been in the meeting all day. No one said anything about Jeremy's book and when Frank tried to prod the staff for any ideas, he didn't get much response. Since then, Frank's been battling uphill on behalf of Jeremy's book, but just can't seem to light a fire under anyone. He lobbied the sales rep for Barnes & Noble to get the book into the Discover program. While the book got a reading at the chain (great!), it was ultimately passed over for the special promotion and the bigger buy that goes with it (oh well). He lobbied the publicity director to put aside a small budget for the book, which she did. But a round of budget cuts initiated by the publisher and the business manager soon eliminated that. When Frank sees the all-too-familiar sales pattern—a slow trickle of small advance orders from bookstores—he starts to detach from his author. Frank's onto the next big book, and this time it's a project that he hopes will get people really excited.

The author: Jeremy can't understand why his editor isn't returning his calls. He enjoyed the editing process with Frank and their occasional lunches. His novel was published one month ago—7,500 copies were printed and most of those shipped, he's been told. The big reviews haven't happened yet, though there was a nice write-up in the hometown paper where Jeremy lived until he went away to college. Whenever he calls, the editorial assistant, who answers Frank's phone, is always very nice to him, but recently he's detected an embarrassed, evasive tone in her voice. Or is he imagining it? His publicist, Kate, returns his calls, though not necessarily on the same day. She's very pleasant but she's also overwhelmed and resists Jeremy's suggestion that she call the editor of the *New York Times Book Review* to see if a review has been scheduled. She can't tell him about the sales because, she says, she doesn't see the sales reports. To top it all off, Jeremy's agent, Francine, is becoming a little testy with him. After she spoke to Frank about the lack of publicity for the book, she reported that there's no budget for the book and not much more that Frank can do. Jeremy asks her why Frank paid him a $35,000 advance if the publishing house isn't promoting the book. Surely the publisher will lose its investment. Francine agrees but points out that that's the nature of this crazy publishing business. After a few more weeks go by, no one at the publishing house is thinking about Jeremy's book. Jeremy himself no longer calls. The book is pretty much dead.

The analysis: Jeremy's situation is by no means unique in the book publishing business, though he was lucky to get a higher advance than most midlist authors. However, a relatively large advance doesn't always guarantee a publisher's support. Many books with advances much higher than his have fallen by the wayside from lack of marketing and publicity attention. Jeremy's real problem is he realized too late that he was not getting the campaign he believed his book deserved. Had he asked the right questions during the months leading up to publication, he would have been in a much better position to influence the course of events. Once a book has been published, it is difficult to start a publicity campaign or hire a freelance publicist, because an unenthusiastic sales force has already distributed the book. In other words, few copies of the book exist in the marketplace, making it difficult for consumers to find the book even if they do read about it in the press. Once a book has been in the marketplace for a couple of months, making the book stand out from the pack is an imposing challenge because of the next wave of new books coming up behind.

An author who thinks like a marketer, and who starts thinking about marketing before the book is even completed, will help the book toward a successful publication. The author is in the best position to offer suggestions for marketing that the house might have overlooked, and sometimes to help bridge any difficult internal relationships among the publishing team that might impede the book's success. (In-house squabbles do happen in the business, and while in a just world they shouldn't interfere with a book's progress, sometimes they do.) Most important, the author can be the catalyst to motivate a house's enthusiasm about a book.

Jeremy could have provided critical information to his editor and publishing house by getting actively involved in his own marketing campaign. He could have come up with leads about speaking opportunities and reporters who cover subjects related to his book; developed sales and publicity angles for his book; set up a meeting for his editor, his publicist, and himself to brainstorm about publicizing the book; assisted with the development of his publisher's marketing materials to help raise his profile in-house; reached out to friends and family across the country to set up local promotions; devised an unusual presentation for bookstore and library appearances; developed an online presence in appropriate newsgroups to help build an audience; assembled a personal database or e-mailing list to market the book; researched any special audiences that might take a particular interest in the book; and so much more.

WHAT ONE AUTHOR DID RIGHT—A 7,000-COPY FIRST PRINTING LEADS TO 185,000 COPIES IN PRINT: A TRUE STORY

James Douglas Barron is the author of *She's Having a Baby—and I'm Having a Breakdown*, a funny and informative gift book for expectant fathers that started with an inauspicious 7,000 copies sold into book-stores. Barron devoted a significant amount of his time and imagination to helping the book succeed. Though his publishing house would not justify devoting significant resources to promote the book, he was very lucky that his publicist, Sharyn Rosenblum, had faith in the book's appealing message and in his own commitment. While Rosenblum set up some media interviews, the author set up some promotional events, special mailings, and special sales, and underwrote the expenses to travel to a few cities, which amounted to several thousand dollars. The result: Within three years the book was in its nineteenth printing and now has more than 185,000 copies in print. Once the book took off, the publisher paid for a larger publicity tour and some print advertising. Barron has since published two more books: *She's Had a Baby—and I'm Having a Meltdown* and *She Wants a Ring—and I Don't Wanna Change a Thing*.

"When I write a book and it's been accepted and all the editing is finished, then I'm only at the fifty-yard line and I have another fifty to go," says James Barron. "And I can't depend on anyone else to get me there. I work harder once I've handed in my manuscript."

For his campaign for *She's Having a Baby*, Barron understood that his publisher simply did not have the time and resources to promote the book to the extent he desired. He decided to invest a certain amount of money as well as an enormous amount of time in creating his own campaign, sometimes logging as many as eleven hours a day on marketing. "I'd worked for years to get a book published," Barron says, "so I wasn't going to stop there."

He sought endorsements from several noted people to put on the book cover. Among them were Michael J. Fox, whom he'd met at a barbecue and to whom he pitched his book; the author of a parenting book bestseller, S. Adams Sullivan; and the actor Tony Randall, who, at seventy-seven, had been in the news when his wife gave birth to their first child. Barron did not know any of these people beforehand; he reached Sullivan and Randall simply by writing to them.

Barron wrote or called everyone he knew and told them about the book. He stopped by specialty stores like maternity shops, toy shops, and hospital gift shops to persuade them to order the book from his publisher to sell to their customers, and provided them with a ready-made sales order form. Barron offered to buy the books back if they could not sell them—but he never had to buy back one copy. He guesses that somewhere between forty and seventy-five stores chose to order the book, sold out and reordered again and again.

Tapping into his charitable involvement with the Children's Museum of Manhattan, he organized a book launch party there. He found a donor to contribute money for the museum's fee for renting the space for the party, and the museum notified its mailing list of 40,000 about the event as well as his own list of 2,000 names. Knowing that the head of Barnes & Noble was also involved with the museum, he wrote him an appealing letter about the book and the event, which translated into significantly increased support for the book from Barnes & Noble.

For a second book event, he worked with a gallery owner whom he knows—Barron is by profession a private art dealer—to throw a party and was able to use the gallery's 8,000-name mailing list. Then he persuaded his publisher to buy a mailing list from ACOG (American College of Obstetricians and Gynecologists) and to send out a complimentary book to doctors. (At a subsequent book event, one doctor reported how he alone was responsible for selling 250 copies of the book.)

Then Barron selected two markets outside of New York City to promote the book: Chicago, his original hometown, and Atlanta, where his wife grew up. He hired publicists in those cities to help set up media and book signings, as well as to go to the same kinds of specialty stores as he did in New York.

Barron called many strangers during his campaign. He simply picked up the phone and made his pitch to people involved with organizations or groups likely to take a natural interest in his book. "I work under the assumption that I'm going to get twelve rejections for every yes," he says. He doesn't mind the rejections because he views them as part of the process of getting to that one yes.

Though Barron puts in an extraordinary amount of effort to promote his books, he also believes that publishers can be great collaborators. He advises that if you work with them in a positive way, you can garner an enormous amount of support. Bottom line, though, he says, is that you have to be realistic about what the publisher is capable of and willing to do, given its limited resources. Your publisher views your book as a business investment, he says, and you should, too. Ask yourself, what time and money are you willing to put into your business venture?

Barron's recent promotional activities on behalf of *She Wants a Ring—and I Don't Wanna Change a Thing* included book signings at jewelry stores in Los Angeles and Las Vegas. That's a very smart marketing idea. Baron has also set up a Web site to promote all of his books: www.jamesbarronbooks.com.

What other authors can learn from Barron is how he used his personal and professional affiliations to market his book, how he understood his target audience and figured out how to reach them, and that he made a conscious decision to commit a certain amount of his time and a little money to try to make his book succeed in the marketplace.

1

BOOK MARKETING BASICS

BOOK marketing is, quite simply, determining how to sell books as fast as possible to as many people as possible. Specifically, book marketing is defining and reaching your potential readership, and then coming up with ways to convince them to buy your book—the more copies they buy and the faster they buy them the better.

Faster is better because when a book achieves a certain level of sales momentum, bookstores steadily reorder copies and, in some cases, will automatically replenish inventory. Also, books that sell in high quantities in a short amount of time have a greater opportunity to hit bestseller lists than books that might sell the same number of copies but over a longer period of time. This is because bookstores report sales on a weekly basis to the bestseller lists.

If your book can't achieve high-speed sales, it still benefits from ongoing small though steady sales. Regular demand for your book will prompt a bookstore to reorder your book from your publisher. A bookstore that has ordered one or two copies of your book is perfectly happy when those books sell out. But the store won't automatically reorder the book. Therefore it is your ardent desire, as well as your publisher's, that the marketing of your book drives consumer demand, which in turn stimulates bookstore reorders.

Advertising, promotions, and publicity are the three core areas of book marketing. Advertising—which refers to paid ads in any form of media—is not particularly effective in driving book sales, and few books receive advertising campaigns. Unless the publisher plans to spend a significant amount of money, an ad campaign alone simply cannot reach enough consumers. When a publisher advertises a book, the strategy is generally meant to accomplish one of two things: to alert readers that a big-name author with a known fan base has just published a new book, or to boost visibility for a book that has already been successfully publicized.

Promotions are the discounts, displays, and co-op funds that publishers offer booksellers. Co-op funds are earned marketing dollars that publishers give to booksellers to promote their books. The amount of co-op available to a bookseller is based on its volume of business with the publisher the previous year. If you're going on a book tour, then booksellers might spend co-op money on posters and newsletters to promote your appearances in their stores. The promotional materials that a publisher might produce include corrugated book displays, posters, bookmarks, and postcards.

Publicity—getting your book mentioned in any form of media—earns you the legitimacy of a third-party editorial endorsement, can reach large audiences, and requires relatively little spending. Publicity is where your greatest opportunity lies to contribute to the shape and scope of your campaign. The right media coverage for your book can stimulate measurable sales results that turn your book into a success.

The challenge for many writers is to think of themselves as marketers. Marketing might at first seem at odds with the creator's side of the business. But with more than 100,000 books published a year, every book needs help to find its market, whether the book is the latest release by a well-known author or an unknown writer's first novel. While your relationship with your editor may focus almost entirely on the editorial quality of the work itself, every good editor is engaged in the act of selling every day, advocating the works of his or her writers. The earlier you engage your editor in conversations about selling the book, the earlier you help your editor promote your work effectively in-house. In other words, editing your book is only one of your editor's jobs: He or she is also responsible for generating in-house enthusiasm for your work and getting the publisher to view the book as worthy of time and money.

Coming up with innovative marketing ideas—or *any* marketing ideas—may at first seem to require a special set of thinking skills. Do not be discouraged. You can acquire and practice this kind of thinking. First, try to recall the skills of persuasion that you used when you got a job you really wanted, or talked your way out of a parking ticket. In those scenarios, most likely, you drew from a deep well of conviction, an important asset that you will tap into throughout your campaign to persuade your publicist and editor to help you.

Other qualities that you need to help you create a marketing success of your book are an open mind, curiosity, polite persistence, and a certain level of boldness. There's no room for shyness in a publicity campaign, a characteristic that some authors have to combat. One helpful idea is to form a small circle of trusted friends, family, and colleagues who would draw you out, and serve as a sounding board for mock interviews or readings.

What you *do not* require is a lot of money. Of course, money helps if you want to hire a freelance publicist or send yourself on a book tour. But you can market your book effectively, or work with your publisher to market your book effectively, without spending an abundance of cash. (Even if you do not intend to spend a lot of money on your marketing campaign, keep an expense log of tax-deductible phone calls, postage, book-related business travel, express mail, Internet service provider fees, and so on.) The resource that you *will* spend extravagantly is your time. Be prepared. If you work a full-time job, save your personal days and vacation time to contribute toward marketing the book as needed.

The best way to start planning your marketing is to develop a well-thought-out marketing plan. Normally a publishing house creates a formal marketing plan only for the top books on its list. Your written marketing plan will help your publisher focus on your book, will prove your own commitment, and will become a valuable reference tool throughout the publishing process. If your publisher elects not to use your marketing plan, then you have created a blueprint to promote the book yourself, or to turn over to a freelance publicist. If you are a self-published author, you should still write a marketing plan. A marketing plan helps any author focus on what needs to be done to reach readers and to organize priorities in the book campaign.

THINK LIKE A MARKETER

What does your book offer readers? Who are those readers? How do you reach them and convince them to spend money on your book? Any marketer has to answer these questions at the start of any campaign. Put in marketing terms, you provide the product, you locate the audience, and then you persuade them to buy.

Actually, you will have several audiences to persuade about the appeal of your book. First, you want the audiences inside your publishing house—the editor, your publicist, the sales reps, and other publishing staff—to get excited about your book's potential. The staff will then convey its enthusiasm to your other target audiences: the booksellers, the media, and then finally, consumers. Considering that each audience has particular interests, your job is to address them in a way that ultimately sells your book.

Here's how it works: Your editor convinces the publishing staff that your book has potential in the market. Following the in-house planning meetings, the marketing, publicity, and sales people begin working on various tasks to launch your book. The subsidiary rights staff sells direct marketing rights to book clubs, like Book-of-the-Month Club, and to foreign publishers. The sales reps promise booksellers that your book will be covered in the media to encourage them to buy large quantities of your book. (And if you're a writer of fiction or quality nonfiction, the reps may also successfully convince the booksellers to read your book. If they like it, you will benefit from handselling, which is when booksellers recommend your book to their customers.) The publicists work with book reviewers and other media to begin to arrange media coverage for your book, which in turn may create ongoing favorable conversations and recommendations among your readers—and stimulate ongoing book sales. At various stages all along the way, you can contribute ideas and enthusiasm.

The Internet gives you access to the news of publishing no matter where you live. To get inside the heads of the people you're now in business with, read what they read. *Publishers Weekly* is the trade magazine for the industry, and you can subscribe to the print edition or read it online at www.publishersweekly.com, where you should also subscribe to the free daily e-newsletter called *PW Daily*. You will learn what the trade press is interested in covering, which will help you come up with media angles for your publicist later. Another source that you might find helpful: an e-newsletter called *Publishers Lunch* that summarizes the daily news in publishing (www.publisherslunch.com). To get a feel for the library market, read *Library Journal*, which you can subscribe to at www.libraryjournal.com or read at your local library. If you're the author of a children's book, read *School Library Journal*, which you can find online at www.slj.com.

Get to know your local booksellers and ask them what books are selling and why. In your visits to the bookstore, notice the books that you are drawn to. Did the vivid jackets and compelling titles catch your eye? Or was it the books' eye-level positioning on bookshelves and special displays? Going to bookstores will teach you about the competition that your book will face. It "is like boot camp for new authors" says marketing expert and literary agent Marly Rusoff, who has masterminded many book campaigns in her career. She sees the visit to the bookstore as an opportunity for authors to recognize the challenge before them in terms of the sheer volume of information and competing books.

Your local bookstores will include branches of the national chains, such as Barnes & Noble, Borders, and the regional southern chain, Books-A-Million, as well as independent booksellers, which are generally single-store businesses. The local chain store receives its books through orders placed with publishers at store headquarters. Store managers do have some discretionary buying power, so becoming familiar to local chain store managers can help you when your book is published. The independent booksellers may place their orders through a publisher's sales rep, who comes to the store, or through a publisher's telemarketing rep or wholesalers. Not all independent booksellers see publishers' reps so they must count on trade reviews and other sources of book news to decide which books to order.

As you become immersed in the marketing of your book, you may be surprised to find that the world views your book as a product. Some authors find this notion difficult to understand and accept, particularly writers of literary fiction. But, for example, in the world of the media, the author is just one more individual competing for airtime (or for ink) to sell a service or a product. A book is simply a form of entertainment or a source of information that a consumer might choose over another entertainment product, such as a movie or computer game. (Yes—your book is competing with *all* other forms of information and entertainment.) And while your publisher may treat your prose with all due respect, the house is also very concerned with your book's net units sold and its contribution to the company's bottom line. The earlier in the publishing process that you understand this thinking, the better, as you will become closer to learning the mind-set of the people you're working with. (It may also surprise you to overhear your publicist or editor referring to you as "my author." It's just the lingo of the trade, so do not be concerned by the implied possessiveness. Be flattered instead!)

To give yourself the best head start, think about your marketing campaign while you write your book. Keep a separate notebook and jot down marketing ideas or reasons why your book stands out from others in its field. When you are ready to create a formal marketing plan, the notes will be valuable.

You may also include marketable ideas within your book itself. For example, print media will often use "Top Ten" lists or other excerpts from how-to books. Include them in yours and you have provided desirable and accessible copy that's easily reproduced by the media. Another example of a marketing hook embedded in a book: One bestselling novelist always includes in his books a character who is a graduate of his alma mater, a school that happens to have an active alumni organization that supports all of his books in the form of promotional events.

Then there is *The Bulgari Connection,* by Fay Weldon, the ne plus ultra of product placement in fiction. The Bulgari jewelry company paid Weldon for prominent mention of the brand in the novel. The media's coverage of the book as the commercialization of art created a buzz and controversy. Literary purists will balk at the notion of placing marketing angles within the text, feeling that it compromises artistic integrity, and that's fine. You will need to make your own determination about what you think is acceptable within the context of your own book and your own field.

A thoroughly respectable way to embed a marketing angle within your book is to invite a noted person in a related field to contribute a foreword. Your book's sales will benefit from the additional draw that his or her name offers.

BRAINSTORM

The most fruitful way to begin to generate marketing ideas is to talk to other people. You must brainstorm with your friends and others about how they think your book will appeal to other readers. You are so close to your book that you may not see marketing opportunities that are obvious to others. Also, as any marketing person knows, the best ideas often emerge from conversation with others.

In my many conversations with authors for this book, the ones who had involved themselves in a writer's group, or other informed support group, seemed confident about their prospects and willing to try their hand at marketing. Beth Bruno, the self-published author of a book on parenting called *Wild Tulips,* credits the Connecticut Authors and Publishers Association (www.aboutcapa.com) as an important source of ideas and support. Type "writer's groups" into your Internet search engine to find organizations in your area, such as the Writers' League of Texas or Rocky Mountain Fiction Writers. They offer regular forums for writers to talk about their craft and to exchange ideas about getting published and finding an audience. Look also at the Shaw Guides, a free online guide to writer's conferences and workshops throughout the United States, at www.shawguides.com/writing.

Like Bruno, romance novelist Mariah Stewart says that the local chapter of Romance Writers of America (www.rwanational.com) was essential to her start as a writer. "They were very generous about sharing information," Stewart says, and cites the organization's ongoing contests as an excellent way to reach her core audience. Look for local chapters of national organizations that focus on your genre, whether romance, mystery (such as Mystery Writers of America, www.mysterywriters.org), science fiction (such as Science Fiction and Fantasy Writers of America, www.sfwa.org), horror (Horror Writers Association, www.horror.org), and more.

If you can't find any relevant local writer's organization, you can start your own, which is not as hard as it sounds. Your local bookstore or library would be more than happy to help you reach out to other writers in your community or host monthly meetings. Don't want to go to that trouble? Then you can reach out to brainstorming communities online. Browse the Internet and you'll come across active online writer's groups that you can join. A good place to start is the book publishing area of www.about.com with many links to organizations and online discussion groups.

An interesting Web-based brainstorming service, one that is designed to teach you to think like a book marketer, is available at www.BuzzYour.com. (Click on the Buzz Your Book icon.) Novelists and Internet marketing specialists M. J. Rose and Doug Clegg created "buzzstorming" to help authors promote their books. In a paid online course, Rose and Clegg teach brainstorming marketing techniques to writers, who complete the class with a marketing plan tailored to his or her own book. If you don't want to take the course, then the accompanying workbook, called *Buzz Your Book*, is available as a downloadable e-book. The book describes top marketing techniques for traditional media and for the Internet, offers advice from PR professionals who specialize in book marketing, links to many useful author Web sites and Web-based services for authors, and much more. Because interacting with others is crucial to your developing marketing ideas, the site offers a free brainstorming (or "buzzstorming") forum. Join in to read ideas about other authors' books and ask questions about your own. The premise is that the more you help other people, the more you can help yourself. This online community strikes a friendly tone and offers terrific advice for writers looking for unconventional or interesting ways to promote their works.

The bottom line is this: Find people to talk to and ask them questions. Then find even more people and ask them questions, too. Don't stop doing this even after your book has been published.

SHARPEN YOUR MARKETING MIND

Learning to think like a marketer is a commonsense process that takes place over time. It is accomplished largely by paying attention to the media and to the marketplace and thinking about how your book fits in. Here's how to start.

- Read the newspaper with the intent to figure out which interest group(s) had a hand in shaping or pitching the story. Nearly every article has one or more advocates behind it who were pushing a particular point of view. Yes, even governments have publicists in the form of lobbyists—everyone has a message to convey, whether it's the author of a new book or the Chinese government.

- Watch television interviews and listen to radio interviews. Which guests effectively convey their points? Which do not, and why?

- Scan for references to books in *Time* or *Newsweek,* in your local newspaper, in *USA Today,* other media—particularly media that you are not already familiar with. Books are covered in feature articles, opinion columns, editorial pages, everywhere—not only in the book review section, which with few exceptions cover only serious fiction and nonfiction. If your book will not fit well on the book review pages, can you identify other opportunities elsewhere in these publications?

- Pay attention to how the media covers books to learn why the media might take an interest in yours. Does the book offer news or information that's useful or important to consumers? Is the book funny or controversial? Or does it represent a special achievement on the part of the author?

■ Pay attention to the names of reporters who regularly cover books outside of the book review sections and make note of their names to share with your publicist later. Start to develop a sense of the reporters' interests. Based on your growing knowledge of their beat, would your book interest them?

■ Attend author readings at local bookstores and libraries. Talk to the authors about their campaigns.

■ Talk to friends and associates to find out if you can tap into their contacts to market or sell your book. Do you know someone with access to an inexpensive party space? Or who has access to organizations that might be willing to sponsor a lecture, or buy your book as a premium to attract new customers?

■ Use the Internet to listen to radio interview programs.

■ Use the Internet to check out newspapers around the United States and Canada, and to research reporters interested in your book topic. (I will tell you about some great sites to do this later in this book, on page 133.)

■ Look for Web sites relevant to your book topic. Start to make contact with the online community interested in your subject to build an online marketing base for your book. (There is a protocol to promoting your own work to online interest groups, which I will address in Chapter Eleven, page 220.)

■ If you think you belong on *The Oprah Winfrey Show*—the ultimate dream for many authors—or *The View, Live with Regis and Kelly, Today,* or *Good Morning America,* then watch the shows faithfully to understand how to position your book to appeal to the shows' producers.

A WRITTEN MARKETING PLAN

If you have never written a marketing plan before, do not be intimidated, but take the challenge seriously. Your final plan need not follow any specified format—you may use the format suggested in the next chapter, or else come up with your own. What's important is that you convey your ideas about how your book will reach and sell to its audience. (If you submitted a marketing plan at the time your book was acquired, then you should plan on updating it, since your thinking will have evolved in the interim.)

If you've got a professional background in marketing at, say, a consumer goods company, then understand that a book marketing plan is far less formal than what you are used to. It's more like a commonsense memo about how to reach your book's audience. You can find marketing plan templates on the Internet, though I've not come across one that's geared toward book promotion. Instead, they use a form of business school–influenced language that is unsuited to book publishing. Avoid them and concentrate instead on getting some smart ideas down on the page.

Publishers have a standard set of promotional tools, some or all of which they will put into use depending on the level of commitment to your book. These might include extra discounts to booksellers, advertising, a publicity tour, signage for bookstores, an unusual and eye-catching jacket, and so on. It's not your job to try to list all of these tools in the marketing plan. What you offer the publisher is more valuable—inside information about your book's potential, and how to define and possibly reach markets that they may not have thought of. The publisher may already be willing to promote your book and have set aside some funds to do so, but perhaps the staff cannot come up with a specific, individualized marketing or publicity plan that makes sense for your book. If the right idea doesn't materialize, then they may spend the money on ideas that do not make sense for your book, or else will divert the funds elsewhere.

The marketing plan will take you a significant amount of time and thought to prepare, but the effort is worthwhile. As you get closer to the publication date, other ideas will strike you as essential to include in your plan. As your plan evolves, alert your editor and publicist about any late-breaking brainstorms.

You will discuss your finished plan with your editor. Ask if he or she thinks it's on target, if your expectations are realistic, if you've missed anything appealing or interesting about the book. Enlist your editor in support of the plan and even to contribute ideas to the plan. Your editor's support will give you leverage in getting your ideas adopted later by others on the publishing team.

Your publisher can use your plan in a variety of ways. Your editor can draw from your book description to write jacket copy for the book, the tip sheet (or title information sheet) copy, and catalog copy. The publicity department can use your marketing plan to create a publicity plan, press releases, and press pitches. Points you raise in the plan might later become the basis of media interviews and provide ways for the sales reps to pitch your book to booksellers. The marketing department might draw on your ideas to create promotions for booksellers, to write catalog marketing copy, and to alert the appropriate sales reps about any local connections you have in their territories. The subsidiary rights department may share parts of the plan with book clubs and foreign publishers to demonstrate the book's potential in the marketplace.

As you begin writing your marketing plan, you will probably be unaware of your relative position on the publisher's list. At this early stage your publisher has probably not decided upon your book's potential in the marketplace. Present the plan about six to seven months before your book's publication. You can present it closer to publication than that, but take advantage of the time you have to build support. To be certain to deliver the plan when it can do the most good, check with your editor about the key publishing dates at your publishing house. You want to deliver the plan to your editor before he or she participates in any key launch or strategy meetings.

BOOK MARKETING BASICS—A SUMMARY

The good news is that your marketing plan can have a genuine impact on the way your publisher decides to publish your book. Learning to think like a marketer for your books means that you will:

- Identify the many target audiences for your book.

- Read the book publishing trade press to understand your publisher's point of view.

- Read and watch the media with an eye to figuring out how your book fits in.

- Brainstorm with others about marketing opportunities; seek out as many brainstorming opportunities as possible.

- Make a commitment to writing a marketing plan.

2

How to Write a Marketing Plan

A marketing plan tells the publishing staff what's interesting, unusual, and special about you and your book and how you think the book can be promoted. To get an idea of your publisher's sensibilities, ask your editor for a copy of the latest catalog. From reading it you can find out how the publisher presents and describes their books. You can use this as a guide for writing about yours.

Don't plan on writing the plan in one sitting. One useful tactic is to begin your plan as a rough draft that you embellish over the course of several weeks, as you develop more ideas about how to market your book.

Make your plan a thrifty one. Focus on promotional ideas that do not require your publisher (or you) to spend a lot of money. If your title is a "midlist" book (i.e., any book not at the top of the publisher's priorities), then you stand little chance of persuading your publisher to spend the kind of money required for print ads and other paid media. Where you stand a better chance of getting some money is for publicity, which is relatively inexpensive. "Publicity" refers to the array of strategies that generate positive (and free) media coverage of your book. This coverage can create the ever desirable word-of-mouth attention—when your book becomes the topic of conversation between friends and colleagues as they recommend your book to one another.

While you're thinking about appropriate publicity strategies, be honest with yourself. You know your own comfort level in public forums. If you are wildly uncomfortable with the idea of doing live interviews or bookstore appearances then do not force yourself. On the other hand, if you're uncomfortable with the idea of giving interviews, but think that with some media or speech training that you could become an effective communicator, then perhaps push for a publicity tour.

A publicity tour—a trip to several cities where you will be interviewed by the media and appear in bookstores—is warranted if your book is topical and makes for interesting conversation on talk shows, which then might draw audiences to attend bookstore signings or talks. A tour also makes sense if your book is controversial, if you have an unusual life story to tell, or followed an unusual path to becoming a writer. On the audience side of the equation, having friends and family in other cities who can help drum up support is an important factor in determining whether you should tour.

If you want to go on a book tour, then let your editor know when your book is acquired or at least before you've turned in a marketing plan. That way your editor can begin to advocate for this in early conversations with the publisher and director of publicity. Do you have friends and family in other cities and free places to stay on tour? That alone is a convincing argument for a book tour. One author traveled with her father on his business trips. While her publishing house paid for her flights, her dad let her crash in his hotel room to help defray the costs of the tour. Many authors stay with friends as a way to decrease hotel expenses for the publisher and divert the savings into the rest of the campaign.

A book tour is merely one tool to promote a book. You will become familiar with many other ways to get the word out about yours. Among them are concentrated press pitches to the national press in New York and Washington, D.C., local book signings and publicity in your hometown, postcard mailings, and even radio interviews conducted by phone. Then of course there's the Internet—a tool for self-promotion as well as an open retail market to sell your book.

Some sections of the marketing plan will duplicate the author's questionnaire that your editor may ask you to complete. However, as the marketing plan specifically addresses how to sell your book, redundancies are expected and forgiven. The marketing plan should include:

- Book title, your name, and contact information

- Goal

- Book description

- Target audience(s)

- A positioning statement—the one or two sentences that capture the essence and appeal of your book

- Why you wrote the book—the background story

- Marketing strategy and campaign

- Sales handles and media angles

- Biography

- Competitive titles/comparative titles

- Personal and professional contacts (who might help in the book launch or who might give you a "blurb" or endorsement)

- Your prior media experience

- Sales leads

- Your top ten media and marketing wish list and ideas how to target them (this last item is optional, but it's really impressive and puts you way ahead of your competition on your publisher's list)

THE TITLE

The title of your book is essential to its effective marketing. Its job is to tell and sell: It needs to tell what the book's about and sell it to your audience.

If your title and subtitle are not satisfactory, your editor will work with you to get them right before the book is first presented to key sales reps and other publishing staff. Your title should be set before catalog copy is finalized. While you can still change your title after the catalog has been printed, you've lost an important opportunity to make the right impression on booksellers and the media. Wrong titles in the catalog have a sneaky way of getting into bookstore computers, which causes confusion once the book is published when booksellers try to reorder the title.

Consider the titles of these novels: *The Mysteries of Pittsburgh, Angela's Ashes,* and *All the Pretty Horses.* Or these works of nonfiction: *The Best and the Brightest, The Cake Mix Doctor, The Liars' Club*, and *Einstein's Dreams.* These books all have great titles that pique a reader's interest to explore further. A good title, in combination with the book jacket, will prompt the bookstore browser to pick up the book. Book reviewers sift through mail sacks filled with books by unknown writers: It is the book with an intriguing title or cover design that's likely to get pulled out of the pile first.

In some cases the title and subtitle might define the audience, making it clear to the prospective customer that this book is for them. For example, a book by Eileen Behan called *Eat Well, Lose Weight While Breastfeeding* targets new mothers, who want to lose the weight they gained during pregnancy; and Sarah Schlesinger's *500 Fat-Free Recipes* targets home cooks looking for no-fat dishes whether for health or dietary reasons. Both books performed exceptionally well.

DEFINE YOUR GOAL

The first important step in writing a plan is to understand and articulate your goal for the book. A goal helps you focus your expectations and forces the publishing team to address its own expectations.

Essentially you need to explain why you wrote your book in one or two lines.

Perhaps you want your book to become a bestseller, or to influence public policy. You might hope to create enough attention with the book's publication to attract paid speaking engagements and consulting assignments, or perhaps earn enough money from your royalties to quit your day job. Perhaps you want to leave something for posterity, or to share your expertise with people who need it. You may even intend to build a long-term writing career.

Make your stated goals realistic so that you appear credible. If you've written a book on a narrow topic and you expect a bestseller, then you've got to produce a convincing marketing plan. It bears repeating: Do not push unrealistic expectations on your publisher.

A DESCRIPTION OF YOUR BOOK

Many people working on promoting or selling your book may never have the time to read it. It is to your absolute advantage to carefully convey what your book is about in two to three tightly written paragraphs. What you write will become the basis of how the publishing staff will describe your book when they go out to sell it. Your description may even be used verbatim throughout the course of your book's publication in all manner of promotional materials—from tip sheets and catalog copy to flap copy and press releases.

DEFINE YOUR TARGET AUDIENCE

Michael Schrage, author of *Serious Play* and *No More Teams!*, says that anything you can do to reduce the ambiguity in your book's marketing is very helpful to your publisher. One approach, he says, is com-

ing up with a reader profile, literally writing down who you think your
readers are, their age group, their personal and professional interests,
and so on. Your definition of your audience will help you and your
publisher to concentrate resources on reaching your largest groups of
readers. To determine who these treasured folks are, ask yourself these
questions:

- While you were writing your book, did you envision a particular
kind of reader?

- Which individuals will benefit from reading your book? Think
broadly, as your book likely has more than one target audience.
(For example, the individuals who might benefit from this book
include authors; editors and agents, who help their authors figure
out how to market themselves; publicists, who need or want additional training; publicity directors, who can give the book to their
authors to help make them an effective part of the publicity process; and small publishers, who need publicity and marketing
advice.)

- Who do you think will buy your novel? If your answer to that is
"all readers of general fiction" then try to further refine your thinking. Among readers of fiction, are they women who enjoy the
Oprah-favored hardship-to-recovery novels, men who enjoy
techno-thrillers, readers of mysteries with crossover mainstream
themes, readers of family dramas, and so on? Beyond fiction readers, could other readers take an interest in your book? For example,
Ship Fever, a short story collection by Andrea Barrett, has characters based on historic individuals in science. The harrowing and
brilliant title story is about the infectious diseases carried by Irish
immigrants to America escaping the famine back home. Several
audiences exist for this book: readers of literary fiction, readers and
practitioners of the biological and ecological sciences, readers of
history and historians, and Irish Americans. Other examples: Tom
Clancy's techno-thriller novels are clearly of potential interest to
past and present members of the armed forces. Publishers of legal

thrillers often market books successfully to the legal community. Less obvious: Your novel has a lovable cat in it? Then let *Cat Fancy* magazine know about it so that you can reach cat lovers. Or you've written a novel of political intrigue set in Berlin? Have your publicist send your book to the foreign correspondents based in the Berlin bureaus in case you can score a mention in their columns or at least get some good word of mouth in their circle. Your novel features recipes? Get the book into the hands of the food editors at the top papers as well as the book reviewers to reach readers interested in food. As you begin to define your audience, ways to reach them will begin to suggest themselves to you.

- Can your book attract readers of books from other genres? For example, Jonathan Harr's nonfiction book, *A Civil Action*, was of interest to readers of crime, law, and politics. Yet the publisher also positioned the book to attract readers of fiction, as it had a strong narrative style.

- What age groups might take interest in your book? If you're writing about midlife themes, then chances are that the young Gen Y readers will not take much interest.

- Are your potential readers located in a particular geographic region? If your book takes place in Iowa, for example, then Iowans should be a particular target of your marketing and publicity campaign.

- Does your book speak to men or to women or both? For example, to define the audience for your diet book, go to health and weight loss Internet sites to find out the size and characteristics (or demographics) of your book's potential audience. You might then target women of certain age groups, who are the most frequent dieters and buyers of diet books and diet products.

- Would your book interest people of a particular ethnic background, whether because of the themes you address or because of your own identity?

■ Would your book appeal to consumers of certain media? If you're unsure how to define your audience, then back into your audience profile through your intuitive sense of what your readers will listen to. For example, if you've written literary fiction, then perhaps your audience is to be found among the highbrow and educated listeners of National Public Radio. Or if you've written a joke book, a sex book, or a book about popular culture, then perhaps reach your readers through the zany zoo morning drive radio shows. (To really refine your understanding of these listeners, access the stations' media kits online to find out the demographic breakdown of your potential readership. Do the listener demographics as outlined in the media kits conform to your sense of who your audience is?)

Remember: By defining your audience, you can figure out which media to approach—or suggest that your publicist approach—to get publicity coverage for your book that will reach your readership.

POSITIONING STATEMENT

When sales reps pitch your book, they need a concise way to talk about your book's content and audience, and why it stands out from all others. The positioning statement is one or two appealing sentences that make the listener curious about the book. The idea behind the positioning statement is to create a way to talk about the book that will appeal to booksellers, the media, and the reading audience.

One way to understand positioning is to consider movie advertising. For example, the successful independent film *Billy Elliot* was positioned as a feel-good movie for general audiences about a young boy from a tough northern English mining town who beats all odds to become a dancer. Actually, the film contained more violence than the advertising suggested, with a plot about labor unrest, as well as a homoerotic subplot. Had the film been positioned as a gritty film about union busting, or as a film for gay audiences, then it probably would not have been as broadly successful with general audiences.

To come up with the positioning statement for your book, think about how you would briefly answer the questions "What's your book about?" and "Who will read it?" *The Hot Zone*, by Richard Preston, was positioned as a true-to-life medical thriller about the ravages of the Ebola virus and its potential threat to us all. The positioning was intended to frighten us into reading the book as well as to capture general fiction readers, and those of quality nonfiction. The book quickly became a bestseller.

A book's positioning might also be tied to the author's authority in the subject, or the topicality or controversial nature of the subject. Comparisons to other authors also help position a book by suggesting that the readers of one author will like the work of the other author. For example the publisher of a young writer whose work is reminiscent of, say, John Irving's early work might position the novel as a similarly impressive debut. When Doubleday published *Faerie Tale* and wanted fantasy novelist Raymond Feist to reach a broad mainstream audience, the house compared his crossover potential to Clive Barker's, who had recently achieved bestseller status. (The publicity department extended the idea even further and booked a segment on ABC's *Good Morning America* with both Clive Barker and Feist.)

In an interview with *New York Magazine*, Little, Brown publisher Michael Pietsch described the strategy behind the marketing campaign for *Infinite Jest*, a literary novel by David Foster Wallace published in 1996. Addressing the challenge of marketing such a long book—it was more than 1,000 pages long—Pietsch had two strategies: to spur jealousy and therefore intense interest among the literary writing community through a word-of-mouth campaign, and to market to readers of literary fiction with the premise "Are you reader enough?" for the book. The campaign worked beautifully, with news of the book first creating a stir in the publishing industry, and then going on to become a *New York Times* bestseller.

Why should we care about your book? The positioning statement answers this question.

WHY YOU WROTE THE BOOK—THE BACKGROUND STORY

A short background piece—a couple of paragraphs or a couple of pages long—about how and why you wrote the book can be extremely useful information for publicists and sales reps. Your path to publication—whether it included fifty rejections before you found a publishing home, or was a beeline from your English professor to your editor—can become part of the promotional story surrounding your book. (Do not assume that an interesting story surrounding the book's acquisition is known or remembered by anyone else in the publishing house other than your editor and perhaps the editor-in-chief. Include it in your written materials.) The piece might also include any unusual events in the creating of the book or specific influences on your work. (And the media loves a good rags-to-riches story, or tales of overnight success, or of many years of dedicated hard work suddenly paying off. If this applies to you, say so.)

If you're unsure about what qualifies as interesting material to include in this section of the plan, start reading profiles of individuals—not just writers—in your local paper, in magazines, on Web sites. Pay attention to how the subject talks about his or her work. Now think about the information or impressions that you were trying to convey to readers through your own work. Did the book require any special research? Did you work part-time jobs while raising your children and yet still managed to find time to write? The details of your writing career might seem mundane to you, but may interest your publicist or the media. Unsurprisingly, one of the most common questions that audiences ask writers at bookstore appearances is "When do you write?" or "How do you find the time to write?" Readers have an endless interest in the process of being or becoming a writer.

During publicity interviews for his memoir, the musician David Crosby said that he became a musician because he wanted to meet women. (Actually he put it more graphically than that, but that's what he meant.) Which is to say that as you write the back story on becoming a writer, you might inject a little humor or self-awareness to leaven what might otherwise come off as ponderous and self-absorbed. Simply put, be aware of the general impression that you create.

What all the background information attempts to get at is what marketer and agent Marly Rusoff calls the "story" about your book, or the way that the book is talked about—both in-house and, it is hoped, among consumers. Your editor will use your "story" to pitch the sales force; your publicist will use it to pitch the media. Bear in mind as you're writing this section of the plan that what you may view as uninteresting may intrigue those working on your marketing campaign.

If an author does not provide information about how the book came to be, a publicist will sometimes talk to the author in an effort to extract an idea of who they are and of the book's background. However, the publicist will do this only if she or the house has decided that your book is worth spending some time on.

THE MARKETING STRATEGY AND CAMPAIGN

The marketing strategy section of your marketing plan addresses how you or your publisher will reach your readership, and will probably require the most time and thought and continual refinement on your part. This section is really the heart of your campaign—the blueprint for how you will reach your target audience. Here are many ideas and examples of successful strategies that you can draw on to develop your own marketing strategy. Not all examples will apply to every book, but they should serve to stimulate the marketing side of your brain.

- Can your book tie in to local or national political campaigns? One publishing house, Addison-Wesley, went right to the core market for a book called *Reinventing Government,* by David Osborne. Intending to get the book in the hands of reporters covering the New Hampshire primaries, the publisher sent staff to New Hampshire to put complimentary copies of books in the local bars where the national political reporters were hanging out. Many of the snowbound journalists wrote about the book. The subsequent cov-

erage and sales launched the book onto the *New York Times* bestseller list.

■ Could your book interest policy makers? Then suggest that your
publisher send copies of the book to public opinion leaders and
opinion columnists, who can become important mouthpieces for
your book. For example, you could send a book that touches on
political or social matters to influential government leaders who
are interested in your subject matter. For a promotion for *The
Tenth Justice,* the bestselling novel by Brad Meltzer about a group
of fictional clerks at the Supreme Court, the publisher sent books
to the current clerks and other members of the Justice Department,
knowing that this audience could help build interest in Washington, D.C.

■ Does your book contain a strong spiritual or social message, in
which case a church or other religious congregation can help
spread the word? Send copies of a self-empowerment book to the
church leaders, for instance, and invite them to share it with their
congregations.

■ Is your book aimed at a specific self-help readership? Then you
might try working through the national media, which offers many
service stories. For instance, a diet book, by definition geared to any
American who thinks he or she is overweight, might be launched by
national television media appearances, as well as excerpts or coverage in women's magazines.

■ Does your book have a niche readership and, if so, what media
vehicles reach that readership? For example, the publisher of a
basic early childhood parenting book would target first-time parents by trying to sell excerpts to parenting magazines, offering
free excerpts to parenting sections of newspapers (which often
can't afford to pay for excerpts), and setting up media interviews
for the authors. A few lucky authors have had their books
excerpted in the promotional brochures of the baby formula man-

ufacturers Similac and Enfamil. Other books have been bought by HMOs, which offer information about preventive medicine to their members.

■ Does your subject matter appeal to a dedicated group of journalists and other professionals who can generate exposure and buzz for your book? For instance, a sports book could be promoted to sportscasters who might mention the book during on-air broadcasts of games. Your publisher might also contact the public relations people at local sports arenas to see if they will put copies of the book in the pressroom at game time.

■ Should you take a grassroots approach to building an audience? Laurie Beth Jones, author of *Jesus, Inc.* and *Jesus CEO,* toured the United States in her RV to reach more cities than a traditional tour could finance (www.lauriebethjones.com).

■ Can you team up with other writers in your genre? Mystery and romance writers sometimes go on the road with other writers to help build one another's audiences and to save on expenses.

■ Can your book tie in with a local or national event? A book about the fashion industry called *Model,* by Michael Gross, coincided with Fashion Week in New York City, when the new collections are launched. The publisher delivered press packets to the hotel rooms of fashion reporters who were in town for the shows. The author was ubiquitous at Fashion Week's parties and events, and was widely quoted everywhere in the fashion press. The publisher also worked with Saks Fifth Avenue, which mounted window displays that were themed around the book.

■ Can you link your book to events in the news? When former First Lady Hillary Clinton professed an admiration for Eleanor Roosevelt, publishers of Roosevelt biographies reprinted works by and about Roosevelt, and positioned their authors as experts on first ladies. Political campaigns, the latest crime statistics, teacher shortages, reading scores, teenage behaviors, caring for aging parents, the economy—whether declining or booming—the environment: Reporters cover all these issues on a continuing basis and need to interview experts. Keep current with what's going on in the world, and if you see an opportunity to tie into the news headlines, then let your publicist know. If you are doing your own publicity, call or e-mail the appropriate reporters to let them know about your book.

Linking to News Events—a Word of Caution

Link to the news in a tasteful manner. A publishing newsletter that appeared a few days after the destruction of the World Trade Center urged readers who had written books about grief, airport security, or skyscraper architecture to get in touch with news organizations to make themselves available for interviews—all legitimate topics. But before you tag onto a catastrophic event, ask yourself if you are providing a public service by letting the media know of your expertise, or merely straining to connect your book to the event. Many public relations people caught flak from the press for attempting far-fetched connections to 9/11 on behalf of their clients. Perhaps there are just some occasions when you shouldn't be thinking about book sales.

- Could your book be part of cultural programs organized by your local department store? For example, Macy's stages hundreds of special events a year and will invite authors to participate as guest lecturers. The store will also offer the authors' books for sale.

- The people that you interviewed for your book may help you promote it. Confirm your sources' willingness to help out and state that fact in the marketing plan. For example, James Hirsch's *Hurricane* is an authorized biography of Rubin "Hurricane" Carter, for which Carter appeared in interviews with the author. A writer of fiction might call upon any intriguing individuals he or she interviewed in doing background research for the novel.

- Can you link your book to a holiday or an anniversary? Check out a directory published every fall called *Chase's Calendar of Events,* which lists all kinds of quirky events, birthdays, celebrations, and anniversaries, such as National Pie Day and American Education Week, among many others. You may find an event to connect to your book's marketing.

- Are you an effective or charismatic public speaker? Then emphasize public appearances and media interviews as a key part of your campaign.

An Author Creates Marketing Events for Her Own Books

Bestselling author Lois Wyse is the author of sixty-five books. A marketer by profession, her success offers lessons for would-be marketers who want to sell their books to readers. Her books all have ready-made, built-in marketing angles. For a book called *How to Take Your Grandmother to the Museum,* she traveled with her coauthor, who happened to be her young granddaughter, to a number of tour cities where the local museums provided the press-worthy local settings for publicity interviews. For *Women Make the Best Friends,* the publisher set up friendship teas and parties in bookstores where women were encouraged to bring a friend. And for *Funny, You Don't Look Like a Grandmother,* Wyse had the idea to set up power breakfasts for grandmothers. The concept created a lot of buzz and print coverage and the book reached number one on the *New York Times* bestseller list.

Wyse's advice for new authors is to look at all your contacts and spend some time brainstorming with them. Ask your friends who they think is the audience for the book, and what in your book will make someone want to buy it. And then, who is that someone?

■ Does your book's success depend on favorable and widespread book review coverage? A campaign for a literary novel or work of serious nonfiction might focus on getting galleys into the hands of book reviewers and influential critics on the board of the National Book Critics Circle, which awards an annual literary prize. To accomplish this you might recommend a higher printing of galleys than usual. (Galleys—a bound paperback-style edition of your book printed three to five months before its publication—allow reviewers who have a long lead time to read and review the book in time for the book's publication.)

■ Are you good-looking or unusual-looking or are you an eccentric? Some publishers promote the author's good looks (Michael Chabon for his first book, *The Mysteries of Pittsburgh*) or outrageous personality (David Sedaris for his collection of essays, *Naked*) alongside the book's literary merits.

■ Can you create a trend story around your book by conducting informal surveys or polls? You do not have to be Gallup. As long as you poll people in a credible way, your results can form the basis of a press pitch for your book. The survey might even provide the basis for your book, as well as offering a marketing angle. For a book called *Married Lust* from Redbook magazine, the author Pamela Lister conducted research through surveys on the very active *Redbook* Web site and got 10,000 responses. What men and women reported about their feelings about sex and marriage became both part of the book's content and its press coverage. If you have a Web site and attract sufficient traffic, then you can conduct your surveys online.

■ Does your book have any strong visuals? A photo insert with just a few stunning photographic images can create significant publicity for a book. State in your marketing plan the nature of the photos that are available to help market the book. Strong visuals can become the basis not only for press coverage but also for striking window displays for booksellers. For David Halberstam's book *The*

Fifties, the publisher created sets of easel-backed photographs of iconic images from the 1950s for displays.

■ Can you create a photo opportunity around the subject of your book? You might stage an event with a compelling visual that local or even national press will want to shoot. A shot of you handing a check to the president of a local charity is not an exciting photo. But a shot of the prizewinners at your costume party to raise money for that charity is a good photo op.

■ Does your book tie into current social trends and concerns? For example, a recent parenting book posited the idea that parents are less important than peers in determining a child's values and behavior. The argument generated a media interest because it tapped into parental anxieties about whether we're raising our children right.

A Book Campaign Connected to News Events That Did Not Sell Books

Shortly after Heidi Fleiss and Sidney Biddle Barrows had been arrested for running call-girl rings, we published a book by Hollywood's Madame Alex. I booked her on a major national talk show for which she procured several call girls for an on-air appearance. (Actually, she provided the phone numbers but I had to do the actual procuring—one of my more bizarre publicity assignments.) The women, some of them in disguise, were interviewed in the New York City studio while Madame Alex appeared live remote from Los Angeles. Well, the Madame couldn't hear the talk show host very well through the studio earpiece, so when he asked her if her girls were "ambitious," she misheard and replied indignantly, "My girls are not bitches." As book promotion segments go, it was hugely funny, but didn't sell many books. In this case the subject matter was interesting to the audience as an amusing media story, but not as a book. The point is, you can reach the potential consumer, but is your book something that they really want? That is the gamble that publishers make every day with every book.

- For any project-based book, you might show finished projects. For a crafts book bring the finished crafts on air on a television demo; for a floral arranging book you might present different styles of floral arrangements. The publicist might offer free excerpts of a project and illustrations to newspapers and Web sites.

- Does your book offer controversial information? If so, you can withhold information until publication date to build interest and suspense among your target audience. The idea behind embargoing content until publication is that the contents will instantly create news headlines that will in turn drive instant book sales. If the information leaks out before publication, then the news value is lost since books are not available for consumers to buy at the very moment when they're most interested in it. Typically books that are published like this are gossipy celebrity books, or exposés. But if your book contains never-before-known information within your field, then alert your publisher to that fact: They are not experts in your subject area and may not recognize the news value in your work.

- Does your book offer a contrary point of view? Then stir up controversy through public or journalistic debate over your position.

- Will your book provoke curiosity among people who think they are in the book? A publicity technique that sometimes works nicely to promote popular biographies and autobiographies, as well as books of a sensational nature, is sending a copy of the book's index to the individuals who are mentioned in the book. This tease gets them talking about the book—just what you want.

- Can you attract guests to a book party who will start serious buzz about your book? Parties can also be useful in the context of an industry trade show, where your publisher can introduce you to key booksellers. They can also work as sales opportunities say, if a friend is throwing you a party and your publisher or a local bookseller brings books to sell to the guests. However, unless a party can achieve some real word of mouth or sales for a book, do not expect your publisher to pay for one just for the sake of it. (Of course, if you simply want to have fun and celebrate your book's publication, then by all means party on.)

The Worthwhile Book Party

Some people in the business think it gauche to sell books at a party; other pragmatic folk will take a sale anytime and anywhere (that's me!); others suggest that friends should buy books at bookstores, not at parties, to help build bookstore reorders. I'm in the "sale is a sale" school of thought, because I'd like to capture the sale for a book at the moment the consumer is interested. You will simply have to make up your own mind about what to do. If you sell the books at your parties or any other events, then buy them at your author discount rate, charge full retail price for the book, and you get to keep the profit. (And depending on your contract, you probably get paid a royalty on those copies.) Many authors will have a friend help sell the books so that they can meet their guests instead of handling a cash box. If your publisher is involved with your party then your publicist can bring books either to sell or give away.

To keep party costs down (and therefore have access to more funds for other elements of your campaign), call a liquor company. Ask to speak to its public relations account manager or publicist about contributing the liquor for a promotional event. Explain what the party is for and offer to fax the guest list including your guests' professional titles. If the size and caliber of the guest list are suitably impressive, you may get a free case of wine or champagne. Ask your book publicist to make this call, if she is willing.

If you throw yourself a party, ask your publicist for the names of the appropriate staff to invite including any book club editors or paperback and audiotape publishers who might be interested in your book. Likewise ask your publicist for a media mailing list, or to send invitations to the media. Even if your publisher is not paying for the party, publicists are often willing to absorb the cost of printing and sending invitations in their budgets.

■ Can you come up with a celebrity angle or a connection to celebrities? Perhaps seek and obtain endorsements from celebrities. This may involve many months of relentless pursuit through their publicists or agents, but is still doable.

■ Can you create an award? When his novel *Secrets* was published, Kelvin Christopher James created an annual writing contest with a cash prize that he presented to three New York City high school students for their essays about "Getting Along in New York." The award angle enabled me to book him on NPR's *Talk of the Nation* along with the first-prizewinning student, as well as to get a column in the *New York Daily News*. The next year, his publicist used the award angle to get a column in the *New York Times*. All this for a literary short story writer and novelist. Another example: Novelist Rona Jaffe has created a foundation through which she administers a grant program for women writers in fiction, poetry, and creative nonfiction. Every year the award's presentation is covered in the media.

■ Can you host a fund-raiser or other charity event to raise your profile? Create a local cause–based event for any institution in need: the public library, a children's day care center, a museum, a literacy program, any organization that has some reasonable connection with the message or intent of your book. Can you get local celebrities involved in your fund-raisers to help attract more media attention? A friend of mine, Lana Turner, has organized many special fund-raising events, some of which promote reading awareness. She arranged for house tours in Hamilton Heights, a prosperous area in Harlem, New York, followed by dinners with authors as the star attraction at each of the homes. The fund-raising campaign received press attention, as well as exposure for the authors. Stage this kind of event in your community and invite other authors to participate.

■ Can you stage a stunt? No, you do not have to dress up like a bunny or a clown. But if you're willing to make yourself the center of attention, and if you make the stunt a visual one, then you've improved the chances that television news crews will want to tell your story. The attention-getting event could be a contest, a fashion show, or a pet parade—anything out of the norm for your community.

- Can you create a quiz around your book's theme? A quiz can provide entertaining material for radio discussion about your book, or else for pickup in the print media. For example, a publisher of a first aid book created a quiz to test the readers' first aid knowledge that was picked up in the *New York Daily News* as well as other publications. A quiz can be serious or light entertainment depending on the nature and tone of your book. To promote *Don't Know Much About the Civil War,* author Kenneth Davis created quizzes and a crossword puzzle. Many of his radio interviews for the book took the form of "Stump the Author" with callers to the shows asking tough questions about the Civil War (www.dontknowmuch.com).

Still having trouble figuring out your strategy? Try some serious brainstorming with your editor, who may even introduce you to a publicist or the publicity director at this early stage. (Later, you will have more brainstorming sessions with the publicist who is formally assigned to your book.) The editor and publicist will have a sense of which stories will interest the media, while you provide insight about your book. But don't stop there. Tackle your friends and family and colleagues to try out your marketing ideas on them. Sometimes the best ideas come out of collaboration: Getting other people's point of view will help you shape your media pitch.

Advertising Versus Publicity: Why Publicity Is More Cost Effective Than Paid Advertising

Your marketing plan should focus on publicity rather than advertising. Most advertising is too expensive to warrant spending on most books. For instance, small black-and-white ads in the *New York Times, Washington Post, San Francisco Chronicle,* or the *New Yorker* cost approximately $8,000 to $12,000. Those short book ads that you hear on National Public Radio? They cost upward of $13,000 for a minimum commitment to twelve fifteen-second spots. Other types of book advertising include bus or subway ads (pricey), television ad campaigns (you've got to spend at least $25,000 on production and then another $50,000 minimum if you're buying network time; less if you're focusing on cable), and radio advertising (around $20,000 or more). Publishers can rarely afford to spend enough on advertising to create a sufficient number of impressions among the target consumers to deliver sales, and most book advertising is bizarrely obscure. Take a look at the book section of the daily *New York Times,* a favorite advertising vehicle for many publishers, where you will frequently see book ads that never actually explain what the book is about: How, then, will the target audience know that the book is for them?

In contrast, you have a much greater chance of reaching and, more important, engaging readers through a publicity campaign. A ten-city tour might cost $20,000 to $30,000. A tightly focused national media campaign—requiring travel to New York and Washington, D.C., will cost your publisher $500 to $4000, depending where you live. If Canada is part of the book's market, then the national media in Toronto might also be included in the national campaign. Typically, book tours cost your publisher between $1,200 and $2,500 a city. Expenses include the hotel room, airfare, ground transportation, and food. The media coverage you can get through publicity is more extensive than what you can buy with the equivalent dollars spent in advertising.

SALES HANDLES AND MEDIA ANGLES

Once they've shared the positioning statement with the buyer and have piqued his or her interest, the reps will talk about the book's sales handles to clinch "the buy." Sales handles are three or more specific points that explain the book's market and why the book will do well. Media angles are the talking points that your publicist will use to convince the media to interview you or to cover your book. Similar to sales handles, the media angles help the publicist clinch the deal with a producer or reporter to get your book covered.

During a sales call, a sales rep may have to present an entire publishing season. Or the rep may have only an hour with the buyer to get through a full month's worth of titles. In other words, there's not much time. The rep needs to convey the heart of your book in a few minutes—or less. This is where the sales handles in your marketing plan will come in.

Sales handles will convey what's new and different about your book—your authority as the writer, the marketplace for your book's topic, its advantages over the competition, and its marketability. For example, for a new dog-care book that focuses on natural health, the sales handles might be as follows (and do not be dismayed by the fact that I've thrown in the kitchen sink for this nonexistent book, as most books do not have quite so much going for them):

1. The author's last book sold 85,000 copies.

2. The author is an established expert on dog care and is a frequent guest on national television.

3. The author is planning to underwrite an aggressive marketing campaign.

4. The book reveals for the first time how a dog owner can increase his or her dog's life span by changing its diet.

5. More than 60 percent of U.S. households own at least one dog and the number grows every year.

6. The book has been endorsed by celebrity animal activist Brigitte Bardot as well as Monty Roberts, the author of *The Man Who Listens to Horses*.

7. *The Washington Post* has compared the author to bestselling author and veterinarian James Herriot.

8. The book includes easy-to-read diagnostic flow charts.

9. The book includes a resource section telling readers where to buy natural dog care products.

Sometimes the sales handles will also serve as media angles, the key points to convey to the media. In coming up with your media angles, think about what your book offers to consumers. Does your book:

- Make people's lives easier?

- Help them make more money?

- Entertain them?

- Get them a date or save their marriage?

- Help them accomplish a goal?

- Enlighten them?

- Help them save time, or decrease stress, or raise their kids?

- Help them improve their health?

By focusing on the end benefit to the consumer, you can come up with the angles that will help your book get media coverage. For example, for the same hypothetical dog-care book, the media angles might be:

- The author can bring animals from his practice onto television shows.

■ The author can talk about how changing the health and diets for the dogs in his practice has changed their lives and the lives of their owners.

In other words, the sales and marketing angles are merely ways to communicate to your core audiences: booksellers and media. Even if your sales and marketing handles are a little off the mark, they are a helpful starting point for a conversation with your publisher about your book's publishing strategy.

One approach to coming up with media angles for your book is to ask yourself the questions you'd like to be asked in your media interviews and then figure out how you would answer them. A twist on this is to ask yourself what one publicist asks all the authors he works with: Name the three reasons the media should interview you. If you can name them, then you've probably just come up with the media angles for your book.

YOUR BIOGRAPHY

Your publisher will use your biography in promotional materials including the book's jacket. Interesting aspects of your past may become the entire basis of the marketing strategy, which is why you've probably heard the story of Mary Higgins Clark, who was widowed as a young mother and turned to fiction writing as a desperate measure to support her family; or of J. K. Rowling's life as a cash-strapped single mother before she hit it big with her Harry Potter novels. Mention your professional credits, any previously published books, personal achievements, notable events in your life, your birthplace, other places where you've lived, and where you attended college.

When she begins a campaign, publicist Meryl Moss of Meryl L. Moss Media Relations has several conversations with her clients to understand the person she is pitching. She tells the writers she works with, "I want to know you in ways that you don't think I want to know you." What she means is that what may seem prosaic to you might become essential information that colors her pitch to the media. There-fore, in creating your biography, spend a little time talking to friends and family to access long-forgotten events of possible interest to the media.

Martin Arnold of the *New York Times* wrote an article on author biographies and a tendency toward cuteness by mentioning the family pets, as in "he lives in Pennsylvania with his wife and two dogs." The lesson: Be aware of the impression you're creating in your author bio. (Do you really want to come off as cute?) Read how other authors describe themselves on their book jackets: Do their bios make them sound accessible and appealing? Use the exercise of writing the bio to get used to the way you will be talked about and perceived during your book's promotion.

Do not be daunted if writing the biography is difficult for you. After all, it's not often that you are called upon to summarize your life. If you've written a novel that's in any way autobiographical, then your author bio offers an opportunity to discuss the parts of the book that are based on your own experiences. Mary Gaitskill's short story collec-tion, *Bad Behavior,* has a character who was a prostitute. Gaitskill's self-declared so-called bad behavior became the basis for the book's publicity campaign—a tricky position for the author to take. But Gait-skill's way of talking and writing about herself made her seem oddly vulnerable, and her personal appeal lay in the intersection of her bravado and her sensitivity.

Other writers feel that admitting to autobiographical elements in their novels diminishes the artistic merit of the work. The extent to which you share aspects of your life is entirely up to you, but if you reveal yourself, prepare yourself for what may seem like harsh public judgment and misunderstandings about you. Public opinion is even worse for memoirists, as critics judge not only their written words but also their lives and how they've lived them.

Although you may feel that your ethnicity is no one's business, cer-tain marketing opportunities are available to you if, for example, you are Jewish or black or Irish American. Many African-American book-stores and Black Expos (or fairs) offer good venues for writers to promote and sell their books. Jewish book fairs and newspapers are happy to promote Jewish writers.

Mention any languages that you speak other than English. The information is helpful to the person in the subrights department who will sell foreign rights. Sufficient international interest might open the opportunity to promote the foreign editions of your book.

BOOKS THAT COMPETE OR COMPARE WITH YOURS

It is important to know what books that are already published cover the same subject area or are written for the same audience. In a sales call, the sales rep will mention comparative titles to the bookseller, who will then check their sales. The thinking is that if the comparative titles sold well to that customer base, then your book could sell well, also. Therefore, in your marketing plan, provide the title, author, publication date, publisher, and ISBN for books in your subject area. If the books on your list are well known in your field, then you should explain how your book offers a different point of view, contains new information or offers something different to the reader. With the continual drive for newness among the media and consumers, many books on the same subject easily coexist in the book marketplace. What matters is that you convey to your publisher, and by extension to booksellers, that your book offers a particular point of view that will help it sell well in its category, despite the competition. Do not throw down every title that's been published in your field on your list of comparative titles. Other books that have sold poorly do not help your sales rep sell your book, unless the rep can convince the bookseller that yours is simply the best book on the subject.

When the sales reps were selling an important cookbook on the Hearst list, their use of comparative titles during the sales call was essential. The buyers naturally compared the book, *The All New Good Housekeeping Cookbook*, to its key competition—other name-brand cookbooks. The booksellers, while aware of the high sales figures for branded cookbooks, wanted to know that book offered something different and special to the consumer. Consequently, our marketing team prepared a detailed chart for the sales reps that compared the *Good Housekeeping* book to all its competition point by point, including page count, trim size, number of recipes, number of color photos, ability to lie flat, and so on. The evidence was overwhelming: The book clearly surpassed its competition in most categories, and the sales reps got the buys they were aiming for.

Comparative titles also help your publicist frame a pitch for the book. By telling a book reviewer that "Jane Doe's new detective will satisfy fans of Hercule Poirot," the publicist helps the book reviewer understand right away that the book is a mystery of a certain category and caliber. Of course your book is an original work. Nonetheless, an apt comparison to another successful book communicates a salable handle for your book.

You might also compare the book to a film or other form of entertainment. In my letters to reviewers, I once compared a first novel by Alexander Stuart called *The War Zone* to the film *Blue Velvet,* in that the surface of the characters' lives cloaked a seamy emotional turmoil. The concept worked and the novel was widely reviewed.

Take your time coming up with comparison titles that will help your sales reps and publicist make the case for your book. This task is often left to the editor or the editorial assistant, but you know the literature in your field better than anyone else does.

PROFESSIONAL AND PERSONAL CONTACTS

Let your publisher know how your contacts can help make the book a success. They may throw you a party, arrange for you to speak at local organizations where they have their own contacts, monitor the presence of your book in stores once it's published, or give you a spare bed when you're in town on your publicity tour. Try to plumb these possibilities before you begin your marketing dialogue with your publisher. The more support you can establish in the early planning stage, the more likely you are to motivate your publisher to get excited about your book's potential.

If your contacts are sufficiently well known at least in their own field, then ask them for a "blurb," or a positive endorsement, for your book. This will appear on your book jacket or book flaps and in the publicity material. The names of the "blurbers" are meant to signal to the consumer that your book is worthy of buying and reading.

If you do not know any suitable blurbers, then simply write a list of names of appropriate potential candidates. Be imaginative. Though you've written a book on design, a novelist or even a filmmaker might give you a quote if your work resonates somehow with their own. Look for blurbers who will trigger positive recognition among your target audience. (The other day a friend told me that she bought a book only because a novelist she admires had endorsed it.) Your editor may approach some of the blurbers you've suggested through his or her own contacts.

Your contacts are also useful for you to create a mailing list database. When you create this list, do not stint yourself. Dig deep into your past friendships and business and academic relationships. People will be happy to hear what you're up to.

Alternately, your database might take the form of an e-mail database. Beyond your own e-mail contacts, tap into the e-mail addresses of your friends and family: Ask them to kindly forward your announcements to anyone they know who might also take an interest in your work.

You will state in your marketing plan your intent to send press releases to your database just as the book arrives in bookstores, to motivate your core audience to buy your book early on. That way your book can start to build some sales momentum and reorders. Your publicist will mail a press release to the list at your request. (If your publicist is truly swamped and unable to get this mailing out on time, offer to stuff and address the releases for her. But ask her if the publisher will pay for the postage and mailing costs.)

Building a database is somewhat time-consuming and somewhat dull, so it is a task best handled over a long period of time, perhaps for fifteen to thirty minutes a day over several weeks or months.

One successful author has mastered the art of marketing among his existing relationships to create a grassroots groundswell of interest in his books. With the assistance of a supportive family, he assembled significant crowds at bookstore readings in ten cities. "Book signings are a way to say thank you," this author says, and acknowledges his friends and family as an essential part of his publishing process. He advises authors who are creating a mailing list not to worry about having a large list, which is expensive to mail to. Instead, he advises that you concentrate on developing a core list of people who care about you and your books.

YOUR PUBLIC SPEAKING AND MEDIA EXPERIENCE

If the media has ever interviewed you, or if you regularly deliver speeches as part of your professional life, tell your publisher. Your level of experience and competence in public speaking and in media appearances will influence the size and scope of the publicity campaign that your publisher puts together.

Attach any significant press clips to the marketing plan. Even better, the names and phone numbers of reporters and producers who have interviewed you is very helpful information for your publicist. If you have videos of your interviews on television, state here that you can make those available upon request. Your publicist will watch the tapes to evaluate your media skills.

YOUR TOP TEN PUBLICITY GOALS

You will most certainly get your publisher's attention if you include your top ten publicity goals in your marketing campaign. By defining what you want, you've given the publisher's publicity and marketing team something to react to and address.

Your goals may very well change or evolve as your book progresses toward publication. That's OK. Just make the first stated set of publicity goals realistic to demonstrate that you understand the media market. For example, if you write commercial fiction, understand that the chance of a review in the more literary book review media is slim.

To know what's within reach, you have to do your homework. Read and watch the media to find out where your book could fit in. It takes practice to understand what the media thinks is a good story.

Often the most desired goal for a successful publishing launch is to get on *The Oprah Winfrey Show,* the single most influential media on book sales for more than a decade. Oprah Winfrey has democratized and demystified the act of reading, and so has encouraged reading— and book buying—among a broad swathe of the population. (As one book marketer says, all publishers should bow down daily in the direction of Chicago, where Oprah's show is taped, and thank her for what she has done for reading and for book sales.) However, no secret formula exists for appearing on *The Oprah Winfrey Show.* A persistent publicist can talk an author onto the show after months and even years of pitching a concept, or sheer fluke and luck of timing might lead to a speedy booking on the first try. And even then, the appearance does not guarantee bestsellerdom. While you should put time and thought into figuring out how your book might interest Oprah's producers (and more on that later), getting on *Oprah* shouldn't be the only focus of your book's campaign strategy. In any case, before you decide what show is right for your book you should familiarize yourself with that show by watching (or taping) and observing. What topics are discussed, what authors are interviewed, how is the interview conducted, and so on.

Beyond Oprah, the following media outlets have influenced book sales for many years:

■ Longer format shows like *Dateline NBC,* or *60 Minutes.*

■ The national evening news on one of the network stations—a supremely difficult placement to get but one that reaches many millions of people.

■ *Today, Good Morning America, The Early Show*—ranked by audience size, the networks' morning television shows offer a great media launch for a book. In Canada, a spot on *Canada AM* is desirable.

■ Television shows with on-air book clubs. Since Oprah ended her book club in 2002, other shows launched book club segments including *Today*, which has a bestselling author choose a book and then invites a reading group on air to talk about the title; *Good Morning America*, which features a different reading group's book club choice for each "Read This" segment; and the monthly "Reading with Ripa" segment on *Live with Regis and Kelly*.

■ National Public Radio's programming, like *All Things Considered*, and national radio shows like *Imus in the Morning*. NPR's shows can help sell quality literary fiction and nonfiction. Don Imus talks about an eclectic assortment of books on his nationally syndicated radio program, ranging from the literary to the quirky. In Canada, the CBC's *This Morning* is national and has an upscale audience. Despite its raunchy content, *Howard Stern* can also be surprisingly productive for authors who want to reach a male audience.

■ A write-up in a nationally syndicated column can reach millions of readers. Columnists who sometimes mention books are William Safire (language, *New York Times Magazine*), Dave Barry (humor, based at the *Miami Herald*), Molly Ivins (a feminist, liberal perspective at the *Ft. Worth Star-Telegram*) are just a few examples. You can find the names of syndicated columnists and sample columns through the Internet. (Chapter Six, page 131, lists the appropriate links.)

■ CNN's *Larry King Live*.

■ PBS's *The Charlie Rose Show*.

■ A feature in the national wire service, the Associated Press.

■ A feature article in one of the nationally distributed newspapers like *USA Today*, the *New York Times*, the *Wall Street Journal*, and, in Canada, the *Globe and Mail*. Also effective is a feature article in a local newspaper—even a small community paper—which gets syndicated through one of the news syndicates like Gannett, Scripps Howard, Cox, or Knight Ridder.

All of these shows have Web sites, which you can easily find through your search engine.

SALES LEADS

Special sales—high volume and generally nonreturnable orders to non-bookstore customers—can be highly profitable. Finding viable leads is one of the most time-consuming parts of the special sales business. Most special sales outlets are unconcerned about the newness of a title and will reorder a book as long as it continues to sell. Unlike bookstores, which buy books based on catalogs, galleys, and sales reps presentations, most special sales channels will consider a book for purchase only after they've seen a finished copy. Even then, some special sales outlets may not commit to a book until they've test-marketed it or until the appropriate buying season.

Special sales accounts include mail-order catalog companies (Signals, Miles Kimball, Jessica's Biscuit); nonbook retailers (T. J. Maxx, gift shops); display marketers (Scholastic, Books Are Fun, Publications International) who set up book displays in schools, hospitals, and businesses and collect bulk orders; gift wholesalers (Cogan Books); and others.

Special sales opportunities exist primarily for nonfiction books, and rarely for fiction. If your book has some connection to a type of product or service, then it is a candidate for special sales. Your book may in fact already include special sales leads in its resource section. For example, if your book is about candle making, then you've probably listed vendors of candle-making materials, which your publisher's special sales reps can approach to sell your book. Cookbooks benefit from many special sales opportunities, as nonbook retailers will frequently offer cookbooks as customer premiums. Books about health are candidates for premium sales to HMOs or to pharmaceutical companies.

THE AUTHOR PHOTO

In some instances, the author photo becomes a significant part of a marketing campaign. Certainly you've seen the pictures of celebrity authors and noted writers: Their images are an important part of their book launch. For unknown authors, an interesting or unconventional author photo can help create a media profile, as newspapers and magazines are more likely to reproduce the image adjacent to a review or interview. Susan Minot's debut novel was promoted alongside her striking author photo. Sebastian Junger's first book, *The Perfect Storm,* was released along with images of the handsome author hoisting logs, presumably shot during his stint as a climber for a tree company. Dennis Lehane's publisher had him photographed to capture a moody noir image just like the atmosphere of his novels. Publishers view the image of the author as a vital part of the marketing campaign, particularly for novels and memoirs.

Your publisher will eventually ask you to provide a photograph of yourself for use on your book jacket and in publicity materials. Ask your editor if the publishing house intends to pay to have you photographed. Publishers will sometimes pay for author photos (an item that may be addressed in your contract). Otherwise you will need to provide a decent jacket photograph on your own dime.

If you do not have a good recent photo of yourself, and if your publisher isn't planning on having one taken, then have an experienced, if not professional photographer take your picture. The photo should be shot in color, giving the publisher the option to print in either color or black and white. Or e-mail your publisher a JPEG file of a photo taken with a digital camera, which can also be handy later for posting on your Web site (if you have one) or for sending your image to publications or Web sites that might want a photo to accompany a review or an interview.

Some authors give their publishers blurry photos or family snapshots for their book jackets. Many people feel ambivalent about their looks, and their anxiety often reveals itself in their choice of author photos. Remember that the consumer will often look at the picture of the author while considering buying a book. And a couple of book critics have told me that as they peruse the pile of books to decide which ones to assign for review, a good-looking author photo "doesn't hurt." One fellow, a book reviewer who was notorious for not returning publicist's phone calls, called me back moments after I left a message that the book I was calling about was written by an attractive blonde of Jewish and Italian descent. I shamelessly played on that critic's particular preferences, but he called me back to talk about the book. Even radio producers will respond to an author's good looks, though the author's appearance can clearly have no effect on listenership. I called one NPR producer to follow up on a pitch about a relatively unknown author. She booked him on the spot, telling me in a knowing voice, "Oh yes, we've all just been looking at his photograph." You have every reason to look your best or most interesting in your author photo.

Every now and then an article appears about the "new" trend of promoting the images of good-looking authors, and usually someone is quoted huffing and puffing about how terrible and debasing to the literary merits of the work this is. This may be true, but it is naïve to pretend that critics and producers do not make any judgments based on someone's appearance.

Again, do your homework. Go to the bookstore and browse the bookshelves for author photos that you think are successful and attention-getting. You will notice how family snapshots rarely make ideal author photos.

BESTSELLER LISTS—HOW IMPORTANT ARE THEY?

Not all lists are created equal, but they can all help your book. The *New York Times* bestseller list used to be the only one that really counted, but its clout has diminished in recent years. The two largest chains, Barnes & Noble and Borders, no longer use the *Times* list, and instead use internal sales rankings to determine bestsellers and the candidates for up-front display and discounting. (Discounting is good, making the book more affordable for more people.) Although it is no longer the only game in town, a spot on the *New York Times* bestseller list gives the sales reps an opportunity to call on their customers and sell-in more copies. Success breeds success: Your appearance on the list gives your publicist another way to pitch your book to the media and earns you another credential.

Other national bestseller lists include the *Wall Street Journal* and *USA Today*, perhaps the most purely democratic of the lists, as it mingles all formats and price points. Books sometimes become regional or local bestsellers before becoming a national bestseller. Many newspapers offer bestseller lists, with the data gathered from local bookstores. These include the *Boston Globe*, the *Rocky Mountain News* (Denver), the *San Francisco Chronicle*, and the *Washington Post*, among others. Others will run lists supplied by *Publishers Weekly* or the *New York Times*. Effective publicity in regional markets can help to drive books onto the local lists quickly.

Some authors have attempted to manipulate the bestseller lists by asking friends and associates to buy multiple copies of their books within the same week. This tactic can work in a limited way only: It is expensive and some booksellers will not report bulk purchases to bestseller lists to eliminate the chances of list manipulation. Before you embark on this strategy, think of the economics. Say you purchase fifty copies of your hardcover book in one market, then you're probably investing about $1,300 just to get onto one local bestseller list for one week, a tactic that may or may not work. For the amount of cash you will have to spend, you may as well enlarge your publicity efforts to extend your reach further, create some real readers and word of mouth, and produce effects that last longer.

Amazon.com has taken bestseller lists to another level by ranking every single title's sales at any given moment. Infuriatingly or wonderfully, any author can find out how his or her book ranks at any time of day. A good television or radio appearance can stimulate immediate sales and send you zooming to the top of Amazon's list or sales ranking. Remember that the ranking is no indication of sales volume—which can be a very low number—but rather a reflection of how your book's sales compare to every other book on this site in that hour.

FOUR GREAT PUBLICITY AND MARKETING WEB SITES

The following sites offer great advice on book marketing and publicity. While three of the sites sell various kinds of services—whether newsletters, books, or consulting—they also offer plenty of good, free information that might help you as you write your marketing plan.

For hundreds of great ideas about how to market your book, go to www.publicityhound.com. Joan Stewart, a.k.a. The Publicity Hound, shares information about how to pitch the media, great Web sites, how to prepare for your interviews, what not to say to reporters, and so on. Her tone is smart, friendly, and inspiring. You can subscribe to a free weekly e-newsletter, which offers tips on publicity and promotion. Not all of them will apply to your book, but you will come away with many good ideas. Print out the extensive archives for previous editions of this newsletter and you will find much of interest. You can also participate in her reasonably priced tele-seminars on various themes, which you'll read about in the newsletter: Recent conferences with a media trainer and a producer have focused on how to get on daytime talk shows like *The Oprah Winfrey Show* and *The View,* and how to get on drive-time radio shows. If you can't participate, then you can buy the transcripts.

Dan Poynter's site, www.parapublishing.com, targets the self-published author and is filled with great links and good information on marketing and promotion resources. The site offers a lot of free information about the media and other aspects of book publishing, as well as a free electronic newsletter. Para Publishing also offers books, tapes, seminars, and consulting on a full range of publishing topics.

The site www.bookzonepro.com offers tips for authors and publishers and other publishing professionals. Here you will find hundreds of articles about marketing, publicity, public speaking, advertising, a very useful calendar of events in publishing, great links to bestseller lists and marketing resources, and more. The site is very well organized, making it easy to find articles related to your interests. Much of the information is geared to small publishers, which also applies to authors involved in their own publicity efforts.

The fourth site is www.readerville.com, a community for readers and writers. While technically it's not a publicity and marketing site, you will find plenty of good information about promoting your book. The site contains hundreds of active discussion groups on nearly any book and publishing related subject you can think of, from interviews with authors and discussions about Harry Potter and Irish literature to forums offering publishing advice and the latest news in publishing.

AN AUTHOR'S MARKETING PLAN IN ACTION

Beth Bruno's marketing plan for her self-published parenting book, *Wild Tulips,* is short and simple. (Actually, it is deceptively simple because it evolved over time, as the author discovered what marketing techniques work and what don't.) While the written plan does not elaborate on specific strategies, it does serve as a constant reminder to Bruno of her overall intent.

The plan is governed by Bruno's knowledge of her core audience, her experience in education, and her understanding of her own capabilities: Bruno is not trying to take on more than she can manage herself. Instead she started in a methodical, grassroots way and built from there.

Marketing Plan: *Wild Tulips*

Audience: mothers, fathers, teachers (pre-K through adult), special educators, mental health professionals, pediatricians and OB-GYN physicians, grandparents, child caregivers, writers, small business owners (which Bruno includes because she networks with local businesspeople at luncheons and other gatherings), homeschoolers, clergy, nonprofit family support organizations, storytellers, and the young at heart.

Media: newspapers, magazines, television, radio, the Internet.

Retail: bookstores (chains and independents), gift shops, other stores.

Wholesalers

Libraries

Corporate and nontraditional markets

General approaches in all markets:
Direct contact—in person or by telephone

E-mail

Regular mail—sales letters to friends, colleagues, and associates

Advertising

Book talks

Book signings

Conference seminars

Seeding (free copies of *Wild Tulips*)

Bruno has implemented her plan in an ongoing and effective campaign. She has nearly sold out of her first printing and is ready to look for a publisher for her book. Some of her marketing efforts included:

- Direct sales efforts to friends, relatives, and colleagues, which "started sales off with a bang," Bruno reports.

- A local librarian was featured in a newspaper article about a "gifts to newborns" program. Bruno contacted the librarian, who then bought eighty copies of the book and will buy more when she gets more funding.

- Appearances at local bookstores and libraries have had good crowds, good book sales, and generated invitations to speak at other events, including at writer's groups about self-publishing.

- A local hair salon agreed to display a poster and copies of the book, as part of a celebration of local artists and authors. The salon sold dozens of books and invited Bruno to return for a fund-raiser later in the year.

▪ Bruno has booked herself into the annual Connecticut Storytelling Festival to present a workshop about the craft of writing stories. (There are local, statewide, and regional storytelling festivals that take place annually around the United States.) Jonesborough, Tennessee, is home to the National Storytelling Festival in October. Bruno contacted The Storytelling Store there and convinced them to offer *Wild Tulips*.

▪ Bruno is developing parenting workshops for preschools. She is also targeting Headstart as a workshop sponsor, her thinking being that relevant organizations with grant money will offer a fruitful way to promote and sell the book.

▪ Online initiatives have included chats and free articles, though Bruno thinks that Internet promotion has delivered less promotional value considering the amount of time invested.

Bruno's experience offers an encouraging example for writers undertaking their own promotions. While she felt shy calling bookstores, her confidence was bolstered after the first few positive responses. "After a few people said yes, it got easier," she says.

HOW TO WRITE A MARKETING PLAN—A SUMMARY

Tackle the marketing plan's individual components to come up with a complete, step-by-step plan for promoting your book. Once you've assessed your own goals for the book as well as your personal resources—such as your contacts—you will define your audiences and figure out how they can benefit from your book. Spend some thoughtful time figuring out your positioning statement and your audience. You can't come up with a meaningful marketing strategy until you know who you are trying to reach and why.

Then you will figure out how to reach your audiences through various strategies such as:

- Connecting to current news trends or creating a controversy

- Conducting a survey

- Creating a celebrity angle

- Joining forces with other authors to set up group events

- Planning for demonstrations or tastings

- Providing interesting visuals

- Public speaking

- Setting up an award

- Staging a fund-raiser, a panel discussion, a party, or a stunt

- Continuing to pay attention to the media to identify opportunities for your book

3

YOU'VE SUBMITTED YOUR MANUSCRIPT. NOW WHAT?

TO work effectively with your publishing house, you must understand the normal sequence of events leading to your book's publication. You need details about who does what and when they do it. For example, some houses require that the publicists make contact with all the authors at least once. Other houses do not. Their publicity staffs have no obligation to contact an author—particularly one whose book has no significant plans. So if you have not heard from your publicist within four months of your book's publication, then ask your editor for her name and politely make contact. This way you can apprehend in good time what, if anything, the house has planned for your book. Then, at least, you have information early enough to self-market and self-promote your work.

THE NUTS AND BOLTS (PART ONE): WHO DOES WHAT

The following job descriptions apply to a large publishing house. In a smaller house or an academic press, the job functions may be shared among a smaller staff. However the nature of the work remains the same for any size house.

Publisher: The decision to acquire a book, how much to pay for it, and the approved marketing budget all fall under the publisher's purview.

The publisher establishes the overall direction of the publishing house and is ultimately responsible for all the decisions that are made about the publishing list. Usually the editorial, sales, and marketing staffs all report to the publisher. In some houses, the sales team reports to another person, perhaps the president, which means that the publisher has less direct control over the sales force.

Editor in Chief/Editor: Your editor most likely reports to the editor in chief who would have endorsed the original acquisition. The editor in chief works in partnership with the publisher and brings in the books that the publisher is willing to publish. Your editor is the point person for all activities surrounding your book. He or she is responsible for conveying everything that the publishing staff needs to know about your book in order to position it in the marketplace and publish it well. The editor is your advocate and representative in-house.

Sales Director, National Account Reps, Field Force, Special Sales Reps, Tele-marketing Sales Force, Canadian Rep Group: Everyone in the sales group sells your book into his or her sales territory. The reps take their direction from the publisher, who sets the house's agenda at sales conferences, and from the sales director, who pushes them to reach their sales targets. A few of the sales reps will work at the publisher's headquarters. These are likely to be the reps that sell the national bookstore chains and special sales reps. Other reps live throughout the United States and Canada and call on accounts in their assigned territories. Some reps are employed by the publishing house. Other reps work on a commission, probably for several publishing houses.

Subsidiary Rights Director: Book club, serial, foreign, audio, large print, and paperback reprint sales are handled in the subrights department. The director may have evaluated the book club and international sales potential of your book before its acquisition. Serial sales are excerpts of your book that appear in magazines or newspapers. First serial refers to excerpts that appear before publication date; second serials run after publication date.

Director of Production and the Production Staff: You may never meet the production manager assigned to your book. This person works with the printer to determine manufacturing costs based on the trim size and extent of your book. He or she buys the paper and other goods and services required to manufacture your book, and sets the press date. If you deliver your manuscript late, the production manager, in tandem with the managing editor, works with the printer to try to accommodate the tardiness and keep your book on schedule.

Art Director: This person may run the jacket design department, and depending on the publishing house, may also run the interior design department. A successful jacket or cover design is of utmost significance to a book's success.

Marketing Director: This person is often involved with acquisition decision-making, particularly during a competitive acquisition that requires the publishing house to produce a marketing plan. The director will set overall advertising and promotion budgets. The marketing staff assembles and distributes all the sales materials such as catalogs and copies of book jackets, handles the preparations for sales conferences, and sets up mailings and promotions to booksellers.

Publicity Director: The person who runs the publicity department formulates the overall strategy for the top titles on the list and supervises a staff of publicists. The directors generally meet with the major media several times a year to present the publishing list. Some directors, particularly in smaller publishing houses, will handle some book campaigns themselves. With a number of talented publicists rising to the top of the publicity department, a publishing house might have several directors, but only one of those runs the entire group. This person will also get involved with competitive acquisitions.

Your Publishing Team

You will work most closely with your editor, your publicist, the editor's assistant, and the publicist's assistant. Yes, everyone else is important, too, but these four people will be among your closest contacts and sources of information. From the moment your book is acquired, you will make friends with your editor's assistant. Underpaid and overworked, these assistants are the unnoticed heroes in any publishing house. Treat your editor's assistant well and you will have a valuable ally in your camp. The assistant can tell you why the editor isn't calling you back, remind the editor to call you, and help generate buzz in the house among all the assistants (who go to parties with assistants from other houses and start to spread the word about you and your book).

Similarly, the publicist's assistant, whom you will meet later, can keep you in the loop when the publicist is too busy to get back to you right away. This person is learning publicity and may set up a few of your bookings. She is probably also taking care of all your travel arrangements if you are touring. Be a friend to this person, too.

Many other people are involved in creating and publishing your book. The managing editor helps keep all the schedules on track, the copyeditor may be the unseen hand that made good suggestions to improve your book, and the sales and marketing administrative staffs put together your sales kit. Take the time to find out their names and drop them thank-you notes. (Never underestimate the power of the handwritten thank-you note. The recipients will remember you.)

NUTS AND BOLTS (PART TWO): THE SEQUENCE OF EVENTS THAT LEAD TO THE PUBLICATION OF YOUR BOOK

Understanding the flow of work that leads to your publication will help you get involved at key junctures to influence your book's success. This is a typical schedule at many publishing houses, but you should check with your editor about your own book's schedule. Here is the sequence:

- Acquisition

- Scheduling of a publication date

- Manuscript submission and editing

- In-house launch meeting where your editor formally presents your book to key sales, publicity, and marketing staffs. (Publishing houses have different names for the launch: It could be called publishing planning, the title meeting, or something else. But the substance of the meetings is the same.)

- Jacket planning and design

- Ongoing publishing planning leading up to the printing of the publisher's catalog and sales conference

- Sales reps make the first early calls on national bookstore chains

- Sales conference or the meeting where your editor (or other staff person) presents your book to the entire sales force. This generally occurs about three months after the launch meeting, and three to eight months preceding your publication date depending on how early or late your book is scheduled in the publishing season.

- Editor sends out bound galleys for advance endorsements (three to five months before publication). Publicist sends galleys to long lead magazines and book reviewers.

- The print run is set (two to three months before publication, longer for illustrated books)

- Publicist books the tour and sends the book to reviewers (four to six weeks before publication date)

- Early trade reviews begin to come in (*Publishers Weekly, Kirkus Reviews, Library Journal, Booklist*, and *The Horn Book* and *School Library Journal* if you've written a children's book)

- Books are shipped to bookstores about two to four weeks before publication date

- The in-store date is when your book is expected to be fully distributed and publicity can start to happen. The publication date itself is generally cosmetic unless there is a marketing reason to choose a specific date

---

A Publishing Time Line from an Author's Point of View

Author Neil Gaiman kept an online diary in the months leading up to and after the publication of his novel *American Gods*. Read it at www.american-gods.com in the journal archives to get an excellent idea of the sort of planning and activities that can take place leading up to a book's publication. The site also offers a good example of how the author creates an ongoing and authentic conversation with his readers.

HELP YOUR EDITOR PREPARE FOR THE LAUNCH MEETING

The publisher, marketing, sales, subrights, art, and publicity directors and some of their staffs attend the editors' presentations for the books planned for publication in a particular season. In a large publishing house the launch meetings take place over several days. During the editor's presentation, the members of the publishing staff are making up their minds about the book's potential, whether it should get a tour or a significant promotion budget, the likely size of the first printing—all of which makes the editor's on-target positioning of the book essential. As an author, you can influence the meeting from afar. The primary task is to get the decision makers as excited and motivated as possible about your book. Truth is that most of them *want* to get excited about books. You just need to show them why they should like yours.

Begin by offering to help your editor prepare the tip sheet, or title information sheet, the working document used at the launch meeting. Every publishing house has its own format for the tip sheet, but it is usually two to three pages long and includes a book description, sales handles, your bio, and main competition. If your editor is willing to let you take a crack at writing the first draft of the tip sheet then ask for an e-mail copy of the house's tip sheet template. (See pages 292–296 for sample tip sheets.)

Some editors come to launch meetings with incomplete tip sheets, often intending to finish them later on in the season—a disservice to the book, as it forces members of the staff to use inadequate information on their early sales calls. For example, the subsidiary rights department needs to pitch the book clubs early in the planning process. The marketing and sales staffs also need informative tip sheets to create their publishing plans. As you can see, it makes good business sense to provide your editor with enough information to create a persuasive tip sheet. Thus you can help your editor be an effective advocate for your book in the launch meeting.

If a marketing reason exists to request a specific publication date, then now is the time to make that point. An obvious example is a book on love that might carry a Valentine's Day publication date. A book that addresses the workplace could be launched on Labor Day. A book on education might be published in August to coincide with the bookstores' back-to-school promotions. Black History Month takes place in February, around which bookstores will set up promotions. Gay Pride Month is in June, which is why some gay-theme titles are published then to afford maximum display exposure in bookstores. A book that ties into a historical anniversary could use that date as publication day. Again, check out *Chase's Calendar of Events* to find a date that might be appropriate.

Publication dates used to serve as concrete guidelines for reviewers for when a book review should run. While book review editors try to schedule a review to appear around the same time as the book's publication date, many book review sections are backlogged. Some reviews appear weeks after a book's publication. Unless the book's publication is highly anticipated—such as Joyce Maynard's memoir that recalled her years with J. D. Salinger—reviews can trickle out over the course of several months. If you choose a publication date that is somehow tied to an event or anniversary, then you might be able encourage timely reviews.

If you think you should tour for your book, then prior to the launch meeting, suggest to your editor that the house avoid publishing the book in television's sweeps months—February, May, and November. During sweeps, the ratings determine how much the stations can charge advertisers. Therefore the programmers and producers schedule the most compelling and sensational shows and guests possible. If your book does not address a hot topic, and if you're not a celebrity, your chances for television bookings are slim. If your book's publication date occurs in a sweeps month, then work with your publicist to schedule your tour during the following month, rather than trying to book you on television during the months of greatest competition.

The launch meeting is an opportunity to distribute additional information about you and your book. This might include any significant press coverage for previous books or achievements, excerpts from past good reviews, a mini biographical essay that entertains and informs, and so on. Concentrate on providing only the most interesting and useful information for your publishing team.

Last, and this idea may sound kooky, but there's nothing better than food to perk up a room full of tired people who have been in a daylong meeting. It gives them a welcome, unanticipated break. And most important for your book, the sugar temporarily raises everyone's energy level. Arrange with your editor and editor's assistant to have cookies and milk (or some tasty something) delivered to the meeting just as your editor is presenting. The participants will remember you, even though you are not present, which is what you want. It doesn't matter if your book is a cookbook or not. This is just plain old bribery by food. (However, bake *tasty* cookies. I attended a meeting where an editor unwittingly served revolting homemade muffins in an effort to sell the in-house staff on a new cookbook. She meant well, but the food actually hurt the cookbook in people's minds because the recipe had come from the book.) Do not be discouraged if your editor objects to having food at the meeting. The approach might not fit his or her style. Go with the flow.

THE RIGHTS GUIDE

The rights guide is an annotated list of upcoming titles that the sub-rights department creates for foreign publishers and book clubs. Again, ask the editorial assistant whether she can use your help in producing the summary paragraph that's required for the guide, or show you what she plans to submit to the subrights department. Very often this task is done in haste and with limited knowledge of your work, so your involvement could make your book's description just that much better.

The subrights department might try to sell foreign rights to your book at the Frankfurt Book Fair. (Publishers from around the world assemble in Frankfurt every October to buy and sell publishing rights to one another. A savvy subrights director can make an array of foreign sales for a book all in the course of the week.) Give your editor as much of the manuscript as possible in September for the rights director to take with her to Frankfurt.

BOOK JACKET DESIGN

Your publisher will schedule jacket design meetings around the time of the launch meetings—either shortly before or after. Help your editor and the jacket designer by outlining several cover concepts. Spend some time in bookstores to understand which jackets are effective and eye-catching. Educate yourself about the competition in your subject area. With more than 50 percent of book-purchasing decisions made at the bookshelf (as opposed to predetermined by the customer before they came into the store) your jacket's selling power is essential. Make a list of the visual elements in your book that could inspire an interesting book jacket design. Your art director will not have time to read every book on the list and will appreciate your notes.

Ask your editor if you can see early drafts of jacket designs. Note that if you do not have jacket consultation rights in your contract, then your publisher is not obliged to show it to you until it's finished. Some publishers are more willing than others to show jackets to the authors. If you do get to see the jacket while it is still a work in progress, first allow yourself to be surprised by an art director's originality. Then listen to why your editor thinks the jacket is effective. If you're not sure if the jacket is right, show the jacket to your agent, your friends and associates, and then get back to your editor within a couple of days with your suggestions. In the end, if you don't like the jacket, do not accept a design that you really dislike. If you're not at the top of the list, the publishing house will not make your jacket a top priority so you and your agent might need to lobby hard for a new design.

Once a front cover design is approved, ask to see the spine and back of the jacket, too. Publishers often forget to embellish the spine of a jacket, which is often the only part of the book that's exposed to consumers in bookstores. If your cover has a graphic element, ask that it be repeated on the spine to help the book stand out. Or if the book has an all-type cover, then eye-catching colors and typeface should be used on the spine.

It is said that verbal people often lack a sense of design. If this is true, then it makes sense that both you and your editor might have trouble figuring out how to direct the jacket designer. Some editors do not know what they want but tell the designer that they will know it when they see it, which does not make the art director's task easy. Conversely, many designers are not as sensitive to the use of type as heavy readers, and make the type treatment on the book jacket subsidiary to the overall design. Be reassured. The jacket for your book will finally emerge despite—perhaps even because of—the tension inherent in these creative relationships. Your can assist the process to your benefit. An easy way to provide input is to let your editor know which jackets (in the same category as your book) you find appealing. Having something to show the art director is very helpful.

A note of advice: Show respect to your jacket designer. His or her ego is on the line, too. Yes, the book is yours, but the design is not: The designer's creativity is on display, just as your own is. Be sensitive to your designer's feelings and you will more likely have a cooperative and willing design partner in creating the ideal jacket for your book.

If the jacket you hate is the one that ends up in the publisher's catalog, it's not too late for the jacket to be redesigned. Most publishers will respond to an author who is truly unhappy with a book's jacket design. As soon as your new jacket design is ready, make sure that your editor follows up with the art department and the sales administrative staff to redistribute revised copies of the jacket to all the sales reps to share with their accounts. Check that your editor has alerted the sales force that the jacket has changed.

PUBLISHING PLANS TAKE SHAPE

The planning season following launch and leading up to sales conference is the most critical stage leading up to your book's publication. This is roughly a three- to four-month period during which you have a real chance to truly convince the publishing team that your book deserves time and money to reach its market.

Just after launch, talk to your editor about the ideal publicist for your book. Encourage your editor to lobby the director of publicity for the publicist of choice. The editor will not always get his or her request, but can sometimes influence the publicity director's decision. Whether the publicist assigned to your book is good, bad, or indifferent, you can make her an essential ally in your campaign. During this period you will also assess whether to hire your own publicist.

At the appropriate time—either shortly before or after launch—your editor should arrange for you to meet key people in the organization. If the editor doesn't mention this to you, then ask when he or she plans to introduce you to the others on your publishing team. The introduction might be informal—you meet the team in passing when you drop by your editor's office. Or your editor might set up a formal planning meeting with your publicist or with the larger publishing team. No matter the size or formality of the meeting, treat it like a sales call, as though you are informing the participants for the first time why they and the buying public should read your book. Do not take offense if no one in the room other than you and your editor has read your book. These people are *busy*. The editor may not have given them your manuscript yet, or they may not have had time to get to it. Do not add to the sense of guilt they already may feel: Most people in publishing have a never-diminishing stack of manuscripts by their bedsides. Instead, view them as the public you will convince to read your book that very night.

Bring copies of your marketing plan for everyone attending the meeting. Do not assume they've seen your plan or have had a chance to read and focus on it. At the meeting, your job is to ingratiate yourself. You are so thrilled to be with these people right now in this room that they can feel your glow. And you will maintain this attitude throughout the campaign because it will motivate your publicist. (I worked with an author whom the writer William Maxwell would have described as "a woman who never draws breath except to complain." Every time I called her, even when I had good news, she managed to turn the conversation to focus on what went wrong that day. Boy, was it hard to keep pitching that woman's novel and not turn my attention instead to the many other titles on our list. A publishing house has no shortage of interesting projects and or work to do. At the end of every working day, a publicist can always choose to make a few last phone calls to the media. You want your publicist to choose to make those calls for you, and not for another author. Remember that you are competing with other authors on your publicist's assignment list for the same resources—whether those resources are money or your publicist's time and interest.)

If you've ever appeared in the media before, whether on television, radio, or in print, bring copies of tapes and clippings to the meeting. (Do not assume your originals will be returned to you.) Your publicist needs videotapes to pitch television interviews, as producers must assess any guest's on-air abilities. Audiotapes of engaging radio interviews or readings are useful for the sales reps to get to know your work better and to share with their customers—the booksellers. The reps appreciate interesting tapes that they can listen to in the cars en route to the next sales call. Newspaper clippings of interviews provide leads to the publicist to pitch a follow-up story, and help the sales rep prove to booksellers that the media is interested in you. I once worked with an author who at our very first meeting produced audiotapes, clippings, and reading schedules—in short, a full background on his literary life. For a new author, he was particularly savvy about the materials and information that would help me to successfully pitch his book.

Talk about your book in a way that demonstrates your understanding of its market. Everyone in the room is evaluating your potential in the media, and your ability to persuade sales reps and booksellers to support your work and consumers to buy your book. They're thinking about whether you should tour, attend a sales conference to meet all the reps, or meet booksellers at specially arranged events.

Do not be alarmed if your publicist appears to be fresh out of college. Her age doesn't mean that she isn't good at her job. Keep an open mind and remember that many of the media people that your publicist is talking to are the same age as she is. If what she lacks in experience she makes up for in genuine enthusiasm and native intelligence then you're in a good situation that you can work to your advantage.

Do something memorable or eccentric in the meeting. Be charming, roguish, sensitive, and generous. Seduce them. Hand out chocolates. (The food trick again, but it works nearly every time.) An author with whom I worked bought many dozens of red roses, brought them to the office, and personally passed out handfuls to our staff members. You can imagine how his favor increased. The moral of the story: You have to make them remember you.

Be forthright about your goals for the book and your expectations for its publication. Ask them what they hope to see happen for the book. Ask them to explain how they intend to achieve that goal. Once they've committed themselves to you verbally, then they will find it hard to go back on their word later. The commitment gives your agent leverage to prod your publisher to honor its promises, should that become necessary. At the same time, bear in mind that you should not come off as too aggressive in meetings like these. The manner will be off-putting to your publishing team and make them think that you'll be one of those authors who will never be satisfied.

Don't bother asking what the budget is for your book. The number will mean very little. If they tell you $10,000, then what does that mean? That they will spend it on a *New Yorker* ad and call it a day? That would be a mistake. Or that they will send you on a publicity tour? That would be potentially more remunerative. So the point is not what the publisher plans to spend, but rather what it plans to do. If you live in New York or Washington, and the budget formally assigned to your book is $1,000, your publicist can still make your book into a media success. It doesn't take money to get on the national media. It does take time and commitment on your publicist's part to pitch you in the right way for the right shows.

You may have your agent present at the meeting, too, which has drawbacks as well as advantages. On the downside, the agent's presence will make the meeting more formal, and the participants may refrain from sharing fresh ideas, as the agent might try to hold them to anything that comes up during brainstorming. But if your agent is a particularly powerful one, you benefit from senior management deciding to attend the meeting. You will command a higher level of attention.

Don't drag the meeting out too long. These people have no time to spare. Instead start the meeting by thanking everyone for taking the time to meet with you and saying that you hope to keep the conversation short and happy. This will set your tone with everyone, and they will appreciate the fact that you're not someone who will waste their time.

Try to assess which of the people present could become your in-house allies. Don't assume that your editor will continue to be your biggest booster. The nature of an author's relationship with his or her editor ranges widely and may change over the course of the publishing experience. Your publicist could become your strongest ally in the house, and may come away from this meeting so wowed by your media potential that she argues for an aggressive campaign. Or the sales director might take up your book's cause and motivate the sales staff to sell in more books. After the meeting the staff that supports your book will be happy to hear from you with any new marketing and publicity ideas and updates. Put your name and contact information on the plan and invite everyone at the meeting to get in touch if they have questions for you.

Some editors stay very close to an author throughout the publishing process, though a hovering editor can sometimes drive a publicist crazy. Other editors recede into the background once the book has been put into production, leaving the author in the publicist's hands. However, an absentee editor makes a publicist feel isolated in dealing with, say, a difficult author or a book with a difficult-to-pitch topic. Ideally, the editor and publicist should have an active partnership in making sure all publicity opportunities are exploited and drawing the author into ongoing publishing planning.

If a book's sales figures are discouraging, your editor might become incommunicado. Do not be surprised if your publicist stops calling you back. Once your editor has dropped you then the publicist is less motivated to deal with you, as well. The best way to keep all these relationships on track is to state clearly the degree of communication you prefer during the course of the book's campaign. For example, do you want your editor or publicist to share bad reviews with you? Do you want them to share discouraging sales figures with you? Talk to your editor and publicist about these issues early in the planning stages: This way, you will eliminate the cringe factor that they might feel if they have bad news for you later on. Further, you keep the channels of communication open, rather than finding an embarrassed wall of silence suddenly erected between you and your publisher.

A final word of advice about your introduction to your publishing team: If you haven't yet met your publicity director, try to arrange for the publicist or editor to introduce you briefly when you're next in the offices. The publicity director is generally the voice of the department, so if you're creating some good ideas for your book's promotion, then telling the director in person helps reinforce your book in her mind. And when a publicity director is asked to cut budgets (which can happen once or twice a year), she will have a harder time cutting funds for your book when she recalls your pleasant personality and good ideas.

Nine Common Mistakes That Authors Make (and How to Avoid Them)

1. **You get involved too late in marketing planning.** Every publishing house has a sense of where any book ranks on its list by four to six months before publication. Find out what your publisher is thinking and get to work.

2. You are polite to your editor, but you condescend to the editorial assistant. The assistants are the grease that keep your wheels moving—never forget that.

3. You assume that what's printed in the catalog is the final marketing plan for the book. The campaign evolves dramatically as the publication date appears—for better or for worse. Stay involved to make sure it's for the better.

4. You wait too long to hear from the publicist. Don't wait. Because publicists are so overloaded, you might never get the call. If you're not sure of the right time to call, ask your editor.

5. You declare in your first meeting with your publishing team or publicist that you are planning to hire your own freelance publicist. Before you show your hand, explore the publisher's willingness to contribute toward paying a freelancer, particularly if it becomes clear that the house's plans don't meet your expectations, or your publicist is either incompetent or swamped with too many projects to do an effective job.

6. You forget to fill out the author questionnaire and lose the opportunity to position the book and present marketing ideas. If you're not writing a marketing plan, then fill out this questionnaire. If your editor forgets to give you one, then ask for a copy.

7. You don't bother having a decent author photograph taken. A poor photo is a lost marketing opportunity.

8. You behave like a big pain in the butt. Complaining about your campaign, gossiping about the publishing staff, and other passive-aggressive behaviors will alienate you from the publishing team.

9. You forget to say thank you for every little thing that someone at your publishing house does for you.

FOLLOW UP AFTER THAT FIRST MEETING

You might leave your first publishing planning meeting with a number of assignments: to send in copies of past reviews, or provide the names of contacts at the television station where you were once interviewed, or write a short essay describing the inspiration behind the book. Produce the information promptly. You want to stay on the minds of these people. The single worst thing that can happen is that the publishing staff simply does not talk about the book—no follow-up queries, no sales director wanting more information or clarification, no editor tugging on the coattails of a publicity director, no nothing.

The strategy here is plain and effective: Suck up to your publicist. Keep the relationship professional, but treat this woman well. After your initial meeting or conversation in which the publicist will probably give you a fair amount of time, keep the follow-up conversations or correspondences short and to the point. The reason for the brevity: Your publicist's workload is an awesome thing. Depending on the publishing house, a publicist might handle the various stages of publicity campaigns for ten to twelve books at any one time. Perhaps two or three of those books have concurrent book tours. So no matter which publicist you're assigned—whether the department star or the rookie starter—you have to ingratiate yourself to get your share of attention.

Currying your publicist's favor should not stop you from asking the right questions to evaluate her abilities and intent. Ask her what media she's thinking of approaching about your book, and whether she has thoughts about the angles to pitch. Remember: At this early stage she may not have had the opportunity to read your book. So draw her out conversationally, rather than make your questions seem accusatory or overly aggressive. And share with her your own thinking about publicity angles. You can certainly ask her the kinds of campaigns she's worked on before and which ones she liked and why. You will be showing an interest in her work, as well as learning how she approaches her job.

While some authors do not push hard enough for attention, others push too hard and alienate or anger the publicist and the rest of the publishing team. You will need to find the right balance. Express your confidence that she can do a great job on your book. At the same time, ask how you can help her. She will be relieved that you view her as a partner, a fine motivating idea when her extra efforts so often go unnoticed. Talk about your book with conviction and enthusiasm and she will feel that she's backed a winner, who—a bonus!—makes her job easier. Frankly, this is but one of a series of motivational hustles that you should initiate. You have to. No one else will. Yes, now and again your agent can step in to broker relationships for you, but at the end of the day you have to be your own fixer.

You might wonder why a publicist's hard work sometimes goes unnoticed. This happens because publishers launch countless books that get good publicity but don't sell. Naturally, most publishing houses really pay attention only after the book starts to sell—which means that the publicist must be willing to keep on trying even after the first few publicity hits have no apparent effect on sales.

If this is the case, then why should the publicist take the extra step for your book? Adrenaline is one answer. This is how it works: When your publicist secures a hard-fought-for media booking, she gets the publicity equivalent of a runner's high. For any publicist, there's nothing quite like the rush of scoring a good media hit, especially when the publicist likes the book and the author. And when that effort leads to increased sales, your publicist feels even finer. Any publicist who takes her work seriously sees your book as an opportunity to do well—to shine and achieve a good reputation, and consequently, better assignments. One hand washes the other, which is why you must convince her that you're worth supporting.

One of the items on your follow-up agenda is finding out from your editor when the sales reps will call on the national accounts—the booksellers that are responsible for the lion's share of bookstore sales. The chains command about a quarter of the book market. The rep's best chance to sell your book to the store buyer is on the first sales call. So a good first impression on the buyer is essential.

Surprisingly, at many publishing houses, the national reps are left scrambling at the last minute for information and jackets to show their buyers. The marketing and editorial departments should treat the national sales call as a top priority, yet the reps are often left short of the materials they need. Many editors are unaware of the dates of pending sales calls. And when important sales calls are scheduled before the sales conference, the reps have not benefited from conversations about the book with their colleagues.

Therefore, give the reps all the information they need to make the best possible pitch for your book. (While you may never meet the sales reps, your editor will pass any appropriate materials along to them—either directly or through the marketing department.) Assemble a small packet of information that will help the rep, and include any new information, anecdotes, or background data that the rep might find interesting or useful. Don't bombard the rep with a deluge of paperwork. In your brief cover letter, hone in on the points that you think will help the rep make a cogent pitch. Tell your editor that you are planning to prepare this information and that you want to get it into the hands of the national sales reps *before* they make their first sales calls.

Some publishing houses discourage direct communication between authors and reps unless specifically sanctioned ahead of time. In fact, once the selling process starts, some houses discourage much communication between the editors and the sales reps, which means your editor will not be fully informed about the progress of the sales calls. This is particularly true of the larger houses where the reps are selling in many lists from various imprints, and simply wouldn't be able to manage the onslaught of communications if the editors and authors were allowed total access. You will simply need to ask about the protocol at your house.

Ask your editor if he or she can follow up with the sales rep after the sales call to see how it went. Though your editor might feel embarrassed to report back to you if the sales call went badly, insist on hearing about it. If the sales rep's sales pitch just didn't go over, then you and your editor have a chance to come up with a new spin, a new angle to help the book sell in better at the other accounts. The Barnes & Noble sales call will likely be the first. If the sales call went well, then have your editor ask the sales director to share the good news with the other reps. (Chances are, a good sales director will have already done that.) If the reps sell the book in well, ask your editor if you can drop the reps an e-mail note to thank them for their efforts. You might simply e-mail your editor a message to pass on to the reps.

Like the sales rep, your director of publicity makes her first calls on the national media prior to sales conference. She, too, needs all the pertinent promotional information in time to make a cogent pitch. Again, check your editor or publicist, if you're already in contact with her, to ensure that the publicity director has everything she needs to make a cogent early pitch to the nationals. (She may not have been privy to any information that you might have already given your publicist.) Or drop a note to her to give her the information you think she needs. Snaring a national interview—such as *Today* or *Good Morning America* or *20/20*—before a sales conference increases excitement among the sales staff. The early bookings give the reps real ammunition for their sales calls. It's not just the celebrity authors that can get booked during these early publicity calls. If the publicity director knows how to pitch your book well, the topic may just grab the morning show producers enough for them to commit early to a booking.

Make the Most of Your Time to Market Your Book, Even If You Have Only Fifteen Minutes a Day

Perhaps you do not have much time to devote to marketing your book. Here are some ideas about how to use a little time to maximum effect. Only fifteen minutes a day becomes nearly two full hours a week that you can use to market your book. First, resolve to do at least one marketing task a day. Then use your time to come up with sales and marketing angles in the following ways:

- Bookmark a list of publishing and marketing sites (referenced throughout this book) that you'll check frequently to get ideas and learn about the publishing business.
- Research the names of reporters who might cover your book by visiting online newspaper Web sites.
- When you read your daily newspaper, pay attention to any leads to companies and organizations that might offer a book marketing opportunity. Then follow up by making a call. Set a goal of finding and contacting two leads a week. For example, a local business leader is interviewed about a new product aimed at young mothers. Your book targets the same audi-

ence, so call the company and suggest that they sponsor a conference or seminar with you and other panelists.

- Identify people in your circle of familiars who can help you. Send a weekly e-mail to them to solicit ideas, asking: How do you think I should pitch my book to television interviewers? Who is the audience for my book and how can I reach them?
- Gradually build your personal database, the list of people to whom you'll send a press release about your book's publication.
- Join an online writer's group or site that has a forum for asking questions and exchanging information. (One way to locate groups is by typing "writers groups" into your Internet search engine, or looking under the "groups" tab on www.Google.com.) Then start asking the group for advice about marketing. You'll find that other people in your group will be happy to help you. Take a moment to dispense advice to others, where you can.
- Look at www.Oprah.com to get ideas about how your book could fit on *The Oprah Winfrey Show*. Go to the sites for other television shows to look at the archives of previous show topics.

HOW TO TREAT YOUR PUBLICIST TO GET THE BEST RESULTS— A FEW POINTERS

It's an old joke among publicists that the best author is a dead author. It is sad but, in some cases, it is true: Some authors are nightmares to work with. The stories of badly behaved authors are legendary: From the former bombshell movie-star "author" who made her publicist hold the phone to her ear when she made calls, to the British politician-cum-novelist well known for verbally abusing his escorts, to the drunk and well-past-his-prime bestselling novelist who invited his publicist to his hotel room to do cocaine, to those who simply will not stop whining and complaining. No matter how experienced your publicist, she's wondering what you will be like to work with.

Publicists like authors who show up for interviews on time; who are helpful in coming up with good angles to promote the book; who get to the point fast and then get off the phone, or else who get to the point fast and then are willing to chat for a while (and you'll have to figure out the right approach); who empathize with a publicist's workload; who are realistic about a book's potential, and who remember to say thank you. Publicists can't stand naggers and complainers; unrealistic second-guessers ("Have you pitched my book to *60 Minutes* yet?"); passive-aggressive types who complain to the agent or editor behind the publicist's back; spendthrifts who squander the publisher's money on tour and so challenge the publicist's ability to manage the budget; authors who show up late for interviews or go AWOL while on tour, which means that the publicist can't slide in that last-minute booking with the local newspaper; authors who e-mail or call several times a day to report, obsessively, on the book's latest sales ranking on Amazon. (While Amazon's rankings provide an immediate gauge of publicity's effectiveness, the data represents only part of the book-buying market and can't be extrapolated.)

Remember: With inconsiderate behavior, you diminish the level of attention the publicist might have been willing to give your book.

Ideally the relationship to cultivate with your publicist is that of a colleague or partner. The best results will come from your teamwork, where you may contribute a significant amount of creative thinking and legwork. No matter how much or little your publicist does for you, creating an open and mutually supportive and respectful relationship that preserves your access is very important. If you believe that your publicist should do all the work, then you are in for disappointment. She may not have the time to mount the campaign that you think your book deserves. You must get involved in a productive rather than an adversarial way.

Many publicists do fabulous jobs despite their limited resources. Don't assume that your publicist is wrong just because she doesn't agree with some of your marketing ideas. She may in fact have a keen handle on what the media is interested in. Ask her why she thinks your ideas will not fly and what she thinks might work instead. As long as you've got a good and thoughtful conversation flowing, you can work together to craft a campaign. Worry instead when there is no conversation at all.

THE WARNING SIGNS OF AN INCOMPETENT
(OR DISINTERESTED OR OVERWORKED) PUBLICIST—
AND WHAT TO DO ABOUT THEM

- She doesn't return phone calls promptly and publication date is three to four months away.

- She doesn't seem to understand what your book is about.

- She's endlessly caught up in process, like tweaking press materials and researching press lists. But then she doesn't seem to know anyone in the media or talk about her ideas for any pitches.

- She speaks in publicity jargon and you don't know what she's talking about.

- She talks to you about other author campaigns that she's working on but not about yours.

- She dismisses any ideas that you come up with but contributes none of her own.

- She pretends she knows more than she does.

- She wants to get you off the phone quickly.

- You get a nasty sinking feeling in your stomach every time you talk to her.

If you recognize these symptoms in your dealings with your publicist, you are absolutely entitled to complain to your editor. If things look bleak, your editor will likely talk to the director of publicity to ask that she reassign your book to another publicist, or at least pay particular attention to how your campaign unfolds. If your editor is unwilling to have this conversation, then call the director of publicity to have a pleasant but concerned conversation about the caliber of your publicist. You can also choose to get your agent involved. Bear in mind that reassignments seldom happen, and you will need to shoulder a larger share of publicity work than perhaps you had anticipated. On a very few occasions, the publicity director will agree to freelance the book.

AN AUTHOR WHO TALKED HIS PUBLISHER INTO A CAMPAIGN

Gavan Daws wrote a book about the Allied prisoners of the Japanese during World War Two called *Prisoners of the Japanese*. Unfortunately, the book's publicist quit on the eve of publication. In addition, the book had no assigned budget, and the publishing house was going through some turmoil with a newly appointed publisher. A group of new people had just been hired, including me, and the book was not at the top of everyone's mind, especially as we were focusing on the next season. Instead of resigning himself to his fate, Daws presented a cohesive and persuasive argument about why the revelations in his book were newsworthy and why his book was important. I assigned the book to a new publicist, who was itching to make his mark in the business. Through the publicist's persistence, and the fact that Daws's book revealed a little known aspect of World War Two, *Prisoners of the Japanese* got some good media attention, including a feature in the *Washington Post*. For a few weeks the book was the house's number one selling title. The key factor in starting this campaign was Daws's own manner—gently but persistently persuasive and deeply committed to his cause.

THE CATALOG

The sales department sends catalogs to booksellers so they can determine which books to buy. The publicity department sends catalogs to the print and electronic media to select the books and authors worthy of review or interviews. The subrights department sends catalogs to buyers in the rights markets.

Ultimately, a full-blown marketing plan is distilled into the tightest possible format—a page in the publisher's catalog that includes a book description, an author bio, and marketing plans. Ask your editor to see the catalog copy before it's turned over to the marketing department and make any changes that seem important to you, even if you're not invited to. If your suggestions improve the book's positioning, your editor will likely accept them. The deadline for copy probably falls a few weeks after the launch meeting, but check with your editor to be certain.

If your editor shows you poorly written catalog copy, take this as an indication that the house isn't fully prepared to market and sell your book. The good news is that catalog copy is written at a stage when you still have plenty of opportunities to help your publisher better understand your book. So rather than take offense at the poor copy, be glad that you've been given a chance to set things right.

The draft catalog copy may not include the marketing plans, as these are often dropped into the copy after the editorial copy deadlines. If you've not spoken to or met your publicist or publicity director at this point, then your publisher is probably not planning to send you on a book tour. Tour cities are always printed in the catalog and rarely does the publicity department determine the cities without consulting the author. If you are convinced that you should go on tour, you must address this with your editor and publicity director before the catalog (and marketing plans) are finalized. Yes, the plans can evolve to include a book tour even after the catalog is printed, but you are in a stronger position with booksellers when they read in the catalog that the publisher is sending you on a tour.

When you read the printed catalog, you may be surprised to find that your book has been assigned a national print campaign or a national media campaign. Do not necessarily believe what you read. These are merely buzz phrases in the business. A "national print campaign" might simply refer to a review copy mailing to reviewers—standard treatment for any book on the list. "National media campaign" might indicate that a publicist will pitch a few media outlets. Don't be lulled into false security by the catalog promise of a $50,000 advertising campaign. Many an ad budget evaporates by the time publication rolls around. Remember that the copy is designed to hype the book to

the bookselling community to get the best possible advance orders. The key to decoding catalog copy is to stay in touch with your editor.

You hope that your editor tells you the truth about what is going on, rather than falsely raising your expectations about what's planned for your book. Publicists meeting authors for the first time are often stunned to hear the author's unrealistic expectations about publicity based on their editor's promises. The editor may have had good intentions, wanting to keep the author in a positive frame of mind while writing the book. Tell your editor that you'd rather know sooner than later what the house is *really* planning. If you know early on, you are in a better position to address the problem, whether that means hiring your own publicist or doing your own publicity.

SALES CONFERENCE

Prior to sales conference, the marketing department sends sales materials to the reps, including tip sheets and selections from some manuscripts. The reps then come to conference prepared to focus on marketing and sales ideas. At sales conference, your editor, or possibly another staffer, will present your book to the entire sales force.

Publishers have ambivalent feelings about sales conferences. What everyone mostly agrees upon is that face-to-face meetings with the sales reps are valuable for the serendipitous ideas that arise, for in-house staff to learn about what's going on in the marketplace, and for the editors and sales reps to get to know one another. The problem with the conference meetings is that they are long and dull, with only so much information that can sink in before everyone's gone glassy-eyed. However, sales conference is not necessarily the most important part of your book's launch. Chances are, the work in selling your book in-house has already been done—at launch meetings, at informal drop-by-the-sales-director's-office meetings, at impromptu conversations among colleagues in the hallways.

After sales conference your publisher may seem to go into a withdrawn, scarily quiet state as though they've forgotten about your book.

You might not hear from anyone for weeks. In fact this deceptively calm period is a critical stage in the publishing of your book. Your publicist plans the details of your campaign, while the sales reps are on the road selling your book, sending information back to the publisher about how the sell-in is proceeding. Your editor may be only partially informed about how the sales calls are going: Many publishing houses limit the sales feedback in order to prevent an irate editorial staff from descending on the sales department. The fact of the matter is that the sales advances that are finally delivered are usually lower than the editor's expectations. That is the reality of the marketplace.

Around the time of sales conference, you may suspect that you will not get the resources your book needs. Tell your agent about your anxieties so that he or she can intercede effectively, but discuss together what your agent intends to ask your publisher. Your agent may counsel you about your unrealistic expectations. But make sure your agent is a realist, as well. Not all agents are practical marketers and an agent's request for print advertising is easily dismissed (due to expense), but a request for specific publicity efforts has a better chance of getting through. Because your editor depends on your agent for the next good submission and wants to preserve a comfortable business relationship, he or she may take your agent's request to the publisher or editor in chief. The agent can always employ the tactic of talking directly to the publisher, who may in fact accede to the agent's request for more spending.

Sitting back and doing nothing is about the worst thing to do in these circumstances. If you suspect that support is not there but hope that it might appear later because "after all, they're the professionals, they must know what they're doing," then you've lost out on getting the most resources possible for your book.

As frustrated or angry as you might feel, tread carefully when you try to push the publishing staff to work harder on your book. As soon as you nag or accuse the staff, whoever it is you've annoyed will make a quick call to your editor, who is obliged to tell you to back off. You need allies. Proceed with caution and respect to preserve your good relationships with the publishing staff. If you decide to hire a freelance publicist, that publicist should be able to coordinate efforts with your in-house publicist, with goodwill on both sides. You also want your publisher to feel favorably disposed to jumping on board once you've created some publicity that leads to sales. As wronged or underserved as you might feel, keep a cool head. The decisions your publisher makes about your book are not personal. Losing your temper will not convince your publisher to give your book a promotional campaign. Worse, if you behave badly, the staff will begin to dodge your calls and keep future contact with you to a minimum.

BOUND GALLEYS AND HOW THEY ARE USED

A limited number of copies of your book are paperbound and sent to book reviewers, some producers, and key bookstore buyers. These copies are called galleys and the text is generally a typeset, but not proofread, version of your book. For the most important books on the publishing list, your publisher will send a large quantity of more elegantly produced galleys called advance reading copies to a wider circle of booksellers and media to pique early interest. Your editor will also send galleys to people who might give your book a positive endorsement to feature on the jacket. Be sure to check with your editor regarding the house's schedule and deadlines for cover endorsements.

Ask your editor to order a few extra galleys to send to people who you feel can help start some buzz about the book. They might include individuals with whom you're trying to book advance speaking engagements, someone you're trying to convince to endorse the book, or a contact at a magazine who might get you some coverage. With other contacts you are better served by sending a copy of the book later. Resist the temptation to send galleys to your friends and family. With galleys costing an average of ten dollars each to produce, that money is better spent on something else.

THE FIRST PRINTING

Your publisher or sales director will announce your book's first printing and sales goals at sales conference. After that, the reps begin their sales calls and orders begin to come in—either higher or lower than the sales targets. Booksellers buy more conservatively now than in the past and may take only a few copies of your book. If and when the book starts to sell, they will reorder more copies either from your publisher or from wholesalers.

A few months before publication and when enough sales orders are in hand, your publisher will set the print quantity for the book. The size of the print run is based on the advance orders and anticipated demand based on the marketing campaign and early publicity commitments. (The exception is children's books and illustrated books that are printed economically overseas. The publisher must set those print runs months before receiving any sell-in data.)

During the sell-in, your publicist and editor feed any additional marketing information to the reps to help boost the numbers. If you've started to work with your own freelance publicist, it is imperative that you or she informs the publisher of any arranged publicity bookings and interviews. This allows the reps to get the best possible sell-in for your book. Remember: The more copies that are sold in, the more money your publisher will be willing to spend to promote the book.

TRADE REVIEWS

Booksellers, librarians, paperback publishers, foreign publishers, and some media read *Publishers Weekly,* the leading trade publication, to help them decide which books to buy or review. *Kirkus Reviews, Library Journal, School Library Journal* and *The Horn Book* (for children's books), and *Booklist* are also important trade review media. A positive review in one or all of these publications can help spur in-house enthusiasm for your book, or give the sales reps and publicist another sales and media angle. Some booksellers rely on these reviews almost exclusively to inform their buy decisions.

Good trade reviews can help stimulate what's known as "pre-pub buzz." The value of pre-publication interest in your book is the possibility of getting a film option, foreign rights sales, and your publisher's commitment to a bigger campaign. Good reviews in the library media can trigger instant orders from the library wholesalers.

A bad review is not a crisis in terms of selling to booksellers because upon reading the review, booksellers will probably not cancel their pending orders. But the review will not stimulate additional orders. A bad review can also deflate the house's enthusiasm for a book. Bear in mind that many books that were panned in the trade publications went on to critical or commercial success.

Not all new hardcover books are reviewed in the trade publications, and even fewer original trade paperbacks are reviewed. Illustrated books including cookbooks and some reference books are not available in the right format in time to earn early trade reviews. Consequently, booksellers don't rely on the trade publications to make buying decisions in these categories. Instead they rely on your publisher's marketing plan.

AWARDS

Your publisher will be aware of the most important awards—such as the PEN awards, the National Book Critics Circle, the National Book Award—but they may not be aware of other smaller awards for which your book might qualify. Depending on the book you have written, you might research appropriate awards. For instance, the Commonwealth Writers Prize is little known in the United States but in fact many U.S.-based authors who are citizens of other countries qualify. (Find out about this prize at www.commonwealthwriters.com.) There's also a good directory called *Grants and Awards Available to American Writers,* published by PEN (www.pen.org) and available through PEN or Poets & Writers www.pw.org).

If you identify the awards for which you might qualify and procure the application forms, your publicist or editor (or their dauntless assistants) will take care of the submissions for you.

TRADE SHOWS

The BEA (BookExpo America) is the publishing industry's annual convention. The show takes place at the end of May or in early June and showcases the fall list. Throughout the three-day events, hundreds of publishers' booths display the upcoming season's wares. There are numerous book signings, press conferences, and breakfasts where star authors appear before a packed ballroom of booksellers.

Your publisher starts to plan for the BEA in December—the deadline to submit authors to be chosen for the breakfast programs. A few months later, in March or so, the publisher begins to focus in earnest on which authors they will bring. Some houses like to throw multiple events—parties and luncheons to introduce authors to booksellers and media. Others are conservative about bringing authors to the show, preferring to concentrate instead on bookseller meetings.

If your publisher does not formally invite you to the BEA and you live in the same city where it is taking place, tell your editor that you would like to drop by and ask if he or she can arrange for an entry badge. At your publisher's booth, the sales reps and marketing and publicity staff will introduce you to key booksellers and media. A tip: Do not stand around at the booth looking sulky because you think no one's paying attention to you. With back-to-back meetings throughout the course of the trade show, your publishing team has a lot of work to do. Expect to be on your own most of the time, and if you're good at initiating contact with people, you can get a lot done by wandering around the floor. Here are some ways to use the opportunity:

- If your publisher's booth is not busy, then find highly trafficked locations where conference attendees are crowding around a focal point and park yourself there. You will get into all kinds of conversations.

- Attend educational sessions that are related to your book topic. Introduce yourself to the panelists and ask questions during the Q&A period.

- Offer to help your publisher at the booth.

- Talk to your publisher's sales reps as much as you can without disrupting their other business. They will introduce you to booksellers who drop by the booth. Be charming without taking up all of their time.

- Ask booksellers and sales reps about the kinds of books that are selling these days. Use the occasion not only to push your own book, but also to find out about the marketplace. Ask them about some of their favorite book promotions.

- Attend any press conferences on topics of strong media interest. You will meet members of the press there.

- Go to the *Publishers Weekly* booth and strike up a conversation with staff there.

- Cadge invitations to parties from your publishing staff. They may give you their personal invitations to events that they are unable to attend. These parties are usually good networking opportunities for you, as well as just being fun.

- Walk the floor to visit other publishers' booths to find out how other publishers are promoting their books. They might stimulate new ideas for your own book's promotion.

One thing you can do at the BEA that will endear you to your publicist forever: offer to get her a cappuccino. (Oh, I know it's such an unsubtle gesture, but rarely does anyone make this sort of gesture at all.) Thank everyone on the publishing team at the show for his or her help and support. Keep notes of the names of everyone you've met from the publisher and send follow-up notes. Remember: Keep yourself in their minds. Unless you happen to visit their territories on your tour, you won't see most of those salespeople again.

The Canadian equivalent of the BEA is the CBA or Canadian Booksellers Association that takes place in June (www.cbabook.org). Do not confuse the Canadian meeting with the Christian Booksellers Association, which has several expos a year as well as an annual international convention (www.cbaonline.org). The Web sites for both organizations will tell you when and where they meet.

Regional book trade shows take place throughout the United States in September. Of these the largest are the shows sponsored by NEBA (New England Booksellers Association, www.newenglandbooks.org) and SEBA (Southeast Booksellers Association, www.sebaweb.org). These shows are considerably smaller than BEA. Publishers set up booths and booksellers drop by to check out the wares and schmooze over the course of a weekend. Publishers throw parties and dinners to introduce authors to booksellers and distribute books and freebies at the booths. Like the BEA, signings and readings provide a good way for an author to gain exposure among the bookseller fairgoers. Publishers will sometimes feature a tour of the regional trade shows as a part of an author's campaign. For a complete listing of the bookseller trade shows go to www.bookweb.org, the site of the American Booksellers Association.

GET TO KNOW YOUR SALES REPS

The reps have a lot of information to absorb about the list they are responsible for selling. Anything to help your book stand out from the rest is a plus, and with the help of your editor you can accomplish this. You might enclose a friendly letter that relates an anecdote or two about the writing of the book. Chances are that the reps will use your comments in their sales calls to add color to their presentation. Even if your editor has shared the same information in launch meetings and sales presentations, repeat any key points to reinforce them in the reps' minds. If you write personal notes to the reps, mention any information that is specific to a particular town or locale in a particular rep's sales territory. Your editor can supply the reps' names, addresses, and territories.

If you're the author of a cookbook, then perhaps send some goodies to the reps at sales conference. Your care package will get them talking to one another about your food and, hence, your book.

Another way to contact the reps is by voice mail. Sales departments have programmed multiple voice mails so, with the blessing of your editor and sales director, record a brief informative greeting to the sales reps for instant transmission to their voice mail. Or your editor can forward your e-mail greeting to the sales director, who will in turn disseminate the message to all the sales reps, as long as the message is short and useful or entertaining.

Near publication, try to meet the telephone sales force. Often overlooked by the rest of the publishing team, the telephone reps are genuinely happy to meet authors. Spend a few minutes with each of them or arrange through your editor or publicist to have a brown-bag lunch with the group. Your meeting helps them shape their sales pitches for your book.

PRE-PUBLICATION BOOKSELLER TOUR

Your publisher may send you on a pre-publication tour to meet bookstore buyers. Pre-pub tours are offered to authors whose books the publisher is trying to "break out," and will involve traveling to the top bookselling markets. The key destinations are New York City (where the Barnes & Noble headquarters and buying office is located), Ann Arbor (where the Borders home office is located), and other cities with a concentration of good independent booksellers. The tour might also include Boston and Washington, D.C., where the local sales rep might organize a lunch or dinner to introduce you to independent booksellers and local chain store managers. A West Coast–based publisher might concentrate on San Francisco or Los Angeles, instead. Another strategic way for publishers to introduce authors to booksellers is by arranging group luncheons with several authors and local booksellers. You might talk to your editor about other authors on the list to see if the house is willing to set up a couple of bookseller lunches or dinners in key markets or else some sort of group event at one of the trade shows.

If your book has a message that will interest booksellers, or if you've had a book published previously that was well received by booksellers, then bookseller meetings may be worthwhile. For instance, C. Britt Beemer's book, *Predatory Marketing,* reveals how to attract customers and to beat the competition. After early marketing meetings where it was decided to reach out to booksellers, Beemer, the chairman of a consumer behavior research and marketing firm, conducted consumer surveys about book buying preferences. The sales director then set up a meeting with executives at Barnes & Noble and Borders where Beemer presented the results of his surveys. Though his book was not a lead title on the list, Beemer's expertise gave his publisher a way to reach out to booksellers, to impress them about his book, and to elevate the book's initial buy-in from those accounts.

YOU'VE SUBMITTED YOUR MANUSCRIPT. NOW WHAT?– A SUMMARY

Find out the sequence of events at your publishing house so that you can understand when to step in and help. Your main tasks during the months leading up to your book's publication are to help your editor do a great job in positioning your book to the publishing team and to develop a good, functioning relationship with your publicist. This is also the key period of assessment, when you will find out exactly what your publisher is planning to do to promote your book.

The key events during this period are:

- Launch meeting where your editor presents your book to the publishing team

- Catalog copy is written

- Meetings with the publishing staff

- The first sales calls

- Your ongoing assessment of your publisher's plans

4

HIRE YOUR OWN PUBLICIST

YOUR publishing house might show little interest in investing time and money to promote your book. Several reasons might explain this inertia, and most of them are beyond your control. It might be that the book falls short of expectations. Perhaps another book on a similar subject was recently published, which preempted the media and consumer market for your book. Maybe the lead titles on the list are crowding the publisher's time and attention. Or the sales force didn't advance as many copies into the field as the publisher had hoped and the publisher has become discouraged. Maybe your editor has little persuasive clout in-house, or has left the company.

A lack of internal support is the number one reason authors hire freelance publicists. Even if your publisher seems very supportive of your book, you may still hire someone to supplement your publisher's efforts. A freelancer can cover a specific aspect of the campaign, like the Internet, or niche media, like business trade publications. Or perhaps your publisher lacks experience in dealing with the national media and you think a freelancer could be useful to secure some national bookings. Or perhaps your book has already been published and the first wave of publisher-sponsored publicity went well, suggesting that more media opportunities may exist. You may be able to get your publisher to pay for this if you are a significant author to the house. If not, you will probably have to foot the bill yourself. (Remember to track all expenses. Any money you spend on promoting your book is tax deductible against your income from royalties.)

Diane Mancher, who runs the book publicity firm One Potata, says that 50 percent of her business comes directly from authors, as compared to 10 percent some ten years ago. Other freelance publicists confirm the trend. Authors have wised up. You are not alone. Sometimes even the big-name authors become frustrated with inadequate publicity efforts. Paul Theroux faxed a masterfully acidic letter of complaint to his publisher when his publicists fell down on the job. (The letter was intercepted before reaching the publisher's desk and was photocopied and circulated widely.) The point is that no author can take a publisher's support for granted.

Once you sense a lack of enthusiasm among the publishing team, you have a critical decision to make. You can default to the publisher's inertia and sit back and complain to everyone who will listen—a tactic certain to doom the book into a swirl of bad feelings on everyone's part. Don't go on and on to your editor about how the publicity director doesn't "get it" or whatever your issue is. Your point may be valid but possibly beyond your editor's influence. Be sensitive to his or her position. The publishing house has its own system in place. Just because you've shown up doesn't mean the place is going to change, or even wants to change. Instead, become proactive on your own behalf. Try to make your editor and your agent your allies, instead of people who would rather avoid your phone calls. Your task is to work within the system when you can still help your book.

If your publication date is just a couple of months away, and you have the financial resources to hire a publicist, then do so. The window of opportunity for making noise around your book launch is not open for long. Do not squander the moment. This is not the time to learn how to set up your own publicity. If you cannot afford a freelancer for a full campaign, consider hiring one for some of the services you need, even if it's on a consulting basis to advise you on your own publicity efforts and provide you with mailing lists.

The ideal time to hire a publicist is four months ahead of publication date if you want your book to have a shot at long-lead magazine coverage; and any time up to a four weeks before publication for publicity that breaks at publication and later. Long-lead magazine coverage may not be critical to your book's positioning in the marketplace and so you may opt for a campaign that concentrates on media that can be booked after the publication date, a strategy that makes sense for many books. The pool of long-lead magazines that could reach your target audience is much smaller than the pool of general media that's available to you once the book has been published. So if you are working with limited resources, then bypass the pre-publication focus on long-lead magazines and spend your money on a campaign that lasts several months beyond your publication date.

Should You Hire Your Own Publicist?

Tracey George, who runs her own PR agency and who previously worked at several major publishers, offers these guidelines for authors to decide when they might hire a freelance publicist:

- Your in-house publicist is planning only a review copy mailing, or is planning a small and/or inadequate campaign.
- You've self-published your book and believe that a significant audience can be found.
- Your publisher's publicity campaign went well and is still generating media requests even after the campaign seems to have been concluded, a good indication that life is left in the media effort.
- Your publisher's publicist did not pitch different angles to varied media outlets—meaning that untapped opportunities still exist. For example, if your book would appeal to women and their teenage daughters, then approach the media in both areas—not just women's media but teen's as well.

    Some authors interview freelancers even when the publisher is already doing a great job. In such cases, the freelance publicist will probably tell the author that it's not worth hiring her.

Once your book has been published, you may still hire a freelancer. If you have published a work of nonfiction in a subject area of perennial interest, then your book can potentially get media coverage well after your publication date. However, if you've written a novel, your prospects are slimmer. Unless your book has strong thematic elements that a publicist can peg to news events, your novel has limited potential for media coverage. Freelance publicists will often tell just-published novelists that they do not want their money, as they can't do much for them. Your best bet is to wait for the paperback edition, then hire a publicist well before that publication date.

BEFORE YOU HIRE A FREELANCER . . .

Carol Fass, who heads Carol Fass Publicity and Public Relations, gives prospective clients a list of questions to ask their publishers. The answers to these questions help her identify how she can create a constructive campaign for the author. All freelancers will ask you variations of the same questions. Follow her advice and find out as many of the answers as possible before you contact any freelancers.

- Will the publisher write any press material for your book? If so, what are they planning to write? What have they already written and may we see it?

- Will the publisher print galleys for your book?

- Will your publisher handle the trade reviewers such as *Library Journal, Publishers Weekly, Kirkus Reviews,* and *Booklist*?

- Will your publisher be approaching long-lead-time magazines with galleys? If no galleys are planned, how is your publisher planning to approach the long leads?

- What is the publisher's timetable for the book? When will books be ready and available at the warehouse? What is the planned publication date?

- Is there a formal publicity plan for the book that has been communicated to you, to booksellers, to your agent? What does it entail?

- If there is no formal publicity plan, what does the publisher intend to do to promote the book?

- Is there any advertising planned?

- Is your publisher sending the book out for endorsements or blurbs?

- Is there a jacket design and may we see it?

- Has flap copy or catalog copy been written and may we see it?

- What is the first printing for your book?

- Is there anything else we need to know?

- Is the publisher willing to pay anything toward the publicity? For example, will they handle the preparation of mailings (i.e., photocopying press releases, collating, stuffing Jiffies, postage)? Will they pay any part of a freelance publicist's fee? Will they contribute to other expenses incurred in doing the publicity?

Fass says that publishers will often contribute at least some monies or services to a freelance campaign, which can significantly reduce an author's expenses. You just need to know what to ask for and when to ask for it. For example, don't ask your publicist if the house will pay for $2,000 in photocopying and mailing expenses. Instead ask if the house is willing to have your press releases photocopied and mailed to the media.

WHAT DOES A FREELANCE PUBLICIST COST?

If you've determined that a tour is important, then take a deep breath: Expect to pay a publicist a fee anywhere between $500 and $3,000 per city, plus expenses (express mail, phone, messengers, photocopying), plus travel costs ($12,000 to $15,000 to cover hotel, travel, media escorts, and so on). There is also a fee for writing press materials. To lessen the financial burden, consider starting with a small tour. Visit two or three cities to test the media response and local sales. Then you can confidently invest in more tour cities, and may even earn some more support from your publisher. And for my money, each tour city should also include a speaking engagement to give you and your publicist a great local media angle and an opportunity to sell books.

There are other cost-effective ways to work with freelance publicists. You may focus on getting a few top-level national appearances. Your top ten wish list might look like this: *The Oprah Winfrey Show, Today* or *Good Morning America, Larry King Live;* a feature article or review in the *New York Times, Los Angeles Times, Washington Post;* a feature on the Associated Press newswire and *People* magazine; and a National Public Radio interview. By defining the publicity efforts, everyone's expectations are clear. The publicist is unlikely to take on the job if she thinks your media prospects are slim. This service might cost you anywhere from $1,500 to $5,000.

A radio phone-interview campaign might interest you. Several public relations companies offer radio satellite tours, where they line up fifteen to twenty-five back-to-back interviews that take place in a studio or by phone. The cost ranges from $3,500 to $5,000. The advantage to this kind of radio campaign is that you reach a lot of top markets in one sitting. An alternative approach is contacting individual radio stations and scheduling interviews over the course of weeks or even months. You may reduce the fees for this service if you ask the freelance publicist to send the initial mailing, and then provide you with the contact lists to allow you to make the follow-up calls. Radio interviews are relatively easy to book, and if you plan to set up interviews on your own behalf on an ongoing basis, then radio offers an excellent arena to learn and hone your publicity skills.

If you're flush and if you think you can be an effective interview subject on television, then spring for the cost of a television satellite tour. Satellite tours run upward of $10,000 and comprise a series of back-to-back television interviews that are conducted in a television studio by satellite. You, the guest, sit in a chair with a single camera trained on you. One station after another links into the studio to conduct the remote interview. Some of these interviews are broadcast live; others are taped for later broadcast.

Some public relations firms will create a campaign that works within your budget and publicity requirements. With a little research you will probably find the firm or publicist who will structure an affordable deal for you. Talion.com is a PR firm that offers an innovative and affordable pricing structure, which allows you to select a limited and targeted media campaign, or a full national media kickoff for your book. Based in Renton, Washington, Talion.com is a terrific resource for anyone looking for a freelance publicist, because you can learn a lot at the site about what publicists do. The site's free reports on publicity are very smart—such as "Top Ten Publicity Blunders" and "How to Market to Associations and Newsletters."

Planned TV Arts offers another useful site at www.plannedtvarts. com. Again, you may not end up hiring this agency, but at least read the Tip Sheet section of the site, which offers interviews with members of the media about what they look for in a guest, dates for holidays that offer publicity tie-ins to your book, and sample media bookings for clients. The tips will help you understand how publicists work.

YOUR BUDGET

What follows is a range of expenses that you might incur in your freelanced publicity campaign. Prices vary widely depending on the freelancer you use and the extent of your campaign. You will need to shop around to find the most value for your money, and in some instances you will perform some of these tasks yourself and eliminate the cost.

Hiring a press release writer:	$50–$350 for one press release
	$500–$1,200 for a full press kit
Photographer for headshot:	$100–$1,000
Creating a Web site:	Free–$10,000

Fees for a freelance publicist:	$1,700–$5,000 for a national media campaign $5,000–$30,000 for a ten-city tour $1,500–$9,000 for a three-city tour $500–$5,000 for consulting
Throwing a publication party:	$250–$1,500
Mailing books to the press:	$2.00–$4.50 per book for postage and Jiffy bags
Photocopying press releases:	Free–$2,500 (depending on your resources and the extent of your press materials)
Television satellite tour:	$10,000–$14,000
Radio satellite tour:	$3,500–$5,000
Tour travel expenses:	$1,200–$2,500 per city if you are flying, staying in hotels, and hiring escorts. $2,500–$3,500 per city for cookbook tours including food prep expenses and food escorts

INTERVIEWING FREELANCE PUBLICISTS

Agencies are quite different from one another. Some focus on particular subject areas, like New Age subjects or serious political nonfiction. Some avoid literary fiction while others have special skill with literary projects. Some agencies will give you weekly updates and provide specific feedback from all pitches. Others will not devote as much energy to keep you informed. Before talking with freelancers, make a list of your expectations and of what you want from the relationship.

Most freelance publicists offer all of the following services: Pitching national and local media, setting up bookstore signings, writing press materials, radio interview campaigns, book review campaigns, events and parties, press conferences, and other press events. Some publicists offer services such as setting up speaking engagements, satellite tours, and Internet publicity. Or you can hire Internet publicists as a separate component to your campaign, or your freelance publicist may have the capability to partner with an Internet specialist to provide you with one-stop shopping. If the freelancer does not normally handle Internet campaigns, then do not have her handle yours. Internet publicity has its own set of protocols and your freelancer shouldn't learn those skills on your dime.

No publicity agency or freelancer holds the secret formula for getting you the coverage you want. Some agencies will understand right away how to market your book. Others will not. A New York City–based agency may be physically closer to the national media based there, but its proximity alone does not guarantee superior results in placing media interviews.

When you start talking to freelancers, you will be asked about your expectations. Share your marketing plan, if you have one, and ask the freelancer what she thinks she can accomplish for you. Be prepared to talk about your budget, as this will naturally be a determining factor in the campaign. Freelance publicists who are good at client management will clearly explain the media possibilities. When Diane Mancher of One Potata talks to potential clients, she likens her work to that of a lawyer, who will try to get the best results for her client, but can't guarantee the outcome. Lynn Goldberg of Goldberg McDuffie Communications will ask about your long-range goals beyond the immediate attention for your book. She then determines how her services will help you achieve those goals.

You may expect to interview freelance publicists and then make your selection from among the group. Keep in mind that the freelancers are also interviewing you to see if you will be a good client and whether they think they can make some media happen for you. Client authors are more time-consuming to work with than client publishers are. Therefore the publicist will evaluate whether you will be worth her time and will avoid an author who seems potentially high maintenance. Once you're signed on as a client, a publicist expects to spend some time educating you about the publicity and publishing process, but not at the expense of getting her job done. Some authors will badger their publicists, calling and e-mailing constantly, all of which can become disruptive to the publicist who is trying to get you some media. Don't become a pest—either to the freelancer or your in-house publicist. If you have a lot of information and enthusiasm and ideas to share, try to take care of them efficiently in one or two phone calls or e-mails.

That said, some freelance publicists themselves qualify as high-maintenance individuals. You might find their behavior high-handed or abrupt, even on the first meeting. They may respond to your questions with answers like "we don't do it like that" or "we don't really set up that kind of appearance." If this happens, it's your clear signal to get out of there! Do not tolerate a publicist who becomes annoyed with you at your very first meeting for coming up with new ideas about your book's promotion. There are plenty of other freelancers to choose from.

Essential Questions to Ask a Freelance Publicist

Among the freelance public relations firms specializing in books are some of the finest publicists in publishing. Because freelance firms are small entrepreneurial businesses, their success depends on excellent staffs to a greater extent than in-house publicity departments: Mediocrity survives longer in-house largely because of corporate inertia. That said, you should still check out a freelance agency's references to ensure that you're spending your money wisely. You can do this by asking the agency for the contact information for past clients who would be willing to talk to you. If an agency won't provide you with references, take that as a bad sign.

Before you enter into a contract with a freelancer, ask the following questions to protect your interests:

- What publicity opportunities do you think there are for my book?
- Have you worked on books like this in the past? What media did you get for them?

- Who do you think is the audience for my book? What do you think is the best way to reach that audience?
- Do you work directly with a lot of authors or is most of your work through publishing houses? Which authors have you worked with and what publicity did you get for them?
- Do you mind if I call every day with questions?
- Will you or a publicist on your staff work on my book? If it will be a staff publicist, then what experience does she have and can I meet her?
- How do you develop a campaign strategy for the books you're working on?
- What are your goals for my book? Do you think my book poses any particular challenges? What are they?
- What can I do to make the book a success? How can I help with publicity?
- Do you recommend a publicity tour for my book? How do you choose the tour cities?
- Do you set up bookstore appearances? Do you set up speaking engagements?
- What happens when the campaign is finished and you receive calls from the media about my book?
- What are some of your favorite past projects and why?
- May I have three references to call about your work?

GOING TO CONTRACT

Once you and the freelance publicist agree to work together, then you will sign a contract or letter of agreement. The contract will require that you pick up expenses and pay a fee in installments. Many a freelance publicist will protect her financial interests by collecting more money up front from client authors than from client publishers. This is because some authors have reneged on their final bills when the publicity results did not meet their expectations. Some freelancers go a step further and require that the author arrange for the publisher to pay the freelancer and the author then reimburses the publisher. Remember: If your publicity campaign and book sales disappoint you, then you still owe the freelancer her fee. (Refusing to pay is, plainly put, theft.) Keep in mind that the final payment should still be large enough to provide incentive for the publicist to do a good job in the second half of the campaign.

You will negotiate the term of contract with the freelancer. The standard duration for a campaign is three to four months. If you believe that your book is going to take a long time to gain attention, you may want an extended period of publicity coverage.

Naturally, freelance publicists have different payment structures. Some offer a fee schedule based on a flat rate per city, per publicity kit, per phone interview campaign, per national media campaign, or even per hour. Others base their fees on how long they will work on a campaign and charge a monthly retainer. Solo freelancers may be more flexible on negotiating a price as they have lower overheads than agencies with a staff. Negotiability will also depend on the freelancer or agency's workflow at any particular time. Their business fluctuates seasonally, with publishers' loaded fall schedules placing a heavier demand on freelancers in the last half of the year. In some years, a notable absence of big books diminishes the freelancers' workload and cash flow. Always negotiate. Creative pricing could work for you and your publicist. You might offer a flat fee for services with bonuses if certain media bookings are achieved. While a somewhat unorthodox approach in the book publicity business, the approach certainly builds in a good incentive for performance. Again, not everyone will be willing to try this, but there's no harm in asking.

What follows is a typical contract between a publicity agency and an author. This particular agreement is for a title to be published on Valentine's Day. The campaign commenced in September and concluded at the end of March. The author felt that long-lead magazine coverage was important, which is why the campaign started so far ahead of publication date.

Letter of Agreement

Date

Dear _____,

This will confirm our agreement concerning our role in publicizing your new book, [title], which [name of your publisher] will publish on [February 14].

Under the terms of this agreement, we shall use our best efforts to bring the book to wide public attention. Our specific responsibilities will include:

—Creating all press materials. This will include a press release, author biography, an author Q&A, and other pieces to be decided.

—Preparing a galley letter and a list of long-lead magazines and reviewers to receive galleys and following up to confirm coverage. Among the long-lead publications we will target for coverage are: *Vogue, Glamour, The New York Times Magazine, Elle, Harper's Bazaar, Vanity Fair, Parade, USA Weekend, Civilization, People, O, The Oprah Magazine, Entertainment Weekly, The Nation, The New Republic, The New Yorker, The Atlantic, and Harper's.*

—Coordinating with your publisher to arrange bookstore appearances in the following cities: New York, Washington, Atlanta, Birmingham, and Chicago.

—Working in advance with the national electronic and print media to secure interviews. Among the national media we will approach are: *Today, Good Morning America, Weekend Today, CBS Sunday Morning, The Charlie Rose Show, The Oprah Winfrey Show, Open Book* C-SPAN, *Fresh Air, All Things Considered, The Diane Rehm Show, USA Today,* Associated Press, the *New York Times, Los Angeles Times,* the *Washington Post, Time,* and *Newsweek.*

—Working with feature and lifestyle editors at the top forty metropolitan daily newspapers to secure coverage in Valentine's Day features.

—Arranging appropriate television, radio, and print interviews in the tour cities.

—Working with the book reviewers at the major metropolitan newspapers to secure timely reviews.

—Coordinating all travel and escort arrangements in each city.

We will begin work on the project in September and will conclude our duties under this agreement on March 31, 2001. We will coordinate our efforts with you and your publisher and will update both parties periodically about our results.

Our fee for the project is $15,000.00, payable as follows: $8,000.00 upon signing the agreement, and $7,000.00 payable on February 1, 2001.

In addition to the retainer fee, you agree to pay expenses incurred in connection with the campaign within fifteen days after receiving a bill from [name of publicity agency]. Examples of these expenses include postage, Federal Express, telephone, messengers, Lexis-Nexis online research, photocopies, and printing. Any single item beyond $250.00 will be preapproved by you.

You understand and agree that payment for our services is based upon our efforts and is not contingent upon results or on specific responses from various media as these cannot be assured.

[Name of publicist] will be the account executive on the project.

If the terms of this agreement as stated herein are agreeable, please sign and return one copy of this letter to me for my records.

Author   Owner
                                                Publicity Firm

_____   _____

_____   _____

Date:_____   Date:_____

HIRING A FREELANCER—SUCCESS STORIES

Andrew Sobel, coauthor of *Clients for Life* (www.andrewsobel.com), started early on his publicity campaign. Though he was a neophyte to book publishing, he has a background in business consulting and marketing strategy and knew he needed to invest some time and money in promoting his book. When he interviewed freelance publicists, he found that they had more extensive promotional possibilities at their fingertips than in-house publicists. Most important, they would have the time to make follow-up calls that the in-house publicists would not.

The campaign he eventually devised with Meryl Moss of Meryl L. Moss Media Relations included a six-month intensive outreach to business trade publications that reached his core audience: Business professionals in the service industries such as accounting, advertising, banking, law, and so on. Moss and her staff researched and pitched all the related trade publications and placed interviews, features, and excerpts in many publications to appear upon his book's publication including *Advertising Age*, *Consulting to Management*, and *Consultants News*. The articles helped leverage appearances for Sobel on several national business shows on CNBC and CNNfn, as well as a review in *USA Today*—a powerful vehicle for business books, as business travelers rely on the publication.

Sobel's advice to authors is to ask yourself, "Who am I trying to reach for this book and what are all the ways I can get in touch with this audience?" Then decide whether you are willing to put the time in to help develop the right materials for the publicist to work with. He cautions that you can't do everything at once and you can't do it all. "I struggled with how to define the universe of available media," he says. "You have to focus on your target media, and reach them in phases during the course of your campaign." Of course the good news about the large size of the media universe is that you have endless opportunities for coverage and, if you choose, you can continue to promote your book for years. Sobel acknowledges that he could not have achieved the level of exposure that he did without the help of the right freelance publicist, or without investing a significant amount of his time.

Romance novelist Mariah Stewart (*The President's Daughter*, www. geocities.com/mariahstewart) took a different approach to her freelanced campaign, choosing instead to concentrate on booksellers. For her first book, Stewart sent bookmarks and personal letters to booksellers, who—seven novels and two novellas later—remain among the core of her most supportive stores. But with a day job and three children, Stewart knew that she wouldn't have the time for such ongoing labor-intensive efforts. She hired a freelancer, Judy Spagnola, to focus on getting the word out to bookstores. Spagnola called stores before the sales reps had called on the accounts, and then followed up to report on any new developments about the book—such as a good review or an award—to keep the book at the top of the booksellers' minds.

Judy Spagnola specializes in romance and mysteries. A former literature buyer for Walden, she is well known to booksellers and has enormous credibility on behalf of her author clients. Her campaigns can comprise single mailings to booksellers and reviewers or a staggered series of mailings that might include three of four pieces of correspondence including bookmarks and postcards. (Romance and mystery writers can contact Judy Spagnola at Judyspags@aol.com.) She encourages her authors to attend the romance conferences and introduce themselves to the booksellers who often attend. "Get to the booksellers," she says. "Introduce yourself, send them signed bookmarks, set up book signings. Don't forget to include your book's ISBN on all promotional material that you send to booksellers. The ISBN makes it very easy for the bookseller to look up information about buying your book."

Only a few freelancers specialize in bookstore outreach. If you want to take this task on yourself, you should start making your phone calls about two months before your publication date. (So you'll need to research your bookstore lists earlier than that.) Persistence is required: The bookstore buyer that you need to speak with will likely be in and out of the store and you'll need to call back until you make contact. Once you reach the buyer, explain who you are and what your book is about, as well as any positive news about the book, like favorable reviews. If you have a Web site, invite the bookseller to visit to get a better sense of your work. Ask if he or she wouldn't mind if you send follow-up information from time to time. What you will have accomplished in the call is the start of a relationship with the bookseller, who, once you follow up, will start to remember your name and your book.

MANAGE THE FREELANCE AND IN-HOUSE RELATIONSHIPS

Upon entering into a relationship with a freelancer, you will ask her to specify the services she will be responsible for. You will also ask your in-house publicist to describe the work that she will handle. All parties—you, your freelancer, your in-house publicist—must know who's doing what. A clearly communicated division of labor and an ongoing dialogue between the freelancer and in-house publicist will eliminate confusion later. When a freelance publicist pitches the media, the in-house publicist commonly manages the book review mailing, keeps the rest of the publishing house informed of your activities, and possibly writes the press materials. The in-house publicist might also agree to send out the media mailing to save your freelancer from charging postage expenses back to you. Most important, she can also let you know if sales are increasing in certain markets as a result of your appearances. If your media appearances generate sales, then you have a case to make that the publisher should help support your efforts in more markets.

Continue to manage the relationship between the in-house publicist and your freelancer. Perhaps you will arrange periodic conference calls. You should serve as a shuttle diplomat for a couple of reasons. First, so that the in-house publicist doesn't drop the ball because she's relying on the efforts of the freelancer. (Your in-house publicist should view the freelancer as an extension of the team, not as a way to abdicate responsibility for your book.) Second, to help preserve your freelancer's access to the house's valuable resources.

Don't expect your freelance publicist to fight any of your battles with your publisher or to tell the publisher what to do. Freelancers do not serve the same function as your agent. Particularly for the New York–based publicists, their livelihood depends on preserving good relationships with publishers. "We are diplomats with the publishers," says one freelancer. "Our role is not to play bad cop, which many authors expect us to do." Resist bad-mouthing your publisher to your publicist, no matter what you feel about the house. You may need your publisher's help later; and your gossip places the freelance publicist uncomfortably in the middle. Nor make the mistake, once you hire a publicist, of sitting back and expecting the publicist to do all the work. The most productive campaigns are those where the author and publicist act like partners in a project, whether that publicist is a freelancer or in-house.

Sometimes an in-house publicist will become offended that you've decided to freelance your book's campaign. She may not tell you that she's offended, but as you move toward publication and beyond, you find yourself losing the benefit of her expertise. Your best move is to bring the in-house publicist into your decision-making process. Clarify that your desire to hire a freelancer has nothing to do with your perception of her talents, but was intended to expand the team working on the book. Reassure her. You need her in your corner. She can help you make a better decision about which freelance publicist to hire and how to best support the in-house campaign.

HIRE YOUR OWN PUBLICIST—A SUMMARY

You'll find an annotated list of publicity firms that specialize in books in the resource section of this book (page 281). Before interviewing publicists:

- Find out what your publisher is planning for your book.

- Determine your budget.

- Shop around for the publicist that fits your goals and with whom you are comfortable.

If you're not sure what kind of campaign is appropriate for your book, talk to a few publicists and listen to what they recommend. Enter into a contract with the freelance publicist so that expectations are clear for both parties, and most of all, plan on becoming an active partner in the campaign.

5

PRESS MATERIALS

THE pitch letter and press release and other written materials should be created and presented in such a manner as to convince a producer, reporter, or book reviewer to cover your book. The materials should be well written, persuasive, concise, attentive to what the media is interested in, and free of spelling errors and typos. Producers and reporters receive giant stacks of mail, as well as hundreds of faxes and e-mails, every day. With such voluminous correspondence to deal with, they will spend little time—perhaps only a few seconds—reading your book's press release before making a decision to pass or to pursue further.

Your publicist will write your press materials based on your manuscript, your marketing plan, and any conversations you've had. She will probably offer to show you the press materials. If not, then ask to read them to verify that they properly represent you and your book. Feel free to edit the press release, but be careful of the publicist's feelings. As you might know, most people are sensitive about their writing. (A publicist who is a poor writer may still have fantastic pitching skills, so do not despair if you see bad prose crossing your desk.) Remember: A good relationship with your publicist is of primary importance. A friend of mine recently rejected the entire press release that the publicist had written. Though grammatically written, the release missed the point of the book and made the book seem dull. His publicist accepted the rewrite because he positioned the new release as making the book more salable, which she recognized would make her job easier.

Various types of press materials are used for different kinds of media pitches. The press release announces news surrounding a book's publication, and is generally sent along with a copy of the book to reviewers, producers, and reporters. Or instead of a press release, your publicist might instead write a personal letter to book reviewers about your book. Her letter might describe your book in a conversational manner, a softer sell than a conventional pitch letter. Pitch letters encapsulate your expertise and the topics that you will talk about in an interview. These are aimed principally at press who will conduct interviews with you about your book and are generally accompanied by the press release as well as a list of suggested interview questions, your bio, and excerpts from the book.

If your publicist is announcing an event—say a press conference—she might send out a media alert. This form of release, which is sometimes also called a media advisory, tells reporters very specific information about the event and the press opportunity it offers. (See the appendices starting on page 292 for samples of all of these formats of press material.) Every single page of any press materials must include the publicist's contact information—or your contact information if you're the one doing the publicity outreach. All of the materials together comprise what's known as a press kit, which might also include any favorable articles or past reviews about you and your work.

THE PRESS RELEASE

The press release (also called a news release) describes in one or two pages the book's news value and content. The release is not a book report—a misconception held by many authors and publicists. The release has a standard format and should mirror the way most news stories are written with the most compelling information at the top of the release and further information provided in descending order of importance. Another common mistake made by neophyte press release writers is to "bury the lead"—placing the most important and interesting information about the book too far down in the press release. A reporter who scans only the first paragraph will miss the news you're trying to convey.

Quotes from you or the book enliven the body of the press release and demonstrate how your expertise could interest a reporter's audience or readership.

Your publicist will send one version of the press release to most media. In markets in which the book has a strong local angle, she should at least customize the headline and the first paragraph of the release for recipients in that market. Another way to customize the release is to attach a separate note that explains the local angle. For example, books that survey the best boarding schools, or the best companies to work for, or the best inns or flea markets all have built-in local angles for their various markets.

The Twenty Rules of Writing an Effective Press Release

Whether you are writing the press release yourself or simply reviewing the release written by your publicist, you should know the rules of press release writing. You can also find sample press releases at www.press-release-writing.com, a press release writing service, or see pages 269–98.

The Rules

1. The words FOR IMMEDIATE RELEASE appear on the top left of the page above the headline.
2. Your contact name, phone number, and e-mail address are stacked in the upper right-hand corner of the first page.
3. Next comes the headline, in capital letters, usually in boldface, and centered on the top of the page to emulate an attention-getting newspaper headline. That headline summarizes why anyone would want to know more about you or your book and announces some item of news interest. This headline is not newsworthy: NEW BOOK ABOUT BICYCLES TO BE

PUBLISHED IN SEPTEMBER. This one is newsworthy: NEW BOOK REVEALS THAT TWO HOURS OF BICYCLING A WEEK CAN REDUCE RISK OF HEART DISEASE.

4. A dateline appears at the start of the first paragraph and also includes the location of the news source, for example: (Charleston, S.C., July 26, 2002).

5. Following the headline, the first paragraph of the release presents the most important information about your book. If you hide the most interesting and salient information deep in the body of the release, then you've likely lost the opportunity to capture the reporter's interest in your book. Present information in descending order of importance.

6. The release should be no longer than two pages. Use double-spacing or at least one-and-a-half-spacing. Do not try to cheat for more space by single-spacing your text, which makes the release hard to read. Use letter-size stationery.

7. Do not use sans-serif typefaces or others that are hard to read. Instead use easy-on-the-eye typefaces like Times New Roman or Garamond. Do not mix different typefaces in the same release, which also makes it hard to read.

8. Customize or target your releases to the media you are pitching where appropriate. Mention any information of local interest in your lead paragraph. A debut book from an author from Cleveland is of greater interest in Cleveland than Minneapolis.

9. Spell every word correctly. Poor spelling and grammar disqualifies your release immediately. Pay particular attention to the proper spelling of names. Proofread the release several times, and verify that all information is accurate.

10. Include any relevant quotes from your book, from you or an expert in your field, that substantiate and reinforce the topic of the release. Think of the release as an encapsulated newspaper article, and write it as such. Many reporters will include parts of press releases in the body of their articles. So familiarize yourself with the tone and style of newspaper articles to present your book in an informative and non-hyped way.

11. Don't use exclamation marks. Apart from making the release hard to read, the style looks huckster-ish and amateurish.

12. Do not use hyperbole. Avoid hyped-up words and phrases like "destined for the bestseller lists," "unique," "best ever," and "fantastic." Write simply and concisely.

13. Keep your sentences short.

14. Edit the press release ruthlessly to eliminate any redundancies or unnecessary text.

15. In their book *Jump Start Your Book Sales*, Marilyn and Tom Ross offer this smart advice: Write all your promotional materials (including your press releases) from a benefit point of view. In other words, clearly convey what the reader or end consumer gets out of your book.

16. After the first mention of your title in the body of the release, include in parentheses the name of the publishing house and the publication date.

17. Book titles are conventionally written all in capital letters.

18. Names are written as Joe Smith the first time he is mentioned, and after that, he is simply referred to as Smith, or, formally, Mr. Smith.

19. At the bottom center of the release, after the body of the text, type -30- or ### to indicate closure.

20. At the end of the release, list the publication date, page count, price, format (hardcover or paperback), publishing house, and ISBN. Also include the Web site address for the book, if any.

A point worth repeating: Some terrific publicists can't express themselves well in writing but can orchestrate a media campaign like no one's business. If editing or rewriting a poorly written press release is slowing you down or making you anxious, be straightforward with your publicist about hiring a freelance writer to fix the release. Publicity departments hire copywriters all the time. If this is not an option for you, then hire a freelance writer yourself.

To find a freelance press release writer:

- Ask your publicist for the names of press release writers frequently hired by the publicity department.

- The site www.elance.com allows you to post your press release project for writers to bid on. The writer's credentials and rates and a feedback and rating system are displayed on the site. Prices are reasonable.

- Contact your local college or university to have your press release assignment posted where communications majors will see it.

- One source of writers is the American Society of Journalists and Authors Web site (www.asja.org). Click onto writer's referrals and for a twenty-five-dollar fee, you can post your project. Potential writers will contact you directly.

- The site www.imediafax.com offers press release critiques, press release writing, as well as a press release distribution service. Writing fees are $200 for one page and $350 for two pages. Press release revision and critiques cost $100 for one hour. The same site sells a downloadable e-book called *Trash Proof News Releases: The Surefire Way to Get Publicity*, by Paul Krupin. The book is a full tutorial on writing effective press releases and press materials, with many samples accompanying the instruction. If you're writing your own press materials, then the instruction provided here will show you what reporters are looking for.

- John Kremer, a book-marketing specialist reachable through his site www.bookmarket.com, will critique and suggest ways to improve your press release for a fee in a ten-minute phone consultation. Through his site you can also sign up for a free e-newsletter offering marketing and publicity tips.

PITCH LETTERS

For a book that's slated for a publicity tour or radio interview mailing, your publicist will write a "Dear Producer," "Dear Editor," or "Dear Interviewer" pitch letter, which offers you for interview and explains what you would talk about. In some cases, particularly for customized pitches for major media like *The Oprah Winfrey Show*, your publicist will personalize the letter to a particular show and producer. (She doesn't need to personalize pitch letters for a mass mailing to local radio, television, and print press: Instead she will address the recipient as Dear Interviewer or Dear Producer. The recipients don't expect personalized correspondence, and it is time consuming for publicists to do mail merges, or make the necessary refinements to truly personalize all correspondence.) A handwritten note that accompanies the pitch also goes a very long way with producers.

While the press release talks generally about the main points in your book, your pitch letter is more directly persuasive. However, it's not the letter alone that will secure the booking. Your publicist will most likely need to follow up with a phone call to reiterate the pitch, or to find another angle to get the show locked in.

When you're reviewing or writing pitch letters, or helping your publicist come up with pitch ideas, bear in mind the following advice from publicity expert Joan Stewart. She says, "The biggest mistake authors make when trying to get onto major radio and television shows is pitching either themselves or their books. Don't pitch authors! Pitch issues. Don't pitch books! Pitch shows.

"Example: If you wrote a book about how children of divorced parents suffer long-term effects well into adulthood, don't try to entice television producers with the book. Entice them with an entire show around the topic of 'Children of divorced parents: Do they ever recover?' Then suggest two or three other guests who might also be interviewed in the same show, with at least one of them on the other side of the issue. Do that and you've just given the producer the guts for an entire show, and they're more likely to bite because you've done their work for them." (Joan Stewart is a professional speaker, trainer, and media relations consultant. Sign up for her free publicity tips of the week at www.publicityhound.com.)

The point is that pitch letters should convey what you and your book offer an audience or readership.

The format for a pitch letter is fairly straightforward. (See page 299 for an example.)

1. Use letter-size stationery and keep the pitch to one page.

2. Set the pitch up like you would any business letter, with the date in the upper-left corner. If you are personalizing the letter, then also include the name of the recipient and address in the upper left, followed by the body of the letter.

3. If you want to personalize the letter but don't know the recipient, use the salutation Dear Mr. or Ms. Otherwise an acceptable salutation is Dear Producer/Interviewer.

4. The lead paragraph gets right to the point: "I am writing to suggest a story about . . ." or "I am writing to suggest an interview with . . ." followed by a compelling reason why the recipient should be interested.

5. The following paragraph gets into the details of what you would talk about in an interview, possibly including some suggested interview topics.

6. Support the pitch with any statistics that bolster your position.

7. If appropriate, the next paragraph should mention any visuals that could support a television interview.

8. The last paragraph includes contact follow-up information.

9. The letter closes with your signature, like any other business letter.

SUGGESTED INTERVIEW QUESTIONS

While your pitch letter will suggest topics for discussion, a separate page with a list of about ten or so suggested questions for interview is also valuable to producers and hosts. With several hours of programming to fill every day, radio and television producers and interviewers find the prompt questions very helpful.

Some publicists like to create an author Q&A, sometimes called a canned interview. Generally speaking, Q&As are too long and dense to be of much value to reporters or interviewers. The exception might be an extraordinarily provocative interview that has news value of its own. If your publicist wants to write a Q&A, explore her reasons and perhaps in your case it is a good idea. But do not push for one if it isn't in the plans. A simple list of questions will suffice.

TOP TEN LISTS AND TOPICAL PRESS RELEASES

In addition to the general press release about your book, your publicist might also write topical releases or articles with content that is easily reprinted by newspapers or read on air by broadcasters. These releases can be included with the first press packet or sent out separately as a follow up to stimulate more press coverage after the initial wave.

"The goal is to produce and package the color around the message," explains PR pro Jeanne Krier, who runs her own publicity business in New York City. By producing what she has nicknamed "lift and sticks" for her press packets—press material that is lifted from the book in a format that's appealing and easy for reporters to use—Krier has generated much press coverage for the books she has publicized. One example is a book called *The Scholarship Advisor,* by Christopher Vuturo, for which her press materials included an article called "Mining for Money You Didn't Know You Were Entitled To" about ten little known sources of scholarship money for college-bound students. She also produced a "lift and stick" for a book called *The Internship Bible,* by Mark Oldman and Samer Hamadeh, on "Famous Former Interns." The list of interns required some additional research on the part of the coauthors beyond what they had included in the book but their effort paid off: Many print media excerpted the list and credited the book in their coverage. In the next edition of the book, the publisher expanded the coverage of famous former interns.

For a book published by Hearst with Esquire Magazine called *Things a Man Should Know About Sex,* the authors included "top ten" lists in the book, knowing that the media loves to pick up quick one-liners and that these would appeal particularly to the morning drive radio show hosts. The lists included things like "The Top 10 Worst

Breakup Lines" and "The Top Ten Worst Pickup Lines," and press materials drew attention to the lists.

Can you use any of the following topical approaches to discuss your book in a press release?

- The Ten Easy Ways to Lose Weight

- The Three Myths About Doctors That You Need to Know

- Take This Quiz to Test Your Survival Skills

- The Ten Secrets to Getting Ahead (That Your Boss Won't Tell You About)

- Ten Great Ways to Save Money

- Shortcuts to Finding a New Job

If you can think of topical releases for your book, then tell your publicist. To get some ideas, simply head to your local newsstand and read the headlines for the monthly magazines. The words Secrets, Myths, Never Before Revealed, Top Ten Ways, Save Money, Tips to . . . , and Behind the Scenes are common attention-grabbing phrases. Use them in your own press releases. If your publicist is unwilling to write another press release, ask if she will edit a release that you write and then send it to her media lists.

ONLINE PRESS KITS

If you have a Web site, put your press materials on the site, making it an easy matter for you or your publicist to include a link when pitching journalists. For examples of some terrific online press kits, go to www. talion.com. The agency's online kits demonstrate savvy thinking about what the media needs to get interested in a book. The kits include multiple story angles, as well as tips from the book that can be excerpted in the press. There are also suggested interview questions, lists of other experts who are also available for interview (making the online press kits very useful to longer-format television talk show producers and to print journalists), and extensive backgrounders on the subject matter and author. Nowhere to be found is the traditional press release, but who cares? Any reporter could find the information here that they need to start to create a good and interesting story. Talion's online kits are solid examples of good press materials: You or your publicist could equally use this agency's approach with the written materials that are mailed to the press.

AUTHOR BIO

Your publicist will distill the biography that you prepared for the marketing plan or author questionnaire into a few lines. The bio may appear at the bottom of the press release or as a separate item in the press materials. If your expertise is an important part of the interview pitch, your publicist might create a longer bio that emphasizes your credentials.

MEDIA ALERTS

You or your publicist may need to invite the media to cover an event that you are staging or sponsoring. It might be a book party at which you will present a check to charity, the launch of a program in your community that brings writers into schools to talk to students, an event at a bookstore, or a press conference. This press announcement is called a media alert or a media advisory and has a specific (and very simple) format that is different from a press release. Your publicist will send a media alert to the following media:

- News assignments desks at local television stations

- Assignment editors at the metro desk of newspapers

- News producers at radio stations

- The Daybook editor at the closest bureau of the Associated Press, who will list events on the local wire for reporters, producers, and assignment editors throughout the area to decide whether to attend. (If you're doing this yourself, go to www.ap.org to find the local AP bureau. Call the bureau and ask for the fax number to send your media alert clearly marked for the Daybook. Do this the day before your event. Follow up with a call to the Daybook editor to make sure your information has been received and whether it will go in the Daybook.)

■ The photo assignment desk of local newspapers. If you are working solo and sending out the announcements yourself, you can find the media contacts with the help of the directories mentioned in Chapter Six, page 133.

The media alert is one page long and states Who, What, Where, When, and Why, as well as whether the occasion offers interview or photo opportunities. The alert should be sent via fax or e-mail to the appropriate stations and newspapers a few days before the event. (See the appendix on page 300 for a sample media alert.)

PHOTOGRAPHS AS PRESS MATERIALS

The press packet might include your photo, but only for the print media. If the book is sent out with the press packet and your photo is already pictured on the book jacket, then your publicist will not send a copy of the photo to television and radio producers.

If your book has a striking jacket, you might ask your publicist to send out a photo of the book jacket rather than your headshot. After all, it's your book's jacket that you want consumers to recognize in the bookstore. The exception is when your image is used as a way to market the book, as previously discussed.

Suggest that your publicist ask the art director for a JPEG of your book's jacket at the beginning of your campaign. These are simply electronic scans. That way she has it on hand for when a reporter on deadline might need it. She can also state at the end of the press materials that a JPEG cover is available upon request. If you're doing some publicity outreach, ask for a copy for yourself. Bear in mind though that publications have different requirements for electronic receipt of art. Also, if you or your publicist can't get hold of a JPEG, and a reporter on deadline needs a copy of your cover, suggest that he or she download it from one of the online retailers.

Publicists for illustrated books can make a selection of photos available to the press. While duplicating photographs is expensive, what seems to work best for many books is preselecting a range of images to have on hand as needed. These can be provided to the media in the form of slides, photos, or, best yet, downloadable electronic files. (Identify the photos that you think promotable even while you are doing the photo research for your book. Clear any photo permissions for promotional use at the same time that you clear the book rights. If you're not sure which images are suitable for promotion, then ask your editor or publicist to help you decide *before* your book goes into production. The images are harder to retrieve once they have been sent to the printer.)

TO PRESS KIT OR NOT TO PRESS KIT

Some publicists like to put all the press materials in a press kit—a fancy two-pocket folder that might have a copy of the book jacket pasted on the cover. They believe that the press kit helps to catch the eye of the producer or reporter. For my money (and more important, yours!—if you're underwriting some of the costs of your campaign), that window dressing is a waste unless the kit is truly an unusual visual knockout. Press packets are more effective and cost-efficient: They are press materials without the expensive folder. Your publicist folds all the press materials together and places the packet inside the front cover of the book.

There are also imaginative ways to package press materials so that they get noticed. When she was publicizing a book called *The Tightwad Gazette,* by Amy Dacyczyn, publicist Grace McQuade came up with an inspired press packet. The book reveals hundreds of imaginative and simple ways for families to save money and became a *New York Times* bestseller. Consistent with the book's penny-pinching philosophy, she mailed out the press packet inside brown paper lunch bags with a sticker of the book's cover pasted on the front. The campaign received a lot of media attention. For a mystery novel by Barbara D'Amato called *Authorized Personnel Only,* the author suggested that her publicist wrap the press materials in yellow police tape, an effective way to catch the eyes of reviewers.

But be cautioned: Do not waste money on expensive giveaways. Unless the item is truly unusual, or very funny, it will go in the garbage.

POSTCARDS

Postcards, with a picture of the cover of your book on one side and advance praise and a description of the book on the back, can be effective press materials. Novelist Laura Van Wormer (www.lauravan-wormer.com) has an instinctive feel for publicity, and has successfully publicized her many books. For *Riverside Drive,* her first novel, she got the publisher to print a couple of thousand postcards with her book jacket on the front and excerpts from her reviews on the back. As the title suggests, the book is set on Riverside Drive in New York City. During her spare moments, Van Wormer would pore through the New York City phone book and write a postcard to anyone with a Riverside Drive address. For those of you unfamiliar with New York, Riverside Drive is an affluent residential neighborhood—a concentrated book-buying community. Indeed, every time Van Wormer sent out a new batch of postcards, the book would sell out at the local bookstore. Of course, she alerted the bookstore about what she was doing so that she could measure the effectiveness of her efforts and so that the bookstore could order books in time for her next mailing.

If you're paying for the postcards, check out the reasonable prices at www.modernpostcard.com. Or if your publisher is paying, tell your publicist about this resource so she can divert the savings elsewhere on your campaign.

PRESS MATERIALS—A SUMMARY

Writing effective press materials means that you or your publicist must convey the essence of your book in an appropriate format. There are different types of press materials that serve specific purposes:

- A press release is a general summary of your book with the most newsworthy or interesting points mentioned up front.

- Pitch letters offer you to interviewers as a guest or interview subject.

- Suggested interview questions make a reporter's job easier by laying out the salient discussion points about your book.

- A media alert informs the press of an event and what's interesting about it.

- A press kit contains all the elements that could interest the media in you, including a pitch letter with story angles, suggested interview questions, a press release, possibly also a topical press release, your bio, and perhaps your photo.

- An online press kit allows you to make your press materials accessible in a most efficient way.

6

The Print Publicity Campaign

MANY publishers send copies of every book to the major book reviewers at newspapers and magazines in the United States and Canada. Then some of those publishers call it a day. For most books, however, a review mailing alone is insufficient. Marketers estimate that a consumer is motivated to buy a book or product only after five to eight exposures to that product. Therefore, unless you're already a well-known writer with an audience anticipating your next book, one favorable review in one market will not drive book sales in significant numbers.

In addition, many books are of no interest to newspaper book reviewers who almost exclusively favor literary fiction or works of serious nonfiction. However, reporters in other sections of newspapers—such as lifestyle, business, health, etc.—should receive your book and be encouraged to write about it. This "off-the-book-page" coverage in feature and other editorial sections of newspapers and magazines can help to stimulate book sales and to generate other media interest in your work.

THE PRINT MEDIA MAILING LISTS

To conduct a review copy mailing, your publicist will create mailing lists from the publicity department's database and send your book to prospective reviewers in two phases: The first is a bound galley mailing to 50 to 100 long-lead publications (monthly magazines that have an

editorial lead time of three to six months), as well as to some book editors at the top daily newspapers and weekly magazines. The second
mailing takes place when your book comes off press. The publicist will
then mail 150 to 300 copies of your book with press materials to newspaper and magazine book review editors.

If you've written a work of fiction or serious nonfiction, because the
book review community has little turnover, the publisher's reviewer
mailing lists should be fairly comprehensive and up-to-date. On the
other hand, less frequently used specialty mailing lists might need some
work. For example, if you have written a cookbook and your publisher
offers only two cookbooks a year, chances are that its food editors
mailing list is not current. Or say your book would interest readers of
military history, you're going to want to look at the publisher's mailing
list in that category to see that it includes the right periodicals in your
field. Your publicist may not have the time to devote to updating the list
for your particular book's mailing. Even if she updates the list by using
the media directories found in most publicity departments, the names
of reporters and editors listed there are often not the appropriate people and still need verification.

This is where your expertise in your book's subject matter comes
into play. Have a frank conversation with your publicist about what
she thinks of the quality of the mailing list she has on your subject and
how often it is used. Offer to spot-check the contacts on the list and ask
her to print out a copy for you including the phone numbers. (If con-
trolling expenses is important to you and you live close to your publishing house, ask to use a spare desk for a day to make the phone calls
from the office.) Plan on doing this at about the same time that the publicist is writing press materials, or a little earlier. Start with the long-
lead specialty publications in your field, because that's the first mailing.
Call and verify the name of the person who handles book review coverage. Get the address at which they prefer to receive mailings. Try to get
an e-mail address, too. Research the book review contact information
for your alumni magazine and any trade publications that might reach
your target audience.

Think broadly about the publications that should be included on your mailing list. If you've written a cookbook, has your publicist got the bridal magazines on her list, which could be appropriate targets? Suppose your book, whether fiction or nonfiction, has a legal theme. *The American Lawyer* should receive a copy. If your book is about graphic design, the many appropriate trade publications should be represented on the publicist's mailing list, and so on. Most of these publications will have book review editors, or an editor who oversees general book coverage.

Give your publicist the name and addresses of appropriate Web reviewers. Many sites review books and you will need to spend some time surfing the Net to identify the ones that seem worthwhile.

Go to the sites of the top newspapers around the United States and in Canada. When you log onto a newspaper site, search for the word *book* to turn up all the stories that mention a book in that day's paper. Pay attention to how the reporters cover books, whether in a general manner or with a local angle? If so, how can you tie your book into a local story? Does your book raise a potentially controversial issue in the community?

To find the names of appropriate publications and reporters:

- Use the published media directories found at your publishing house and then call to verify the contacts covering your field.

- Go to www.publicrelations.about.com and find the media guides section of the site. There are plenty of resources here to help you track down publications relevant to your campaign.

- Go to www.newspaperlinks.com, a terrific portal that links to 1,200 U.S. daily newspapers, 885 weekly papers, 1,100 Canadian and international papers, 90 newspaper groups, 64 associations, and 23 media organizations.

- Go to www.publist.com, a free database of 150,000 magazines, newspapers, journals, newsletters, and periodicals worldwide. The site provides contact information including Web site addresses and e-mail addresses. Search by topic or individual publications.

- Go to www.newpages.com, for alternative newspapers and literary periodicals in the United States and Canada.

- Go to www.usnewspapers.about.com, a portal to dailies and weeklies, which categorizes papers by subject, making it an easy task to locate special interest publications such as Irish-American or Afro-American papers. The site also has a good listing of college papers.

- Go to www.blueagle.com and www.headlinespot.com/opinion/columnists, portals that link to the sites of syndicated columnists.

- Go to www.literarymarketplace.com. The advertising and marketing section offers publicity resources including lists of radio, television, and print media including producers' names, phone numbers, addresses, and e-mail addresses.

- Go to www.bookweb.org for the names and contact information for book review editors in nineteen U.S. cities. Click on the professional development area, and then on "marketing tools."

- Use a search engine to look for your subject. For example, a quick search on Google (www.google.com) for the word "collectibles" turned up an article on the subject that had been nationally syndicated through the Universal Press Syndicate. If I were an author or publisher of a decorating book, I would track down the reporter to find out if they want to see other books on interior design.

If you're not touring, chances are that the publicist has not considered pitching feature reporters at newspapers around the country about your book. This is because the house has not positioned the book big enough to prompt her to that way of thinking, or she hasn't been able to come up with a pitch that would interest feature writers. If you and your publicist can come up with a strong local angle for that market, pitch the market even if you have no plans to visit there. Reporters can always interview you by phone. Ask your publicist if she will pitch feature editors in markets where you are not traveling.

Your "Big Mouth" Mailing

As long as you're in a mailing list frame of mind, put together a short list of "big mouths"—people who should get a free copy of your book at publication because they will talk it up. If you give these names to your editor's assistant, he or she will happily send out copies of the book, especially if you provide the names on labels. Do not send free copies to your friends and family, no matter how tempted you might be. They should *buy* copies of your book. (Well, of course, you should give one to your mother.)

Sometimes publicists will handle this mailing for you. Freelance publicist Jeanne Krier will send a press kit and book to the author's big-mouth list along with a note that says "Dear so and so, This book is being sent to you with the compliments of the publisher and the author. We hope you recommend it to your friends and associates and that it will reach a broad audience. We welcome your comments."

Your big mouths might not even be people that you know—they are simply people who could spread the word about your book. For example, I once promoted a comic novel about hairdressing by sending complimentary copies to the top hairdressers in town along with a note asking that they put the book in their salons. I knew the campaign was working because, by coincidence, I found myself at dinner with a woman who'd had her hair done in one of the salons who started talking to me about the book. Recently the author Philip Howard did a neat trick to get word of mouth going for his book *The Lost Art of Drawing the Line: How Fairness Went Too Far*, about our litigious culture. Through his agent, he arranged for the management of the Four Seasons restaurant in New York City to put a complimentary copy of his book on every table at lunchtime. The restaurant plays host to a daily power-lunch crowd in entertainment, law, media, and finance, and the book generated a lot of buzz.

Here are examples of off-the-book-page articles from recent editions of newspapers:

- The *New York Times* ran a piece about Michael Ledwidge, an Irish-American telephone cable splicer who works for the Verizon phone company. He had written a thriller called *Bad Connection* featuring, yes, you guessed it, an Irish-American telephone cable splicer.

- An article about a book called *Playful Parenting,* by a Boston-based psychologist, Lawrence Cohen, ran in the *Seattle Post-Intelligencer* and was syndicated to other papers including the *Chicago Tribune*. The book was positioned as an antidote to other parenting books that focus on drumming out children's obnoxious behaviors.

- Like many newspaper sections, the Health section of the *Detroit News* runs "briefs" or brief news items that often mention books. A recent brief mentioned a book called *Self-Coaching: How to Heal Anxiety and Depression,* by Joseph Luciani.

- The Living Smart section of the *Oregonian* interviewed James Mulholland, author of *Praying Like Jesus,* a book that promotes the forgiveness and sacrifice reflected in the Lord's Prayer as opposed to the popularized, self-centered prayer of Jabez.

- The Workplace section of the *Los Angeles Times* ran an article on interviewing strategies based on a book by Dr. Mark Goulston called *Get Out of Your Own Way: Overcoming Self-Defeating Behaviors.*

Look for articles in your subject area and keep a record of the reporters' names. You should also peruse opinion columns. These writers cover any subject that interests them, and often reflect the mood of their communities. Check out the metro section of the newspapers if your book covers topics of local news interest. Call the newspapers to confirm the names of the editor or reporter of the beat that concerns your book. You will notice that in certain sections of the newspaper, several reporters will cover the same subject area. Note the name of anyone who might take an interest in your book, as your publicist can pitch more than one reporter at a newspaper. Spell all names correctly. Give the list—including names, addresses, and phone numbers—to your publicist to include in the press mailing and to make follow-up calls.

Special newspaper sections offer a great booking opportunity and are often overlooked by publicists, partly because they appear irregularly on topics that the publicists aren't pitching frequently. Local and national newspapers and magazines run special sections on topics like career, education, personal finance, and so on. Newspapers often run the sections on a Sunday, the day of the week with the highest circulation. Special section editors work with a two- to three-month lead time. You can get their names from the Bacon's media directory and you should call the contacts listed there to verify the up-to-date contact information. (You will find Bacon's at your local library or you can buy it online at www.bacons.com. Each media directory—Radio/TV/Cable, Newspaper/Magazine—costs about $350. If you are planning to book a lot of your own media on an ongoing basis, and you do not have access to media directories nor time to gather media leads, then the directories are a good investment.) Another, less expensive way to find out what special sections are planned is locating the newspapers' Web sites through your search engine and to look for the online editorial calendar. The calendar is generally posted in the advertising section of the site, as a way to prompt advertisers to buy space in the publication adjacent to specific editorial content. The site will also provide phone numbers so you can then call the editorial department to find out the name of the contact for the special section. If the editorial calendar is not posted then call the advertising department and ask them to send one to you.

Suppose you come across a special section on a subject about which you could be quoted as an expert or that's related to your book. Send the editor a press packet and a letter that explains your credentials. Include some of the issues in your field that you could address in an article. Follow up with a call. (Of course you can ask your publicist to do this, but if your campaign is over, then you can pitch the editors yourself.)

If you have only a little time to devote to your publicity campaign, then a finite assignment that might contribute to your book's success is finding appropriate reporters who might cover your book. Set aside perhaps thirty minutes a day over the course of a few months. Use this time to research and read out-of-town newspaper sites to target the reporters that your publicist should go after. Most likely you will come up with a rich contact list of leads that your publicist can follow up on.

A Booking Tip for Your Publicist—Leads to Reporters Looking for Experts to Interview

Do your publicist a huge favor and let her know about ProfNet (www. profnet.com), a service that notifies publicists of dozens of press leads twice daily by e-mail. The leads are queries from reporters who are on deadline and looking for experts to interview on all kinds of topics. The subscription is expensive for an individual but certainly affordable for a publicity department or for several departments to share in a larger publishing house.

DEBUT SHORT STORY WRITER MANAGES HIS OWN BOOK REVIEW CAMPAIGN

David Lida is the author of a short story collection called *Travel Advisory*. Because he wanted the book to receive as much attention as possible, he knew that he would get heavily involved in the publicity planning for the book. "I thought I'd have to do a lot, but didn't know how much work it would really be," he says now. He worked for a full six months, pretty much full-time, on generating publicity for his book.

A freelance travel writer, he caught a lucky break and traveled to Cancún, Mexico, for a story. His visit coincided with a writer's conference that was held at the local Club Med. There he met some book review editors, who later assigned his book for review. However, having connections and sending out a galley or a copy of his book did not guarantee coverage. He says that every contact required several tactful follow-up calls to generate the coverage he was seeking. Ultimately, he garnered a number of good reviews from leading book review publications, but they took a lot of hard work to get on his part.

He also had some success setting up appearances at universities in the Latin American Studies departments. He counsels that setting up university appearances takes perseverance to catch a professor during office hours, and the booking may take several calls to firm up. Some universities offered him an honorarium. He also got himself invited to the Inter-American Book Fair in San Antonio and to the *Los Angeles Times* Book Fair. The same perseverance paid off with interviews in several newspapers and Web sites.

For the next book, he says, he will look into hiring a publicist to make sure that the reviewers and independent booksellers are aware of his book. Bottom-line advice from Lida to writers who are planning to get involved in their publicity campaigns: "You have to be willing to do what it takes, to take responsibility to do things that shouldn't necessarily be the writer's responsibility."

CORRESPOND WITH BOOK REVIEWERS

Generally, with a few exceptions for the leading titles on the list, in-house publicists do not follow up with book reviewers after a review copy mailing. Some publicists are reluctant to place follow-up calls that might "bother" the book reviewers. At worst, book reviewers will refuse to take the call or will behave in a snappish manner on the phone. But without follow-up calls, many worthy books would never get noticed or reviewed. Even for the big books on the list, follow-ups are important to inform book reviewers of the publication date so they can schedule reviews accordingly. (Unlike in-house publicists, if they've been hired to handle the book review campaign then freelancers will call most of the book reviewers on the mailing list.)

Before pursuing reviewers, be gut-honest with yourself. Does your book really belong on the book review pages? If you've written a self-help book, newspaper book reviewers are simply not going to take an interest. Don't expect your publicist to call reviewers about your diet book, your cookbook, your craft book, your twelve-step recovery program book, and so on.

As a publicist I found it sobering to visit newspaper book review editors in their offices, which were often cubbies surrounded by stacks of books and unopened packages from publishers. I learned in my follow-up phone calls to identify a book by saying something like, "It's the thick one with the yellow spine," and asking the editor to put it at the top of their pile to take a look at. With more than 100,000 titles published a year—there were actually 122,108 books published in 2000—your book is up against an enormous playing field. A newspaper might review 260 books a year in its daily pages and another 150 to 1,200 a year in its Sunday pages, depending on the size of the paper. To pique interest, your publicist's calls or correspondence to the book editor must be dead on target.

You can negotiate with a publicist who is reluctant to make follow-up calls. Perhaps she'd be willing to send e-mails to the reviewers. Perhaps you can convince her to follow up with ten of them. When I was a publicist, if I truly believed in the literary merits of a book then those phone calls were easy to make. So try to make your publicist believe in your book—regardless of what she thought about the book when (and if) she read it. Part of your job is to make your publicist a convinced and therefore convincing salesperson.

Finally, if you believe that your book is worth attention on the book review pages, and your publicist will not make any phone calls, bite the bullet and pick up the phone yourself. But before you even dream of contacting a book review editor, or any reporter for that matter, study his or her section of the paper, which you will find online. In any of your own publicity efforts, you will stand a better chance of success if you take the time and trouble to learn about the media you're pitching.

If you prefer not to cold-call the book reviewers, first drop them a short note or e-mail about your book. If you have a Web site, include the link in your e-mail and invite the book reviewer to read the first chapter, perhaps, that you have posted. The immediacy of the link will encourage the reviewer to check out your work. Invite the reviewer to e-mail you for another copy of the book, if necessary. You may also follow up with a polite call to see if they need a copy of the book. Your publicist can give you the mailing addresses, phone numbers, and e-mail addresses. If she won't share the contact information with you, you can easily search for the newspapers' Web sites.

When you tell your publicist about your plans to contact the reviewers you might be surprised at her reaction. She might suddenly seem motivated to make those calls after all. Due to fear of embarrassment, some publicists dread the thought of their authors calling the media. Everyone in the business has stories of authors harassing book review editors and bad-mouthing their publishing houses.

You might experience anxiety once the reviews start coming in. However much you might want to avoid reading reviews, keep an eye out for the good ones. As a way to prompt more review coverage, your publicist can send them to other publications that have not yet covered your book. Even better, a quick e-mail note with a link to the review you want them to see is an efficient way to alert book editors. Coverage in other publications sometimes prompts a reviewer to take a second look at a book they passed over.

If you get bad reviews that you feel are unwarranted or unjustified, then you have a small measure of recourse: Write a letter to the editor. Refrain from writing in anger because your letter will most likely sound hysterical and foolish. Be specific, not personal, about your complaint. Once you've sent the letter, it may run with a response in the publication.

A Booking Tip for Your Publicist—Getting a Syndicated or Wire Service Feature Article

Several newspaper companies own multiple newspapers, as well as other media interests, such as Gannett (ninety local papers and *USA Today*, www.gannett.com), Cox (seventeen local dailies, www.coxnews.com), Scripps Howard (twenty-one dailies, www.scripps.com), and Knight Ridder (thirty-two dailies, www.kri.com). What this means is that if your publicist is able to get you an interview in one of these papers—and they range from large urban papers like the *Atlanta Journal-Constitution* to small circulation town papers like the *Ocean County Observer* in Toms River, New Jersey—she has a shot at getting you serious national exposure if the article runs in all newspapers in the syndicate. Here's how she can try to influence the chances of national pickup.

Once the interview is secured and scheduled, your publicist should call the national office of the newspaper service and talk to the book or features editor. This is the person who assigns stories and selects articles from the local papers to run nationally. Your publicist should pitch that editor to run the local story in the other papers owned by the chain. Another approach is to ask the local reporter to offer the story for the national feed, which they don't do automatically for all stories. A prompt sometimes helps.

The Web sites of the large media companies list all the local papers that they own. If one of the papers is located near you, then, by using a strong local angle, you have a good shot at scoring an interview that runs nationally.

Similar to the news syndicates, the Associated Press wire service can create an enormous amount of coverage from just one press hit. If your book has a strong local angle or a compelling story to tell then pitch your local Associated Press bureau. (See www.ap.org.) Recently the AP ran a long feature story about a book on reflexology by a Hollywood massage therapist. Though the story came out of the Connecticut bureau, the article had no discernable local angle. If the author was originally from Connecticut, that fact didn't make it into the final article.

The wires will also run book reviews. I once tracked down a reporter in the AP bureau in Kentucky because someone had mentioned that he liked to read thrillers. I suggested that he review the thriller I was promoting, and he did. Tracking down the right reporter can take some sleuthing, but the payoff can be big. In this case it was a favorable review that was syndicated and printed in newspapers nationwide.

GOSSIP COLUMNS

Gossip columns, many of which are syndicated, afford a significant opportunity to launch a book. Gossip columnists are looking for celebrity news (is your novel under consideration for a film option?), for sensational exposés, for speculation about the real inspiration for the characters in your roman à clef. Liz Smith tells publicists how to get an item into her nationally syndicated column by:

- Reading her column so you know what she likes.

- Writing an item in the style of the column.

- Faxing it to her office on an exclusive basis (meaning that you've given the item to no one else, and that you've stated on your fax "EXCLUSIVE TO LIZ SMITH").

Many other gossip columns are syndicated nationally and appear online. Check them out to come up with an angle.

Smith's advice about reading her column first so you know what she likes is the first lesson in publicity. Publicists hit dead ends when they pitch ideas that are inappropriate for a particular writer's column or magazine. Knowledge of the media is essential to get the book coverage you want—and I know I've stated this point before—but it is an often overlooked publicity fundamental.

Here's an example of the power of gossip columns. Some years ago I sent Liz Smith an item about Wilt Chamberlain's autobiography, *A View from Above*. Through the instant exposure afforded by Liz's column and the fact that the other media assiduously read her column, the notorious sound bite from that book became household knowledge overnight. The sound bite in question is of course Wilt's statement that he'd had sexual relationships with 20,000 women. Never have I received so many calls from (male) producers and reporters wanting to know if this fact was true and if so how did Wilt arrive at that number because "we've just been figuring this out on the calculator and . . ."

THE OP-ED PAGES

Your local newspaper and national newspapers offer another print publicity opportunity for your book. Op-ed pieces range from the extremely serious to the tongue-in-cheek, but they always connect to current events or current trends.

Apart from timeliness, writing and placing op-eds depends on your authority on a subject. For example, an author of terrorist thrillers known for his scrupulous research might have legitimate comments on the increase in worldwide terrorist activities.Other examples:

- When the American Academy of Pediatrics recently announced that television viewing was found to be detrimental to children, a children's book author or an educator might have written an op-ed piece about their own position on the issue.

- The author of a book on interior design could have written a piece in connection with Senator Hillary Clinton's move to a fancy, new furniture-less house in Westchester, New York.

- The author of a book on work and labor could have written a piece after George W. Bush departed for his monthlong vacation in his first year as president.

- Barbara Ehrenreich, author of *Nickel and Dimed: On (Not) Getting By in America,* wrote an op-ed for the *New York Times* shortly after it was announced that Wal-Mart employees were suing the company for forcing them to work unpaid hours. In her book she wrote about working at Wal-Mart as part of her effort to understand how the working poor live.

Before you tackle an op-ed piece, read your target paper's op-ed section to get a feel for the tone of argument and the length of the op-eds that the newspaper publishes. Most run between 500 and 800 words. Submission guidelines may be mentioned on the op-ed page or perhaps on the newspaper's Web site. (See the *Washington Post*'s Web site for an example at www.washingtonpost.com.) Clarify the point of your argument in your mind before setting to the task of writing the essay. If your essay is reacting to a news event, then turn it in within a day or two of that event. Otherwise the op-ed is out-of-date and irrelevant to a daily newspaper. Submit your op-ed essay to newspapers one at a time. In other words, don't submit your op-ed simultaneously to many papers.

Some op-eds may be of general topical interest rather than strictly time sensitive. Novelist Cameron Stracher recently wrote an op-ed for the *New York Times* about moving to the suburbs because his apartment in the city had become too small for his growing family. The essay's point was about regretting growing older and having to make the mature decision to leave Manhattan. The piece reflected a general trend in New York City and so was not pegged specifically to the news; it gave the author a chance to display his writing and have his novel mentioned in his byline.

A subject that sometimes crops up on op-ed pages is what it's like to go on a publicity tour. Newspapers seem to revisit this idea from time to time: Pitch the idea to your local newspaper's op-ed page.

WHAT HAPPENS WHEN A BOOK ON THE SAME SUBJECT AS YOURS IS COMING OUT AT THE SAME TIME?

This isn't always bad news because two books on the same subject coming out at the same time usually create a greater level of attention than either book would have received alone. That said, your publicist will need to work double time to convey the outstanding merits of your book and to make the media as aware of your book as the competition.

In your interviews, resist the urge to bad-mouth the competition. When you're asked point-blank how you think the two books are different, then honestly point out the distinctions without being derogatory. Otherwise you run the risk of starting a mudslinging match or looking graceless.

If you're aware of another writer working in your subject area, then try to reach the marketplace first, or at least simultaneously with your competition. With the first book to market probably preempting all media interest in the topic, publishing months later could be disastrous.

THE PRINT PUBLICITY CAMPAIGN—A SUMMARY

Print coverage for your book can take several forms:

- Book reviews

- Off-the-book-page coverage or feature coverage

- Item mentions in gossip columns or more thoughtful coverage from more serious-minded columnists

- Op-ed pieces

Use the Internet to gather leads for your publicist. You can research more appropriate columnists and reporters than she will ever have time for.

7

THE PUBLICITY TOUR

A publicity tour normally involves visiting between three and ten cities, over the course of one to three weeks. During a tour, you will go to local television and radio stations for live or taped interviews, meet print reporters at your hotel or other locales for interviews, and give readings or talks at bookstores and other venues. A media escort will probably meet you at the airport to take you to as many as six to eight appointments in one day—all prearranged by your publicist. In between you will stop by bookstores to meet store managers and sign copies of your book.

Publishers have reduced the average number of cities for their tours, because local media programming has been displaced by national shows. Noonday television talk shows that once provided good media opportunities are gone in many markets. (Though local television news shows will still cover books.) Instead publishers are forced to depend on national media, confining many publicity tours to New York, Washington, D.C., and Los Angeles—the three U.S. cities where most of the national television media is located—and to Toronto, the major national media market in Canada. In turn, greater competition makes a national media booking more difficult to secure than in the past. As novelist Jane Heller points out, celebrities have become more accessible to the media and have further depleted the airtime available to everyone else. If a television show has a choice between booking an author and booking a celebrity, then guess who gets the booking.

To improve your chances, you might get to know the national media and the kinds of author guests that they book on their shows. In other words, watch the shows to understand how you might fit on them. Check out the shows' archives on their Web sites. The site www.govspot. com/pulse/talkshows.htm includes links to some of the top national talk shows like *The Charlie Rose Show, Larry King Live,* and so on.

The more limited media opportunities in local markets, as compared to the past, means that you and your publicist have to get more creative about finding a strong local angle for each city. Local print, radio, and television news need a compelling hook. A good way to accomplish this is to anchor your visit to a city with a speaking engagement at a local university, corporation, or other venue. (See Chapter Ten, page 194, for a discussion about setting up speaking appearances.)

A publicity tour can be an experience of extremes—your greatest highs, your lowest lows. You might have some terrific interviews with smart reporters who really seem to understand and like your book. Then your next interview could be an encounter with someone who misses the point of your book entirely. One day you might have a crowded bookstore appearance, an empty event the next. Your goal for the tour is to help your publicist create as many positive bookselling opportunities as possible.

BOOKING THE TOUR

Your publicist will consult you about your schedule to set your tour dates about twelve weeks before the tour begins. (If you have particular scheduling requirements you can set the dates even earlier.) She will set up your local bookstore appearances six to twelve weeks ahead of your tour so that the bookstores can include your event in their promotional calendars. Six to eight weeks in advance, she will pitch you to the top local television shows in your tour cities, which tend to make their commitments to author interviews earlier than other media. When your books come off press—about four weeks before the tour starts—she will send books and press materials to pitch the rest of the media in the tour markets.

Try to stretch your tour dollars by researching cheaper fares. Technically your publicist is the one who should do this, but publicists often wait to book flights until about thirty days before the first tour city. Come up with some bargain fares and you might be able to convince your publisher to spring for booking some extra tour cities without straining its funds.

Some publishers schedule tours tighter than the four-week booking lead. In other words, the bound books arrive at the publishing house only three weeks before a tour is due to start. This might be due to a production delay, or perhaps the need to promote the book beginning on a certain date. This chain of events means that by the time the producers and potential interviewers receive their review copies, the publicist has only two weeks to book the tour. By then many of the top media slots have already been taken.

Remember, the publicist is competing not only with other publishers sending authors to the same tour cities, but also with local celebrities, spokespeople, doctors, and business leaders who also want to appear in the local media. A head start is crucial.

Some producers and interviewers will set up an interview without seeing the book. This allows the publicist to book interviews using only the press materials. However, many interviewers prefer to see the book before committing to an interview. Make smart use of your time. If you suspect that the tour is being booked too late to create an effective schedule, then suggest that the publicist postpone the tour by a couple of weeks. Unless you have prearranged book signings or other appearances that are not easily rescheduled, a delay is good strategy.

Get involved in the planning of the cities and the tour dates. If you think that a particular city should be included on your tour then say so and be prepared to explain why. Ask the publicist for the expected date of the book's arrival in-house. Ask, as well, if the house tends to receive the books promptly from the printer or the warehouse. Opt for the tour to occur five to six weeks (rather than three to four weeks) after the bound book date. The extra time between bound book date and tour date will give your publicist the cushion she will need for booking a full media schedule, even if there are delays in the book's production or delivery. You can control the dates of your tour because without you, there is no tour. Of course, if there is a fixed date to which your book's promotion is connected, like Valentine's Day, then you will not have as much flexibility.

Even with an exceptionally short lead time, publicists can readily create media tours for at least three kinds of books: Books that are controversial; books by celebrities, for which producers will always make room on short notice; and sports books, because sports producers and writers schedule interviews closer to a tour date than general media interviewers.

Your publicist selects your tour cities based on several criteria:

- Whether your subject matter has potential appeal to television and radio talk shows

- Whether you have the capability to handle national talk show appearances or need some practice in local markets first

- The subject matter of your book; for example, Atlanta is known as a good cookbook market because local television will book cookbook demo segments and local cooking schools will host author events

- Where you have contacts—i.e., friends, family, or associates who can put you up and help deliver audiences for book signings

- Whether you travel frequently on business and can do publicity en route

- Where booksellers have a good track record at hosting successful author events

- The size and demographics of the media market

Once the cities and dates have been locked in, your publicist will select her media lists and send ten to fifteen books in each market to the media contacts there. She will begin following up with the media about a week later. Your publicist will probably experience what I think of as "booking karma." Some booking days go very well where producers and reporters jump to say "yes" to the publicity pitch. "When can we have your author in our studio?" they eagerly ask. Those are the great days that give a publicist a booking high that fuels creative pitching for the rest of the day.

But other days might begin with a series of "nos" and boy, those are frustrating! When I ran into days like that, I'd stop altogether, retool my pitch, and then wait until the next day before picking up the phone again.

All publicists have personal techniques by which they pump themselves up during pitching time. Still, when some pitches inevitably go bad, most publicists feel rotten. Many are embarrassed as they watch the tour dates getting closer and have few bookings to show for their efforts. This is when they may become incommunicado or evasive with the author.

However, because of the good relationship you will nurture with your publicist, you will be ensured of hearing the bad news along with the good. Once she begins booking your tour, you will contact your publicist frequently. Having previously discussed the pitch with you, she's not as likely to feel defensive about the results. If the bookings are not going well, you will offer to help rethink the approach. Being a partner in the process saves you from nasty surprises later, like flying to a city to do only one or two meager interviews.

> ### A Booking Tip for Your Publicist:
> ### Use a Media Booking to Leverage More
>
> Publicists routinely send booking alerts by e-mail to in-house staff. When the booking is significant—like a major national television show—one publicist I know will blind copy other producers who haven't yet committed to doing an interview. Some producers object to receiving an obvious mass e-mail. But usually, the e-mails prompt other producers to quickly book the author.

Despite your publicist's efforts, she may have to cancel a tour city or two because of too few interviews with top local or national media. If your tour schedule looks thin, suggest that the publicist try the top stations in a couple of other "replacement" cities to see if the pitch works better. Tour markets can be inconsistent, with jam-packed days, say, in Pittsburgh and little to do in Nashville. Be careful at this stage how to involve your editor. If you tell your editor that the publicity bookings are going badly, clarify that you believe that your publicist is trying her best (if that's what you believe). That way the editor will not make the publicist feel defensive in any follow-up conversations between them. Authors who tattle behind a publicist's back are extremely annoying if not threatening, especially if the editor and the publicist are not on the best of terms, or if the publicist is relatively junior in the organization. You can't know those internal politics, so stay out of them. They can hurt your book.

Your publicist might show you the evolving tour schedule. She will certainly show you a finished schedule a few days before you leave in order for you to plan for any interview requirements and to pack appropriate clothes. The schedule may even change after you've hit the road, with last-minute interviews falling into place or sudden cancellations. The tour schedule should itemize every detail about your tour days: The name, address, and location of your hotel; name and numbers of your escorts; home and office phone numbers for your publicist and editor; arrival time and start time for your interviews; whether the interviews are live or taped and if taped, the anticipated airdates; any particular information to mention in your interviews such as the time and location of the book signing in town that same day so that listeners can attend; your publisher's 800 number for radio stations to mention on air so listeners can order the book; the time you will depart for the airport and, always helpful, a comment about how long it will take you to reach the airport from your last appearance. Your escorts will also receive a copy of the itinerary. (See the appendix, page 301, for a sample tour schedule.)

A Booking Tip for Your Publicist—Work the Weekend Shift

"Make it big, make it loud, make it Saturday," is advice from one media professional. The idea is to announce your news on a weekend when fewer news events compete with yours. The tactic is particularly effective with softer news that might not get as much attention during the week when it faces more competition from hard news.

One book publicist got savvy about working with the local press after his brief sojourn at an aggressive public relations agency. The weekend assignment editor, in a slow news week, looks for ideas for coverage that the weekly assignment editor might not feel so hungry for. The weekenders also have fewer calls to field from publicists so the caller is more likely to get a hearing. This publicist learned to time his press pitches for the weekends when the more receptive weekend assignment editors were on duty, and was successful in planting a number of stories that ended up on the front pages of the local tabloids. During the week, those same stories might have been buried inside the paper. Of course what he was pitching had genuine news value, but his method of handling the publicity gave the books the best shot at maximum coverage.

WHAT TO PACK FOR THE TOUR

Pack a minimum of clothes. Take clothes that you've worn before so that you are comfortable wearing them. Take lightweight clothes that don't wrinkle easily. You will wear a jacket for your television interviews—the television studios are cold, and the jacket will give you a tailored professional look. Don't take outfits that are inappropriate to wear on television, i.e., no striped patterns or bright whites that will "vibrate" on camera. In the weeks leading up to your tour, watch morning television and pay attention to what the hosts wear: tailored jackets in solid colors for the women and men. Wear clothes that can be hand-washed at night and line-dried for morning's wear, if necessary. Avoid blouses or shirts with tight collars that make you look like you're choking.

Think about the topic of your book: Doing a cookbook demo? Then have an apron stamped with the title of your book on the bib and wear it on the set. Your topic is informal? Then wear something informal (though not a T-shirt!) rather than a jacket and tie or stiffly tailored clothing. You will soon get a sense of what dress styles are effective from watching author interviews.

If you're not appearing on television, then your radio and print interviews have no particular dress requirement. Still, remember that some print reporters will describe the way you look in an article and may bring a photographer. You don't want to look like a slob (or smell bad, like one of my authors did. The way he smelled made me reluctant to book any face-to-face interviews for him. No kidding!).

You will also want a good book for the plane ride. If you're like me you will take five books for fear of running out of reading material. But really, take only one or two books if you are appearing at bookstores. Very often, a bookstore owner will thank you by offering you a complimentary book. You will have plenty of opportunity to pick up books along the tour—don't weigh yourself down.

THE TOUR

The tour is exhausting and exhilarating. You set off from home to arrive at your first destination, where you might arrive late evening at your hotel. Early the next morning your media escort will meet you in the lobby to drive you to your appointments all day and get you to the airport at night. You will be the subject of a series of radio, television, and print interviews through the course of the day, where everyone will ask you the same questions about your book. You will meet some interviewers who seem genuinely enthusiastic about your work, and you will meet others who seem just plain bored. The occasional interviewers who ask you different questions from the others will strike you as geniuses. As the road show begins to become a blur, in some interviews you will literally forget if you've already talked about one of your points a few minutes before. One of the challenges in doing a tour is remembering what you've said to what interviewer. Stay vigilant. After completing your evening bookstore reading, you will take an evening or night flight heading to your next tour city. If you don't fly out that night, then you will likely go back to your hotel room alone with your adrenaline still pumping, feeling like you're all dressed up with no place to go. But you'd better get to sleep because you've got an early flight in the morning.

When you are on tour, get the full names and addresses of all the interviewers, producers, and booksellers. Travel with a pack of note cards to write thank-you notes while they are all fresh in your mind, and you in theirs. While many people have bemoaned the decline of the art of personal correspondence in the age of e-mail, let's not kid ourselves. Personal letters were well on the decline before our correspondence became electronic. If anything, e-mail has helped restore written personal dialogue. Still, your simple handwritten note to a reporter or bookseller will create a lasting impression and remind the recipient of you and your book.

Stay in touch with your editor and publicist while you're on the road. If your schedule is too crammed to allow time for contact during the day, then leave an informative message on their voice mailboxes after hours so they hear it as soon as they arrive at work in the morning. Report any good news right away—large turnouts at bookstores, a good guess (or real tally) at the number of copies sold at an event, or aspects of the book that seemed to particularly interest the media. Your publicist can feed this information to producers in upcoming cities or to set up more interviews. If the tour is going well, the editor and publicist can use that information to advocate for more advertising or more tour cities for your book. Your good news keeps the publishing staff focused on sales and inventory levels for your book. If you are underwriting the cost of the tour, you could earn some unanticipated support in the form of funding to expand your efforts.

Your publisher will probably ask your escort to arrange "drop-ins" or informal book signings. Your publicist might call bookstores a couple of weeks before you arrive in town to ask if you can drop by to sign stock. Very often the stores will order more books. The books that you sign are then marked as specially autographed by the author. The value of doing this beyond creating consumer appeal is that a store manager notices you and your books get better display. You certainly do not need a publicist to set up informal drop-ins. Simply call the stores yourself and ask for the store manager.

If you do not have the lead time to call the store ahead of your visit, drop into stores and ask to meet the manager. Politely introduce yourself and ask if you may sign copies of your book. The manager will be happy to oblige you and will put "Signed by the Author" stickers on your book and move the book to the front of the store. (Signed copies make great gifts.) Then thank the store manager. This advice might seem obvious, but you'd be surprised. One bookseller praised a friend of mine, an author, for being so polite when he dropped by the store. The previous author who'd swung by had been rude, signing his books and moving them to the front of the store without asking first. As soon as that author left the store, the bookseller moved the book right to the back. Remember, you're on the bookseller's turf, so don't act with impunity or entitlement.

A bestselling author advises, "Visit every bookstore that you can." When you arrive in a tour city, ask your escort to take you to bookstores in between your scheduled interviews and signings. Introduce yourself to store managers. Get to know them. Carry "Signed by the Author" stickers around with you. Some stores are too small to be regular stops on the author trail, and may not be prepared for authors who drop in to sign stock. The store managers will be grateful that you have stickers and will place your book up front. You can have the stickers made by a local printing store in your neighborhood, or you can find similar services online.

AN AUTHOR DREAMS UP AN IDEA FOR A LOCAL TOUR THAT LEADS TO NATIONAL PRESS COVERAGE

Novelist Jane Heller was in a funk because *Publishers Weekly* had given her first novel, *Cha Cha Cha,* a bad review. "I took to my bed," she said, but then realized that she couldn't let one bad review knock her off her plan to become a full-time writer. Instead, she says, the review motivated her to create a real success. When *People* magazine called the novel the "Beach Book of the Week," Heller saw her chance at vindication and came up with a plan for the "first-ever beach tour." Her publisher agreed and Heller got to work. She lived in Connecticut at the time and called a number of the larger state beaches and parks in her area to get permits. Then she worked with local bookstores to have them sell books at her beach events. Then she took her folding table, display poster and books to the beach, and set up shop. While the booksellers sold some books, she says that the tour's real value was the publicity it generated. At every beach she visited, the local media covered her event, including print, radio, and television. Ultimately, the beach tour was one of the hooks that grabbed *Today*, which interviewed Heller shortly afterward.

Heller says that writers need to understand that "the Cinderella story is not the way publishing works." In other words, the fantastic stories about writers who are swept into the limelight for their first novels and catapulted onto national bestseller lists are rare occurrences. "The biggest reality," says Heller, "is that marketing your book is a constant battle. Your publisher will turn down many of your ideas, but sometimes they will say yes." At work on her tenth novel, Heller's book contracts now stipulate that she has marketing consultation on her books.

CREATE BROADCAST NEWS COVERAGE FOR A NOVEL

Publicist Justin Loeber threw himself heart and soul into the campaign for a debut novelist named Diane McKinney-Whetstone (www.mckinney-whetstone.com). *Tumbling* became a house favorite, because the publishing staff really enjoyed the book and adored the author. Loeber not only secured widespread book review coverage for this literary novel, but he also managed to book the author on CBS's *This Morning* (the forerunner of the current CBS *The Early Show*) and *The Geraldo Rivera Show*. He got the CBS booking by pitching hard, politely, and persistently: He pitched the triumphant success story of a woman, who was a public affairs officer for the Department of Agriculture Forest Service and wrote fiction by night, all while raising a family. *The Geraldo Rivera Show* happened because he pitched the idea of "Dreams Can Come True," all of which demonstrates that the positioning or packaging of an author is everything when it comes to trying to book the media.

Loeber's advice for authors is to research a show and try to visualize why a segment on your book would interest the show's audience. Very often, when a show turns him down, he will talk to the author to try to figure out another angle so he can pitch the book another way. "A publicist would be lying," Loeber says, "if he claimed to be an authority on every subject." When he starts out on a campaign, he asks the author for two or three reasons why producers and viewers should be interested in a segment on the book.

An author who is passionate and knowledgeable about his or her subject area and who is actively engaged with the marketing of the book is Loeber's idea of the perfect author to work with.

MEDIA ESCORTS

Nicknamed "author-haulers" by humorist and writer Calvin Trillin, media escorts provide a valuable service to authors on tour, though one of my authors was seriously disappointed to discover that these escorts aren't the sexy kind. Your escort is your best friend and ally in each of your tour cities. They will meet you at the airport or at your hotel and troubleshoot any glitches that come up during the day. They keep your day running smoothly, get you to your interviews on time, and arrange last minute drop-ins to bookstores that are carrying your book. Joy Delf in Seattle meets her clients with a care basket in her backseat, filled with sundry items needed through the day, such as energy boosters and water and even dry socks on a rainy day. Some escorts are delightfully indiscreet and will tell you stories about other authors they have driven around. This, of course, is entertaining gossip, but should remind you to behave nicely unless you want to become a tour legend yourself.

Naturally the escorts know the local media very well. Most of them keep an active up-to-date media list for their city and the surrounding suburbs. Every time I booked a tour, my first calls were to the escorts in the tour cities to talk about any new media opportunities. This always gave me confidence in my knowledge of the local media market before I started booking. Talking to the escorts also alerted me to reschedule the tour dates to avoid any major local events—like a football game— that might siphon off bookstore event attendees. For authors who are setting up their own tours, the escorts are extremely helpful. When you reserve a day of media escorting, the escort will give you a media list to work with. Some escorts have recently started to book publicity in their markets. Ask your publicist for the contact information for the escorts in your tour cities. (See page 272 for a list of escorts.)

The escorts can help identify opportunities for off-the-beaten-track author appearances. If you and your publicist lock into your tour cities early on, then ask your publicist to brainstorm with the escort about speaking venues such as universities, libraries, and local clubs. (Or ask if you can call the escort.) Because speaking events sometimes require a longer lead time to set up, you and your publicist will want to have this information as early in the booking process as possible.

Some escorts specialize in cookbook author tours. Called food escorts, they will buy the groceries for your demo segment, and will prepare any food that needs to be cooked in advance for the set. If necessary, they will also help you set up your demo on set before you are interviewed.

TROUBLESHOOTING ON TOUR

Your publicist sends you the itinerary the day before you're supposed to leave, and it's filled with mistakes and long empty stretches of time with few interviews scheduled.

If there are gaps in the schedule, then ask the local escort to take you to every bookstore possible in the region, to build recognition among store managers for you and your book. Next time, though, stay in frequent contact with your publicist while she's booking your tour to redirect the tour into other cities or marketing.

You've just appeared on the city's number one noontime live radio talk show. You stop off at the local bookstore on the way to your next interview. They do not have any copies of your book and in fact have never carried the book.

This is a common plight for author and bookstore alike. Sometimes books are delayed in shipping from the printer or from the warehouse. Sometimes the bookstore didn't order the book on time or the order got lost. Sometimes the publicist didn't alert the sales department of the tour city appearance or the sales rep didn't get around to alerting their customers. There's not much you can do about the city you're in, but call your publicist and ask that she and the sales reps contact booksellers in later tour cities. The booksellers will stock up on extra copies of your book in anticipation of your media interviews in their town.

You show up at the bookstore for your evening reading to discover that the bookstore sold out of your book following your noon radio interview.

This is good news—proof that your publicity appearances are effective in generating sales. In this situation, a bookstore will take orders for customers who've arrived to see you and you will sign bookplates for them to insert in their books later. The bookstore will reorder copies of your book and, because of your sales success, is likely to put the book in the front of the store.

You show up at a television station for your appointed early-morning live interview and the producer tells you that you weren't expected until tomorrow. (Or tells you that you weren't expected at all.)

Ask your escort to quickly call the producers and reporters for any interviews left in the day to reconfirm your itinerary. A publicist usually reconfirms all publicity appearances a day or two before you show up, but some publicists forget and producers make mistakes, too. Call your publicist to check that she's reconfirmed the interviews for the rest of the schedule.

You arrive late in a city, show up at the hotel, and find they have no record of your reservation. Or they have a reservation but the room charge won't be billed directly to the publishing house. The hotel clerk asks you for your credit card.

Hotels are legendary for screwing up reservations, and the mix-up is probably not your publicist's fault. Be calm but insistent at the check-in desk, and ask to talk to the manager. If the hotel still refuses to directly bill your publisher, then have the charge put on your credit card. Then leave a message for your publicist at her office number and have her instruct the travel agency to redirect the billing for future hotel stays. The travel agency can sometimes even straighten this out before checkout. *Don't* call your publicist or your editor at home about this.

You have a major national media campaign all lined up. But then there's major breaking news—such as the death of Princess Diana or the Gulf War or the destruction of the World Trade Center. Your interviews are cancelled for the foreseeable future.

The publicist will have trouble rescheduling these interviews. Even though the television stations booked your interview in the belief that you will make an interesting guest, when the publicist tries to rebook you, the station may consider your book old news. Also, rescheduling you would require the producer to cancel or postpone other previously scheduled guests, which they are unwilling to do unless your book story is particularly compelling. Some of your interviews will be salvaged, some may be taped for later airing, but many will be lost and there's little that you can do about it. The larger the disaster, the longer it takes for the media and the public to return to their normal daily interests.

In a disaster, other books and authors will come to the fore. For example, in the immediate aftermath of the World Trade Center attacks, the major media interviewed Tom Clancy because of his authority as a writer of techno-thrillers and Eric Darton about his recent book, *Divided We Stand: A Biography of New York City's World Trade Center.*

Your media escort fails to show up to take you to your interview.

This is an unlikely event, though within the realm of the possible— perhaps her car got towed, which did happen to one of my author's escorts. First try calling the contact numbers for the escort, who usually has a cell phone. Then get in touch with your publicist. If you can't reach either person, arrange backup transit immediately through your hotel. If the publisher is already underwriting your tour then don't worry about the cost. Your goal is to get to your interviews promptly. Leave a message with your publicist and with the escort's voice mail as to your whereabouts. Your escort has a copy of your itinerary and will probably catch up to you at a later stop in your day.

Your tour schedule tells you that you should take a taxi to your next interview but a taxi will not stop for you and you are now going to be late for your live interview downtown.

This happened to one of my authors. Taxis wouldn't stop for him and he finally managed to get to the radio station with only one minute to spare. If this happens to you and you don't have time to call a car service, find a pay phone (or use your cell phone) in a quiet place and call the producer. A radio station can conduct the interview live by phone.

Any author might have trouble getting a taxi, but it can be a particular challenge for authors of color. Your publicist, who is likely white, may not realize or may forget that getting a cab could be a hassle for you, so politely insist on a car service or a media escort to get to your interviews. Similarly, in cities that are unfamiliar to you where you might feel uncomfortable trying to get a taxi, ask your publicist to schedule car services for you.

Your flight is canceled and you will miss the event scheduled in your next tour city tonight.

See if you can get on the next available flight or try to switch airlines. Call your publicist so that she can decide how to handle the missed interviews and to reschedule the flight. She might reroute you to your next city and skip the day that had been planned, or she might try to juggle that day until the end of your schedule. If this happens after your publicist has gone home, then call her at home. If you can't reach her there, call the twenty-four-hour emergency travel agency number that should be part of your itinerary. You should also call the media escort in the destination city to alert her to your delay. If that does not work, call the producer or bookseller who's expecting you so that they can make alternate arrangements and let customers know of the change in plans. Leave a message about your revised plans for your publicist.

Your publicist leaves the company at the beginning of your tour.

Get on the phone right away with your editor and the director of publicity. What is the contingency plan? If the plan seems inadequate, say so. You may need to get your agent involved and ask that your editor step in to advocate on your behalf.

If the publicity director plans to reassign the title to another publicist on staff, ask the director about the number of other titles that publicist is working on. Ask also if the director will instruct the new publicist that your tour is a priority. Ask if the publicity director would consider hiring a freelancer immediately to work on the tour. Ask how the new in-house publicist will handle the additional workload and suggest that a freelance publicist be hired for certain tour cities (if your tour is a big one) or for national media bookings. These are expenses that houses are often willing to assume when they're suddenly short-staffed.

You're in the middle of an interview and the reporter seems disconcertingly hostile toward you.

Even if your book is uncontroversial, you may encounter hostile reporters. Some reporters use an edgy approach to goad their interview subjects into letting their guard down. If the reporter's manner is making you uncomfortable, you might ask—unemotionally—why he or she is so angry with you. The reporter will be surprised to be confronted and may back down. But if you don't think you can persuade the reporter to see your point of view fairly, then feel free to end the interview politely.

A radio host's style may be normally aggressive and you may find yourself taking part in a live hostile interview. In other words, you've become part of an act. Keep your cool, and do not rise to the bait. Try to stick to your message and display your good manners and humor, and perhaps bemusement at the antics going on around you. And remember that this, too, shall pass.

You're in the middle of an interview and all seems to be going well when the reporter suddenly asks you about that embarrassing police incident in your past that you wish no one knew about.

The best way to handle tough questions about personal or controversial events in your life is to prepare for them. Chances are you will never hear the question you fear, but tell your publicist about your concerns, and work with her to shape the appropriate response. Practice that response so that you're able to get your point across with ease.

TOUR WITH OTHER AUTHORS

Increase your exposure by traveling with another author, even if you have different publishers. Generally, authors who tour together already know one another, and are prepared to spend many hours on the road driving from store to store, from town to town. Sometimes their publishers foot the bill; sometimes they pay their own way. The advantages of a shared author tour are reduced expenses, companionship to embolden you to make yourselves noticed in a bookstore, and a two-for-one lineup that appeals to booksellers and audiences. For an effective road trip, plan well in advance, and allow for more time than you think you will need for road travel so that you arrive on time at your bookings.

Check out www.nmomysteries.com, a group site for four mystery writers Lee Harris, Jonnie Jacobs, Lora Roberts, and Valerie Wolzien, who have teamed up in their promotion efforts. They tour together, produce group ads and promotional material, and publish a newsletter. They offer an account on their site of how they set up their book tours and how on one tour, they visited seventeen bookstores and libraries in nine days. They've discovered that they all benefit from one another's readers, by enlarging the size of the audiences and exposing their work to new readers. Because two of them live in the East and two in the West, they've also enlarged one another's geographical fan base.

"We've gone on the road six times in as many years," they report. "One person does the initial—and most difficult—job of contacting stores and mapping the itinerary. Ideally any day that doesn't involve long hours traveling contains at least two events. While mystery and independent bookstores are the backbone of our trips, we've spoken at libraries, luncheons, local conferences, and on radio shows. Groups such as these enjoy having a 'ready-made' panel of authors. And the local press feels it's getting more bang for its buck with four of us so we do well with publicity."

The *Sisters in Crime* newsletter reported on two other formalized groups of touring mystery authors: The Deadly Divas and The Red-Headed League. Touring with other authors works particularly well for genre writers, as they share the same target audience. If you write mystery, science fiction, fantasy, romance, or children's books, consider partnering with another writer in your field. If you don't know any other writers in your field, reach out to writers that you think appropriate to start building collegial and cooperative marketing friendships. Even if no formalized marketing program results from your outreach, you can learn from your colleagues.

THE AUTHOR OF A FIRST LADY BIOGRAPHY TAKES TO THE ROAD AND CREATES A NATIONAL MEDIA CAMPAIGN

Carl Sferrazza Anthony's biography *Florence Harding: The First Lady, the Jazz Age, and the Death of America's Most Scandalous President* was not at first a book of obvious interest for the talk shows. However, the author had spent many years working on the book—a true labor of love—and wanted to give it a fighting chance at success. "I felt that this was a great person who had been ignored unfairly," he says of Florence Harding. "I felt an odd obligation to honor her and her memory, to give her the right kind of PR [that she never had when she was alive]."

Undeniably, as you will see in the story that follows, Anthony had some breaks. But as the old saying goes, luck smiles on those who are prepared. And Anthony worked hard to create his own luck.

Several months before the book's publication, Anthony started planning a media tour that followed the path of the Hardings' cross-country tour that had taken place seventy-five years earlier, at the end of which President Harding died at San Francisco's Palace Hotel. He intended to underwrite the cost of the tour, or to find sponsors, knowing that his publisher would be unlikely to finance a tour for a book about a first lady who had been dead for many decades. He arranged for a meeting with his publicist and director of publicity, where he promised that he would pay for the tour and devote himself to the book's promotion if they would back him up and help to book local media in the cities he planned to visit. They agreed to do so, as well as to underwrite the costs of his hotels. Anthony then approached museums and historical societies along the route to set up speaking engagements. Anthony created a video from old newsreel footage of the Hardings' trip and offered to customize his talks for each location. During his research into speaking venues, he was referred to the Alaska Railroad, for which President Harding had driven in the golden spike and which was now planning a seventy-fifth anniversary celebration. The railroad invited Anthony to participate and eventually sent him on a two-week tour of Alaska.

Then events in the news framed an even broader context for Anthony's book. Just around the time the book was published, the Monica Lewinsky scandal broke and the author, who has written other books on first ladies, found himself in demand by the media to talk about how a first lady might cope with an adulterous husband. *Time* magazine had already run a photo of Florence Harding drawing a comparison between her and First Lady Hillary Clinton.

While the news climate was propitious for Anthony's book, and his idea for the media tour was very smart, and while he was fortunate enough to have a publicist who was willing to book a lot of the media for the tour, Anthony nevertheless dedicated two and a half months setting up his campaign. Later he spent eight weeks on the actual tour where he estimates that he visited twenty-five cities and towns. While he paid for the air travel—unless he had found local sponsorship—the publisher kicked in monies toward local travel and accommodation.

Once the book's sales started to take off, and the media interest became more intense, the publisher began to pay for larger expenses as well. Ultimately, Anthony appeared on NPR's *Fresh Air,* ABC's *World News Tonight,* NBC's *Weekend Today,* and CNN's *Inside Politics,* as well as countless local media outlets. Anthony's tour was capped by a lecture at the Palace Hotel in San Francisco on the seventy-fifth anniversary of the night President Harding had died. A local historical society helped to promote the event.

Anthony's success points to a few lessons. First, if you plan to get involved in your campaign, then you will invest a significant amount of your time. Second, as Anthony comments now on his campaign, try to get a meeting with the director of publicity, even if your book has already been assigned to one of the publicists on the staff. Make that meeting worthwhile—one in which you convince the director of publicity of your dedication and intent—and you will have garnered important support from the top.

BOOK FAIRS AND BOOK AND AUTHOR LUNCHEONS

A number of annual book fairs take place in many cities. You might appear at one or more of these as part of your book tour, or as separate trips during the year. (My favorite fairs are the Miami Book Fair International [November] and the *Los Angeles Times* Book Fair [April], which are among the highest attended fairs and offer a wide variety of author talks and readings.) The fairs are wonderful venues for all kinds of authors, with panels, readings, and signings throughout the day. The fairs are well supported by local media, guaranteeing a level of exposure for all the authors who attend. Publishers sponsor booths at some of the fairs, which give authors a home base manned by sales reps.

Your publicist usually books events at the larger fairs. However, if you are a self-published author, or if your publisher does not plan to send you to the fairs, there is nothing to stop you from pitching yourself to the fair organizers. Just be prepared to pay your own transport and accommodations if you are working independently of your publisher. (Though they may agree to pay your way once you snag the booking—ask your publicist or editor.) Bear in mind that the fairs are interested in hosting authors whose books have been published recently in hardcover or paperback, i.e., within eight to ten months preceding the fair.

Another wonderful fair is the Harbourfront festival in Toronto, which takes place in October. A friend of mine calls Harbourfront "hog's heaven for writers" because of the large book-buying audiences, the extent of media coverage, and the generous array of planned activities and dinners for the authors. Harbourfront sponsors author readings throughout the year, but the annual festival is a gathering of top-flight authors, with a skew toward literary writers. Publicists will pitch their authors to the director of the festival, but in truth, many U.S.-based publicists are unaware of the Harbourfront opportunity, which can sell a lot of books. Check out the Web site (www.readings. org) to see if you think your book would be a good fit at the festival. Then ask your publicist to pitch you.

Besides providing a promotional opportunity for your book, the big book fairs are great fun to attend. Every hour offers a selection of many author events to choose from, and some offer a "green room" or meeting place for authors. There the author has the chance to meet and hang out with many other writers, creating a great community over the course of the few days of the book fair, with useful contacts made for the future.

Other book festivals and fairs offer terrific promotional opportunities. These include the Northwest Bookfest in Seattle, the Rocky Mountain Book Festival, the San Francisco Bay Area Book Festival, the Santa Fe Festival of the Book, the *St. Petersburg Times* Festival of Reading in St. Petersburg and the Sarasota Reading Festival (which are both timed to take place just before the Miami Book Fair International so that authors can do a clean sweep of the Florida book fairs all in one trip), and so on. (See page 264 for a listing of fairs.)

Jewish book fairs take place throughout the United States and in Toronto in November. They take place in close sequence so that an author can make the rounds of the book fairs, with each fair paying a one-way transportation for the author to get to the next fair until the round trip among cities like Atlanta, Baltimore, Columbus, Detroit, Houston, Kansas City, Los Angeles, Miami, Orlando, St. Louis, Toronto, and Washington, D.C., is completed. Administered by local Jewish Community Centers (JCCs), which you can locate online, the fairs showcase a wide range of books, which are sold to customers. These annual fairs welcome authors whose books have been published within the year preceding the fair. Again, a publicist usually sets up these events for authors, but there is nothing to stop you from contacting the fairs' organizers if you think your book fits in.

If your publisher is not underwriting a tour and you qualify for the Jewish book fairs, then put together a tour around the fairs that will cover most of your airplane expenses, though you will probably need to find your own accommodations. The fairs allow enough time in each city for you to do bookstore appearances and media interviews. You should also reach out to the Jewish Book Council, whose mission is to promote Judaica and which will sponsor book tours for select authors. Ask your publicist to send a galley to the director of the council, which is based in New York City.

In addition to the book fairs, annual book and author luncheons take place throughout the United States and Canada and are sponsored by local newspapers and charities. The luncheons invite five or six authors to appear before an audience that buys tickets in advance to attend. Each author speaks for about ten minutes, answers questions from the audience, and then signs books. Several of the luncheons are listed in the resource section. You can find others by turning to the Internet and typing "Book and Author Luncheon" into your search engine.

CORPORATE SPONSORSHIP FOR THE PUBLICITY TOUR

In some instances, corporations use authors as spokespeople. If your book topic helps promote the corporation's own interests, then you are a natural vehicle for it to gain publicity. This happens fairly frequently with cookbooks, where the author of, say, an Italian cookbook can help promote a particular brand of olive oil: The olive oil company underwrites the tour. The USA Rice Council is another organization that has promoted books as part of its campaign to promote rice consumption. The council underwrote some of the publisher's book tour costs for *The Healthy Firehouse Cookbook,* by Joe Bonanno. In exchange, Bonanno prepared rice recipes in his television demos.

EIGHT GREAT THINGS THAT CAN HAPPEN ON TOUR

- Your book sells out and the publisher goes back to press.

- You meet friends from the past who surprise you by showing up to readings.

- You have some really smart conversations with hosts/reporters who've read and genuinely like your book.

- Strangers show up at your reading because they heard you on the radio or read your book or read a good review.

- You give a talk or reading and know that you've got a happy audience in the palm of your hand.

- Someone who hears you interviewed invites you to speak at his or her organization.

- You get the idea for your next book from your encounters on the road.

- Your publisher extends your tour.

THE PUBLICITY TOUR—A SUMMARY

Your tour might include print, radio, and television interviews, as well as appearances at bookstores, book fairs, and other venues. Stay in close partnership with your publicist during the crucial stage of booking the tour. You can become productively involved in several ways:

- If your book does not offer a natural or obvious subject for touring, and if you can come up with a plan to make it so, share the idea with your publisher several months before your book is published so that a tour can be organized in a timely fashion.

- Alert your publicist of the cities where you have contacts to help create successful media stops.

- Research fares to stretch your tour dollars.

- Help brainstorm pitch ideas so that your publicist is well equipped to get you the bookings you want.

- Look into ways to create a hook for your tour, like touring with other authors and linking to events in the news.

Once you're on the road, stay in close contact with your publicist and editor to keep them informed of your progress.

8

GET ON *THE OPRAH WINFREY SHOW*

NOTWITHSTANDING the infamous exception of one novelist who disdained the idea of going on the show, the dream of most authors is to be invited to appear on *The Oprah Winfrey Show*. Exposure on this television show can sometimes propel a book onto bestseller lists. However, few authors really understand the show's requirements. *Oprah*'s format is one hour long and generally speaking she's concerned with uplifting and positive messages for women. Few authors—unless they are celebrities or high-profile, colorful experts with the gift of the gab—appear for the full hour. With some exceptions, noncelebrity authors appear on *Oprah* as a small part of a larger theme show. Nor do many authors realize how difficult it is to secure a booking on *Oprah*. Let's look at the numbers: *Oprah*'s producers are creating some 200 hours of television a year. They are booking between 180 and 225 featured experts a year on the main part of the show. In the past the show has also offered special segments called "Your Spirit" that ran during the last five minutes of the show and focused on a spiritual awakening in someone's life. That venue offered another 200 or so opportunities for a guest booking. Thus a fair estimate of annual combined bookings is 225 to 450, at most.

The stark reality is this: With more than 100,000 books published a year, and with many thousands of individuals from other fields competing for those same spots, the chances of getting on Oprah's show are very slim. But do not despair. Folks who did get on did not give up. Most probably they succeeded because they took care of the pertinent factors that made it happen: a strong pitch, the ability to prove that you will be a strong guest, persistence, and plain old luck.

Here's where you start: You can improve your chances by studying the show and coming up with angles that could help persuade the producers that you are worthy. If you do not have time to tape and watch *Oprah* every day, check out www.oprah.com, which lists past show topics. For example, past shows include "Overweight Children," "Wives Who Don't Want Sex," "How to Set Personal Boundaries," "Understanding Your Emotional Style," "I Was An Abandoned Child," and so on. If you're really serious about getting on *Oprah,* make it your business to thoroughly understand the show and therefore how to come up with show ideas that are related to your book.

IMPROVE THE ODDS: STUDY THE SHOW TO COME UP WITH SHOW IDEAS FOR YOUR BOOK

The Oprah Winfrey Show has a variety of formats. Sometimes a single guest appears, usually a celebrity or one of a number of regular high-wattage personality guests such as relationship expert Dr. Phil McGraw. Or the show may comprise a string of pretaped segments about a particular theme. Or the show may center on one guest expert, who discusses the problems of a panel of guests who have firsthand experience of the topic at hand.

As reported on the *Wall Street Journal*'s Web site, author Jan Yager campaigned for a couple of years to get on *Oprah* (and finally did) for a book called *Friendshifts: The Power of Friendship and How It Shapes Our Lives.* She got on because she understood that her job as a guest on *The Oprah Winfrey Show* was *not* to sell her book. She knew that the producers would be looking for a guest to create an interesting and entertaining show on a topic that the audience can identify and empathize with.

Justin Loeber, as director of publicity for HarperCollins, pitched Anthony Bourdain, author of *Kitchen Confidential,* in many different ways. He placed one of his follow-up calls when the producers happened to be working on a show called "Profession Confessions" about behind-the-scenes trade secrets of various jobs. Loeber pushed for the producer to watch a videotape of the author and, believing that the author would make an effective guest, persuaded her to conduct a preinterview. This tape and the phone interview clinched the deal. The author appeared on the show to talk about what really goes on in restaurants, when not to order fish, what sort of restaurants to avoid, how the bread on the table is recycled, and so on. The other guests on the show included four other authors: Marcy Blum (*Weddings for Dummies*), Peter Greenburg (*The Travel Detective*), Teri Agins (*The End of Fashion*), and Ellen Phillips (*Shocked, Appalled, and Dismayed,* which is about writing complaint letters).

Lynn Goldberg of Goldberg McDuffie Communications says that when her publicists pitch *Oprah,* they offer a range of story ideas surrounding the author's expertise. They frame their pitches as concepts for television programming rather than as straight book interviews. Then of course, Goldberg says, the onus is on the guest to follow through with a passionate and energetic presentation that also manages to convey the book's message.

You improve your chances of getting on *Oprah* by coming up with several pitches that will help your publicist position your expertise with the show's producers. The only way to do this is to watch and study *Oprah.* If you work during the day, tape the show, or watch the evening reruns. To get on *The Oprah Winfrey Show,* you *must* understand what the producers are looking for: dramatic stories that offer viewers hope, paths to recovery, life-affirming values, entertainment. Unless your topic is extremely compelling, and your personality energetic and engaging, chances are that you could not sustain a full hour on *Oprah.* Therefore, think about show topics that can incorporate other guests. For example, a show called "Make Your Dreams Come True" featured a Hearst book called *The Business of Bliss: How to Profit from Doing What You Love,* which is about women entrepreneurs. It took a full six months for the publicist to get one of the entrepreneurs on the show, after relentless pitching and follow-up calls.

Some shows are based entirely on books. "The Marriage Sabbatical" featured women who had taken a sabbatical from their families to pursue their personal quests. They discussed how their time off improved their marriages and family lives. The main guest was author Cheryl Jarvis, author of, that's right, a book called *The Marriage Sabbatical*. A show called *Messy Home Makeovers* offered ideas for removing clutter from your life. The guest was Julie Morgenstern, an "organizing expert" and author of two books called *Time Management from the Inside Out* and *Organizing from the Inside Out*. Another example: The producers used a book called *Ordinary People, Extraordinary Wealth,* by Ric Edelman, to create a show by the same name. The show, like the book, revealed the secrets of ordinary people who have achieved great wealth. Of course the ideal scenario is having a show title named for your book—another important reason to come up with a punchy title for your book that conveys its core message.

All these shows have short, to-the-point titles and introduce the show's theme in a sound bite. As you develop your book's show idea, try to present the message of your book in the form of one punchy line, a sound bite, one that you can imagine Oprah using for her next show's preview announcement.

Common to many *Oprah* shows is the topic of the American Dream—some variation on how you can improve your life. It might be how to find happiness and personal satisfaction, triumph over adversity, mend a marriage or other relationship, find meaning in life, or achieve your dreams. The majority of *Oprah*'s shows reflect this positive philosophy.

Getting on *Oprah* does not guarantee you a bestseller. But it sure improves your chances. On hearing the news of an *Oprah* booking, sales forces can leverage more copies into bookstores in anticipation of the show. Savvy booksellers will ask how long a segment you will get. The booksellers will stock up on more copies of your book on the eventuality that the show translates into sales: The size of the reorders will depend on what the publisher tells the booksellers about the known extent of your appearance. Therefore, as the planning of your show takes shape and you find out from the producer that you are playing a larger part in the show than originally thought, then let your publicist know. She will alert the sales reps, who in turn will tell the booksellers. Because Oprah and her producers might even change the lineup mid-show, you never really know how much time you will end up getting until the show is taped.

Oprah has a staff of many producers, all working on different stories at once. This allows for publicists to develop a variety of approaches when pitching the show. Some have found that it pays to send the book and pitch to several producers at once. To prevent two producers from showing up to an *Oprah* pitch meeting with the same idea, the publicists state in the cover letter the names of the other producers to whom they have also sent the book. Other publicists prefer to cultivate a relationship with one producer. This person should be a mid- to senior-level producer, who will refer the idea to other production teams at the show.

Lynn Goldberg notes that a successful print campaign can favorably influence *Oprah*'s producers. A big plus is high-profile feature coverage in national print media like the glossy monthly magazines or leading newspapers. If you've been lucky enough to score such coverage in the national print media, then those articles should accompany your pitch to *The Oprah Winfrey Show.* Charles Cook, a former producer for the show, says, "Any good producer spends weekends reading through stacks of magazines. Producers are voracious readers of what's topical, looking for what their audience is interested in, always looking for new ideas."

There may come that amazing day when your publicist calls to set up a "preinterview" with one of *Oprah*'s producers. Many potential guests are screened by telephone and flunk the phone call. In other words, the preinterview is actually an audition. Therefore, get ready for this call—it's your big moment. Refresh yourself about your book's salient points. Prepare vivid analogies and anecdotes to illustrate those points. Talk about the show idea with your publicist so that you're fluent in elaborating on it. During the preinterview—and many national television shows other than *Oprah* conduct preinterviews—the producer will decide whether you have the potential to be an interesting guest. The producer will also assess the size of your role in the show—whether you should have, say, a five-minute spot, or whether you could command the attention to take the stage for the full hour.

If your publicist is no longer pitching *Oprah,* then you can take up the cause and pitch the show yourself. Ask your publicist for a copy of her correspondence with the show. Get the name and number of the producer she was pitching. If you're starting from scratch without a producer's name, you might choose producers who have worked on shows with themes compatible with your own book. Find out their names by watching the credits at the end of the show. You won't get the name of the appropriate producer by calling the show's switchboard. You will simply be told to send in your idea for a show, and that the show will contact you if there is any interest. (It's a little like trying to find a publisher by sending your manuscript in blind. Once in a while it can work, but very rarely.)

After you get turned down by the producer, which is more likely to happen than not, keep your cool. Be polite and ask if you might call again with a new show idea. As evident from what a former producer for the show has to say, you can pitch the show again and again until you finally give up or get on.

INSIGHT FROM A VETERAN TALK SHOW PRODUCER AND FORMER *OPRAH* PRODUCER

Charles Cook worked at *The Oprah Winfrey Show* for two years. He has worked as well at other daytime talk shows, and he offers the following suggestions to authors. His advice is equally applicable to other talk shows, particularly the longer-format "magazine" shows. First, Cook says that the show will accept pitch ideas directly from authors. The producers believe that good ideas can come from anywhere, and they are not always predisposed to deal with a book's publicist. The constant hunt for good show ideas means that yours are welcome, especially if you present them cogently and with an understanding for what's current in the culture. The more ideas you have, the better. If you gain access to a producer, Cook recommends that you use your

time on the phone well. From the phone conversation alone the producer can tell if you have guest potential.

Producers look for someone who can give concise answers that will
appeal to the audience and who relates to the woman at home who
watches the show. Cook states that the worst guest is a professional
expert who talks down to viewers. The best guest is someone who
comes across as warm and accessible. During the preinterview, just pretend you're talking to your friends. That way you create an intimate
but informative impression. The other thing the producer is looking for,
says Cook, is the "take-home advice. What I want to know is what are
the top three things that this author is going to tell me, what advice will
I be able to use." In other words, the ability to be prescriptive is an
important quality.

So remember: If you don't get on the show on the first attempt,
don't give up. According to Cook, as long as you can come up with
new ideas about positioning your book, then keep pitching. The show's
production moves fast. New shows go into development all the time.
Whether you are an author or a publicist, try to get a dialogue going
with one producer to improve your access and to get noticed. Send
handwritten notes to the producer. Fax clippings related to your pitch.
Call periodically to touch base and float an idea. Do anything you can
to cultivate that relationship, says Cook.

Also keep in mind that your package has a better chance of being
opened first if it stands out. The show's producers receive carton-loads
of books—most packaged in brown Jiffy bags, most looking the same.
"You get so much stuff that you can't see straight," Cook says. So
whatever else you do, if you want to get on *The Oprah Winfrey Show,*
"Get on the phone! Pitch a producer!"

GET ON *THE OPRAH WINFREY SHOW*—A SUMMARY

Like any show that you want to appear on, *The Oprah Winfrey Show*
has specific formats and requirements of its guests. Watch the show and
study it to learn how to shape a pitch based on your book. Review the
show's archives on its Web site to see what book segments have run in

the past. Keep in mind that producers will take an interest in you if you reveal a strong potential to be an interesting, lively, and entertaining guest. The producers must create good television, and they are not deeply concerned about selling your book. Your challenge, and your publicist's challenge, is to offer viable television programming themed around your book's topic or else your expertise.

9

MEDIA TRAINING: HOW TO GIVE A GREAT INTERVIEW

SOMETIMES television appearances are part of a book's promotion. If you have seldom or never appeared on television, then urge your publisher to send you for media training to teach you interviewing skills, help you hone your message, and build your confidence.

At a training session, a media trainer, who has read your book, will simulate an interview with you—sometimes in a real television studio—by taking the role of the television host. The mock interview is videotaped and then replayed so that the trainer can give you pointers on how to improve your interview techniques. The trainer will cover everything from how you should sit (slightly forward on the seat so that you appear alert) to the color of your clothing to steering the interview in the direction you choose.

Businesspeople and politicians often hire media trainers to refine their presentation of complicated or controversial messages. Similarly, to ensure good appearances, publishers often hire them for important authors preparing for national television interviews. Authors with television interview experience might need a "touch-up"—a short session that refreshes their skills just before their new book comes out. Media training is not confined to television skills: Trainers can also prepare you for radio interviews.

During a real interview, you may find that the talk show host has not read your book. This is not unusual, considering the demands of the job. A host may interview up to five authors a week. They don't have time to read the books, watch the movies, or listen to the music of every guest. Hosts have different styles. Some are terrific at keeping a conversation flowing, while others are not. Hosts may be warm and friendly, or sharply interrogative, or goofy. Media training helps you become adept at handling any type of interviewer that you might encounter.

Many authors want to know if they can media train themselves. You can, but you must take your self-training seriously and take every opportunity to understand what the media is looking for. For critical evaluation, you should practice with others and invest serious time to ensure that you know what to do once you're on air. Help yourself by studying the media. Pay attention to the manner and content of interview questions. Identify and practice the techniques employed by the most impressive guests.

Even if you have appeared on the media before, practice for your upcoming interviews. Do not think that you can get away without honing your message. I once worked on a book by a famous media trainer and political consultant. We both assumed, wrongly as it turned out, that his appearance on *Today* would be a cinch. Instead, he got sidetracked on unrelated issues and failed to convey the points of interest in his book. The main problem was that the book was not fresh in his mind. He probably hadn't looked at it since he'd handed in the manuscript ten months earlier. He was simply not prepared.

If your publisher is unwilling to underwrite the costs of media training, then you may choose to hire a media trainer yourself. Media training for television may cost from $2,000 to $3,000 for a full day, or $1,200 to $1,800 for a half day. You can find media trainers through an online search and I have listed several of them in the resource section of this book.

WHAT IS MEDIA TRAINING AND WHAT WILL IT ACCOMPLISH?

According to Bill Parkhurst, who runs a media training company called Parkhurst Communications in New York City, authors have some misconceptions about interviews. The main one is that they need a string of prepackaged sound bites to sell books. Parkhurst feels that appearing on a television talk show is about creating a connection with the audience through the host. Only indirectly is it about selling. He explains that the audience remembers an overall impression of a television guest, not his or her words. These are soon forgotten. He advises, therefore, to concentrate on conveying your passion rather than a core set of sound bites. During a training session, Parkhurst first seeks the author's core passion—what stirred that person to spend such time and effort writing a book.

Parkhurst says that successful interviewing requires a set of taught skills, and that local interviews on local cable or radio provide the opportunity to practice those skills. "No interview is too small to do, at least not at the beginning of your career as a writer," he says. "They give you that valuable chance to practice in a real interview situation and to boost your confidence and competence." Learning to give good interviews requires you to spend time watching the media or listening to radio shows. "If all you listen to is National Public Radio," says Parkhurst, "then you need to listen to other radio interview shows to understand what is really going on in this media. Once you understand the media, you know where you fit in.

"I put the author through every kind of interview that they're going to get to teach them that an interview is a proactive experience," says Parkhurst. For interviews where the host fails to address a book's core subject, he teaches "bridging" techniques that allow you to steer the interview in the direction you prefer. For example, you might respond to a question that leads you away from your book's message by saying, "Good question, and what I've always thought is . . ." or "What I think is important is . . ."

He teaches that you should refer to your book indirectly. Instead of responding to a question with, "In my book . . .", you might say, "As I was doing research on my book I found that . . ." or "I have a chapter on such a subject that explains . . ." The idea is to sound natural and conversational rather than like a pitchman. Parkhurst spends a lot of time with authors working on the "topper"—the answer to that usual first question, which is always some form of "Why did you write this book?" During his training sessions, he has authors answer that question in a variety of ways, and in several different styles of interviews. Thus, the authors become comfortable conveying the book's key message in any situation.

Eight Ways to Mention Your Book Naturally During an Interview

"What I learned while I was researching my book was . . ."

"It was so interesting when I was working on my book to discover that . . ."

"When I sat down to write the book, I learned that . . ."

"People told me when I was working on my book that . . ."

"When I started the book I thought that. . . . But instead I found that . . ."

"What I think people will really learn from my book is that . . ."

"It was important for me to write this book because . . ."

"Many people that I interviewed for my book said that . . ."

Just don't use all eight in one interview or you'll sound like a huckster.

I saw a good example of bridging the other day in an interview with former President Jimmy Carter about his new book. The show was *The Diane Rehm Show,* an NPR program in Washington, D.C., that often interviews authors. This radio show is sometimes taped by C-SPAN. Carter had discussed his racially integrated childhood and Rehm followed up with an oddly redundant question. Carter, with great warmth, acknowledged her question and went on to talk about something else entirely. He saved her face, talked about what he wanted, and handled the transition gracefully.

During an interview, you may feel contempt at a host's dumb questions. However, whatever else you do, *never* condescend or try to "best" the host to show the audience how smart you are. Remember: The audience is loyal to that host. You are there for mere minutes. Your task as a guest is to redirect the interview, gently. Take it where you want it to go.

WHEN THE INTERVIEW IS A DEMO

Some interviews take the form of demos, in other words, demonstrations of, say, a cooking or gardening technique. For my own book *Reckless Appetites: A Culinary Romance,* I had to demonstrate how to make a recipe for champagne punch on *Today.* I had never performed a demo on television before, and so I spent the full two months leading up to the interview practicing the demo anywhere and everywhere. I did it in the back of taxis. I did it alone in elevators—holding imaginary equipment and ingredients while I spoke about the recipe and my book. At home, of course, I practiced with the real ingredients. It came to a point I could do it in my sleep. The results: My perfecting every word and motion helped my appearance run smoothly. The physical logistics of mixing and pouring ingredients never got in the way of my message.

Publicist Caitlin Connelly often coaches cookbook authors for their television demos and interviews. First she asks the author to name the three most important talking points about the book. "Sometimes what the authors think are the key message points are not, in fact, what would appeal to journalists," she says. By keeping to three points, she believes that authors can carry the book's main message effectively. She finds that too many message points can lead to an interview that goes "off message."

She also works with the author to identify dishes that are appropriate for demonstration on air. These recipes should be seasonal, colorful (to show up nicely on camera), and non-wilting (as the food will often sit under hot studio lights for several hours). "You need to pick a recipe that's easily broken down into stages," she says, "because you want to show some of the process, but you don't want to create the entire recipe. This would take too long for a television segment." It is enough that the author presents the dish in different stages of preparation, and then shows a finished dish. Connelly insists that the author reread and practice the recipe before any interviews. She wants the process and ingredients to be fresh in the author's mind.

Another consideration of recipe choice is the host's preference. Try to find out if the host has any allergies or a favorite food. If your host has a jones for chocolate, then cater to that taste. You are more likely to get that host excited about your food. Find out too if the host will taste the food on the set: Some hosts will not taste food on air. You don't want to push a host to try your food only to be turned down on live TV.

Find out how the set will be decorated. Some shows have set stylists, many do not. If the studio is not providing set decorations, then bring along flowers, pretty serving dishes, a tablecloth. Remember to iron it first. Brand-new cloths have creases that look bad on camera.

Plan on preparing other complementary dishes to display with the recipe you are demonstrating: As well as dressing the set, the array of dishes provides a chance to mention other recipes in your book.

ACE YOUR TELEVISION OR RADIO INTERVIEWS—THE RULES

Here are the rules for your successful broadcast interviews. They apply to both television and radio, unless otherwise indicated.

- Reread or skim your book before your first interview so it is fresh in your mind. Reread the pitch letter and press materials that your publicist sent to the media, as interviewers may use the press packet for all their questions.

- Research your interviewer's background, and understand who the audience is. (Or ask your publicist to get this information for you.) Your knowledge will help you shape your responses to appeal to his or her interests.

■ Know the several points you have to get across no matter what questions you are asked. Remember that the audience has probably never heard about your book.

■ Be alert to the host's mentioning of the book's title. In short television and radio interviews you don't need to mention the title again, and doing so will alienate the audience. In longer format radio interviews, pay attention to the host's introductions after each commercial break. Chances are that he or she will say something like, "With me today is So-and-So, author of a new book called *Such-and-Such*." When you hear this cue, you can relax and not worry about mentioning the title. If the host doesn't mention the book title, then mention it once every segment, so that new listeners know what you are talking about.

■ Be prepared to complete an interview in two to three minutes. In that time you must convey what your book is about and why the audience will find the book appealing or useful. You might get more time but be prepared for the short form.

■ Make a list of all the questions that you might be asked in an interview. Then come up with punchy answers to all of them. Before any interviews, practice answering the questions out loud and refine your message points so that they are interesting and succinct.

■ If you have reason to anticipate challenging questions, then practice the responses that will diffuse any controversy (which of course you've discussed with your publicist).

■ Use vivid anecdotes and examples to illustrate your points, particularly on radio.

■ Reveal facts and figures that support your book's message. (If I were marketing this book on television, I might lead with the fact that more than one hundred thousand books are published every year, so how can an author stand out in the crowd.)

■ Practice your segues or bridges. In other words, if the interviewer gets stuck on one topic too long, then practice shifting the conversation, perhaps by saying, "That's only one aspect of my book that can help people. The other thing I've found is that . . ." Another good segue is, "The most important thing to remember here is . . . ," or "What your listeners will really want to know is . . . ," or "Sometimes people ask me . . . ," and then go on to ask yourself the question you wish the interviewer had asked.

■ One of the worst answers to the host's question about the book's content is a coy "Well, you'll have to read it in the book." While an intriguing answer might stimulate the audience to buy the book, your refusal to answer the question is a turnoff.

■ Do not talk too fast, even though you may be tempted because television moves so quickly and you have a very short time to deliver your message.

■ Be energetic and upbeat. Listen to the high-wattage on-air performance styles of interviewers. They like to hear the same level of energy in their guests. Guests who project low energy seem bored or indifferent.

■ Before you start your radio or cable television interview, mention to the producer and to the host that you'd like to share an 800 number where listeners can buy your book or find out further information. The producer will put the number on the TelePrompTer for the host to read aloud at some point in the interview. On cable television, the producer may run the 800 number at the bottom of the screen. (Network television generally will not do this, but they will take your 800 number to give to any callers to the switchboard who want to get in touch with you.)

■ Similarly, tell the producer that you'd like to mention your Web site on air to share with listeners.

- Show up early for the interview and always bring a copy of your book with you. The studio copy sometimes gets misplaced, and the host may need to refer to the book or the television crew may shoot the jacket for an opening shot.

- Use the host's name to personalize the interview. (Check with the producer before the interview to find out what the host likes to be called on air.) Remember that the listening audience is loyal to that host, so buddying up with that host helps the audience identify with you.

- If the show takes call-ins and you get a hostile caller, maintain an even tone. Your politeness will present you as a professional; the caller will merely seem crazy. By ignoring the caller's anger, you also increase the chance that the producer will cut them off faster to move on to the next call. Once you engage with a caller's anger, you've created explosive entertainment, and depending on the show's style, the producer and host might prolong the call.

- In television interviews, sit perched on the edge of your chair, which will keep you upright and make you seem energetic. If you sit toward the back of the chair seat then you will look slumped. Funnily enough, the same advice applies to your radio interviews. By sitting alert, you will sound alert. Slouching can induce a slower-paced interview, even though the audience can't see you.

- Don't fidget during the interview, or swing your chair, or tap your foot. All of those tics distract the viewer, as well as the television or radio host.

- After the interview, send a thank-you note to the interviewer and the producer. You might get a callback for a follow-up interview on the subject, which you can even suggest in your note.

For Television Interviews Only

- If your book has photographs or other visuals that support your story, then ask your publicist to offer them to the television producer, and bring them along if needed. The producer may shoot them just before your interview to include as still frames throughout the segment.

- Get over nervousness by following this very good advice from Clarence Jones's book, *How to Speak TV*. During your interview, think of your audience as one or two people in a living room, and direct your conversation toward them to create a feeling of intimacy.

- Accept makeup if it is offered. The makeup artists will blot the shine on your nose and forehead. If you have a light skin color, then they will probably also use a darker tone of blush and foundation than you are used to so that you don't appear washed out on camera. In case the show has no makeup artists on staff, carry some blush and foundation and a makeup sponge with you. This applies also to men who may not realize that their four o'clock shadow may look positively gangster-like without some cover-up. If you're not sure what to do then talk to the producer or your publicist ahead of time.

- If you are wearing a tailored jacket, tug the hem underneath you and sit on it to keep the jacket uncreased and in place as you talk.

- Unless you are an experienced guest, you may not know for certain when the camera starts rolling. Assume that you're on air as soon as you are in place, and keep a bright, engaged look on your face. When you answer the questions, look at the host and never at the camera.

- Wear solid colors but avoid all white or all black, or loud patterns. No heavy jewelry (unless this is the subject of your book).

- Wear your glasses if you wear them every day. Changing routine for the television interview will add another unfamiliar element to your experience. Also you may need to be able to read a graphic on the television monitor during your segment, say if the host asks you to read a phone number.

The Exception to the Rules

The two television stations on which you must abandon all restraint are HSN (Home Shopping Network) and QVC. If you are booked onto one of these, your job is to be as aggressive and hyped up in your on-air performance as possible. The segments are all about selling as much product as possible, whether it is a book or a piece of jewelry. Off camera, the station is measuring the dollars-per-minute for the segment. Your job is to sell and to sell hard.

For Radio Interviews Taking Place by Phone, Rather Than in Studio

- Do not use a cell phone for the call. They are unreliable. Turn off any cell phones or second phone lines in proximity during the interview.

- Turn off the radio because leaving it on will produce feedback.

- Eliminate all possible distractions: Lock your pets well out of earshot, have your young kids well looked after in another part of your home, and deactivate call-waiting. If you live near a busy street, then sirens or other traffic noise can spoil your interview: Take your phone into a quiet closet if you have to, or arrange to go to a friend's quieter home or office. If you're doing radio phone interviews in your hotel room, alert the hotel operator to hold any calls when you're on the other line.

- Sight unseen, you can refer to your notes. Keep a short list of your key points in front of you. Have a pen and paper handy to jot down any points to cover later in the interview. Have your book and press materials nearby to remind yourself of your book's content during commercial breaks.

- As soon as you've connected with the radio station, unless the host tells you otherwise assume that you are on air. You will not necessarily know when you go live.

- Have a glass of water at hand, but do not sip and swallow with your mouth adjacent to the mouthpiece or at the moment you're expected to answer a question.

SOME TIPS ON PRINT INTERVIEWS

Interviews in the print media are quite different from radio or television interviews and might take place by phone, in person, or even via e-mail. The pressure of time is lifted—you do not have to squeeze your message into a few minutes—and the reporter is likely to have read your book. You may have a thoughtful discussion, which can be most gratifying if the reporter likes your work. Whatever the situation, keep your answers on point and engaging.

First ask what the article is about. The piece might not be about your book alone, but rather part of a larger theme piece in which your book will get a small mention. Spell your name and title of your book for the reporter. Find out the reporter's deadline and contact information. This allows you to send any relevant follow-up information after the interview has concluded.

During the interview, do not fall for flattery. The reporter is softening you up to get a relaxed interview. Get too relaxed and you may say something you will regret later after it shows up in print. Good reporters can lull you into a sense of ease where you let your guard down. I know one writer who fell for a reporter's apparent interest in his work. He gave a frank and forthcoming interview, and was later stunned by the reporter's negative article. Another reporter's tactic is asking a provocative question intended to make you angry and reactive. Try to recognize when a reporter is trying to goad you and keep your cool while making your point.

Look out for reporters who have an agenda, who have already decided what to say about you. In an interview for my book *Reckless Appetites*, a reporter from a major metropolitan newspaper wanted me to come out with a theory about the relationship between food and sex. He wanted an explicit answer and finally told me that if I said something really provocative, then he'd run the article "above the fold," meaning on the top half of the page. I refused to oblige him: I felt railroaded and found his manner sleazy. In the end, the article never ran, but I didn't mind because I didn't compromise myself. In another situation, one author who had written about recovering from bulimia found herself under attack by a reporter who thought her a spoiled rich girl. The reporter was rude enough to go into her kitchen and open the refrigerator to see what food she had in the house. Unless the reporter is someone whose reputation has been vetted for you by a publicist you trust, or who is known personally, don't allow him or her into your home.

These cautionary tales are not meant to put you on the defensive during interviews. Rather they are intended to prepare you to handle reporters. The reporter's job is not to be your friend or to be on your side. Their job is to get a good story for their readers. They are looking for angles in everything you say and do.

Remember that unless you have a long-standing relationship with the reporter and can trust them, there really is no such thing as "off the record." Why tell the reporter a confidence? If you do not want to see your words in print, then do not utter them.

At the end of the interview, reiterate your most important points. Ask the reporter, "Do you have everything you need?" or "Before you go, shall I go over anything for you?" Then ask the reporter the deadline for the story, and for his or her best contact information in case you come up with more information to share.

After the article runs, drop a friendly note of thanks. If you don't like what the reporter has written, then try to put it out of mind: You gain little by sending a note of complaint. If you really believe that you've been wronged, then write a letter to the editor to point out the factual errors or misleading statements in the piece.

The first few interviews that you do in any format—whether print or broadcast—may be challenging and nerve-wracking. Once you've put a few behind you, you will have a sudden burst of confidence and may take great pleasure in giving interviews. Hit your stride and you will find that the nerves and jitters will be vastly diminished or disappear altogether.

MEDIA TRAINING: HOW TO GIVE A GREAT INTERVIEW— A SUMMARY

Whether you undergo formal media training or prepare for interviews on your own, you must practice your interview skills so that you can deliver an effective, selling interview about your book. There are many rules about giving a good interview, but with repetition you can master them until they become second nature. The major elements of good interviewing to keep in mind are:

- Know your book's content—reread the book if you need to.

- Know the top three messages that you want to convey.

- Practice your bridging techniques so that you can redirect an interview that goes astray.

- Prepare anecdotes and facts that illustrate your points.

- Rehearse your interview responses until they feel natural and comfortable.

10

BOOKSTORE APPEARANCES AND SPEAKING ENGAGEMENTS

SETTING up local bookstore appearances and other speaking engagements can be a productive way to get involved in your campaign. Even if you have a publicist who is active on your behalf, you can track down leads that she probably won't have time to research.

Bookstore events are an important part of building your readership. Even if the events are not heavily attended—they average as few as ten to fifteen people—the book still enjoys visibility through displays and store promotions leading up to the event. Your book also benefits from increased awareness among store managers, which can lead to hand-selling. And you've begun to develop an audience as the people who attend the event talk about your book. In fact, for children's authors, who find access to the media more limited than for authors of topical adult books, bookstore tours done in combination with school visits are the essential way to build readership. Admittedly this type of grass-roots effort is time-consuming, but if you are an unknown writer, here's where you can start to build your readership.

Speaking engagements at non-bookstore venues can also deliver larger audiences for you. Host organizations might include universities, corporations, libraries, museums, YMCAs, garden clubs, fraternal groups, and so on. Usually, these require a longer booking lead time than bookstores, so start your research and outreach five to six months before you expect to visit a particular market. Of course, some speaking engagements can be set up with a shorter lead time, but if you have the luxury of time, then use it to your advantage.

A word of advice if you are setting up your own bookstore and other appearances: Make sure to schedule them to take place *after* your book has been published so that books can be sold at the events.

HOW TO SET UP BOOKSTORE SIGNINGS

According to *Publishers Weekly,* publicists work through the home offices of Barnes & Noble and Borders to set up six thousand chain bookstore events a year. In addition independent booksellers and the chains' local store managers set up thousands more.

Your publicist will probably set up some bookstore appearances for you. But you can continue to appear at bookstores after your official campaign is over. You may supplement your publicist's efforts by setting up events for which she will not have time. Be aware that bookstore chains do not pay for travel or serve as a publicist.

Once you obtain a list of stores to contact—see the box about bookstore directories later in this chapter on page 197 to identify bookstores—send the information to your publicist to find out if your choices are appropriate. After checking with the sales reps, the publicist will give you her assessment whether the stores are capable of mounting good events. Give your publicist at least a week to get back to you with this information. If you hear nothing from her, proceed in setting up your own events. Also ask your publicist to provide you with copies of the press release and extra book jackets: You'll probably need one or two jackets for every signing you set up.

When you're ready to set up the events, contact the local stores directly. (Don't bother contacting the home offices of the major chains, as the events planners prefer to work directly with the publishers.) Ask the store's events coordinator if you can schedule an event at the store. Describe the appearance you envision for your book, whether a reading, a lecture, a question-and-answer session, a slide show, or a how-to cooking or crafts demonstration. Avoid bookstore events where all you do is sign books. Unless you create some kind of talk or event surrounding your appearance, you're unlikely to draw many people. Say how long you are prepared to talk. It's best to plan for a twenty-minute presentation followed by questions and answers. Let the events manager know if you have a local mailing list, which makes you a more attractive candidate.

Once you've booked an event, follow up promptly with a letter or an e-mail confirming the arrangements, accompanied by a press release, a photograph of yourself, a book jacket, and any other information that the bookstore can use in displays or mailings and other promotions. Tell your publicist about the forthcoming event. She should then in turn notify the local sales rep. Better yet, inform the publicist by e-mail so that she can easily forward the information to the appropriate sales rep.

Set up the bookstore events six weeks to three months before your appearance. This allows the events coordinator sufficient time to list your event in the store's newsletter and calendar. The events coordinator may ask you if co-op money is available to promote the event. (Co-op monies are matching promotional funds paid by publishers to booksellers. The amount of co-op funds that a bookstore is entitled to depends on how much business they transacted with your publisher during the previous year.) Because you cannot know what co-op is available, ask the events coordinator to get in touch with the publisher's sales rep. Your publisher may allow a small amount of money to be spent on co-op programs, which might include a newsletter mailing to store customers (costing as little as fifty dollars), a small store-produced ad in the local paper or on the radio, or refreshments at the signing. As you might expect, publishers are less liberal about co-op spending during times of economic recession. If the funds are not available, the store might not cancel the event if it's already made a commitment to you, though it will not have as many resources for promotion. If the store asks you to pay the co-op charge, politely decline the opportunity. Co-op marketing is a way for booksellers to get money out of publishers: Authors shouldn't have to foot this bill.

If you're planning to appear in all the local bookstores in your proximity, schedule your events far apart so that you're not appearing at a chain store a couple of days before you appear at the independent bookseller down the street, or vice versa. Because booksellers are competitive, timing events too closely will only anger them and that will not help your book. Separate your appearances by weeks or months.

Bookstore Directories

You have several options to locate addresses and phone numbers for bookstores.

- Talk to your publicist. She can contact the local and national sales reps for a list of appropriate stores.
- Go to www.bookweb.org, which has a directory of bookstores that are members of the trade group, the American Booksellers Association. The site includes addresses and bookstore Web sites.
- Go to www.booksense.com, the site of independent booksellers, and use the zip code locator there to find stores. The list will include independents only, not chains.
- Go to the store-finders sections at the sites of the national chains, www. bn.com, www.booksamillion.com, and www.borders.com, to locate stores. The sites include maps as well as store contact information.

Let us suppose that you set up a hometown bookstore appearance. You probably know many people in your area and can provide the store with a good-sized mailing list. Give the store a copy of the list on labels to send out notices about your appearance. If the store is not prepared to take care of the mailing, make up a simple flyer and send it out yourself. You can use your mailing list more than once. Some authors will list all of their appearances in one flyer. Others will send sequential mailings.

Ask the bookstore's events coordinator if he or she plans to contact the local newspapers and other publications to get the event mentioned in the listings section. If not, ask for a copy of the store's media list and make the calls yourself. Getting listed is a pretty straightforward procedure. Call the local papers and ask for the calendar or listings editor. Then fax, mail, or e-mail the information as the editor specifies. Ask if the paper can use a photo, and if so send one.

Go to the professional development area of www.bookweb.org, the site for independent booksellers. Click on "marketing" and you will find information about promoting bookstore events, sample media and calendar listings alerts, and pitch letter templates. Then check out www.netread.com. The site e-mails a free calendar of author events in any zip code you desire. Even if you have a good and active publicist, take the time to list your own events. Trusting the bookstores to properly market the event to calendar listings, publicists concentrate instead on securing feature interviews.

Setting Up a Bookstore Event—a Checklist

- Prepare your mailing lists to invite attendees. Work with your personal acquaintances in your tour cities to see if they can provide contacts of their own.
- Plan the format of your appearance and remember, if you're not a well-known writer then a topical discussion is more marketable than a straight reading.
- Contact the bookstore and ask for the events coordinator.
- Describe the proposed format of your appearance and the size of your mailing list.
- Suggest any local organizations that might be approached to attend your talk. The bookstore may already have ties with them, and if not, contact them yourself.
- Ask the events coordinator if he or she will need a press release, book jacket, and photo to promote the event.
- Let your publicist know about the event.
- Ask if the store will order books directly from the publisher or a wholesaler, and provide them with the phone and fax numbers for your publisher's order department.

- Ten days (approximately) before the event, call the events coordinator and reconfirm. Ask if the store has received its order of books for the event. If the order is late, ask when it is expected and follow up again then. If books still do not arrive, then notify your publicist. Sometimes she can help get books shipped to your event in time.
- Ask the events coordinator if he or she is planning to pitch your appearance to the calendar listings of the local media. If not, ask for a copy of the store's media list and send out a media alert.

Bookstores often have ties to community groups. Ask the events coordinator the names of local groups or associations that the store will notify about your appearance. If you have ideas about specific groups in the area that might be drawn to your event, then contact them directly. Ask if they are willing to notify their members about your event. Pitch them the idea of cosponsoring the event (at no charge). If they go for it, ask for a copy of their mailing list (on labels), which you will give to the store to send invitations. The invitations should, of course, mention the name of the cosponsoring organization. In this instance, everyone gains an audience.

MAKE YOUR APPEARANCE A SUCCESS

Your principle obligation as a speaker is to engage your audience. You want to inform and entertain—and ultimately motivate listeners to buy a copy of your book. Use humor or eloquence, surprise or pathos—anything that will capture your audience's attention. Whatever you do, do not bore.

Unless you are a brilliant spontaneous speaker, you should practice what you are going to say before you appear at a lecture or reading. Some authors speak for too long. Some deliver lengthy passages in a monotone, dulling the audience. Instead consider your audience's interests. If your book is a novel, read short segments of your text and, in between, discuss various aspects of your book's development. If your book is nonfiction, then create a short talk based on the key themes of your work: A straight reading of nonfiction almost never works. These approaches will help you connect with the audience. No matter the content you select for your appearances, remember to look up and make eye contact. Raise your voice so that the person farthest away from you will be able to hear you. Remember that the carpeting and surrounding books can absorb or mute your voice.

Prior to your events, you might listen to tapes of writers whose readings of their work you admire. Practice your own presentation style until it sounds as smooth, natural and entertaining. Another sensible tactic is to attend bookstore readings and evaluate what you find effective in others authors' presentations.

The novelist Edna O'Brien has a gorgeous resonant voice and an Irish accent. She is a dramatic and mesmerizing reader. So is Toni Morrison, who creates a charged atmosphere at her readings. Nikki Giovanni is an impassioned reader of her poetry. Frank McCourt and T. C. Boyle are successful and engaging speakers. For utmost effect and beauty, first prize goes to Dylan Thomas. Listen to an audiotape of his captivating and resonant voice presenting his poetry. This sort of private education is essential if you are planning an extended reading tour and have little experience in giving readings.

Relax about the prospect of bookstore appearances. Even if you are unpracticed at public speaking, you will eventually hit your stride with audiences. The old saying is true: No two audiences are alike. Each has a distinct, individual personality. The trick to managing them is to be yourself. Then there will come that magnificent moment when, as you stand in front of a room of strangers—whether a handful of people or a crowd—and as you speak about your book, you will feel their pulse of avid interest in what you are saying. Their engagement will be palpable. They will be putty in your hands—and made to laugh or cry or sigh in empathy with your characters or with you. When this magical moment arrives, you have to be strong. Do not be greedy and speak for too long. It is best to cut your talk a little short. Leave the audience wanting a little more, which is of course the art of the seducer—as well as the art of a successful author on tour.

Apart from giving a straight talk and discussion about your book, create other types of appealing bookstore events, such as:

- A presentation that includes other writers in your genre—say, an evening of mysteries or horror stories.

- A singles' night, where you talk to the crowd about your book of any topic that singles might take an interest in from health and cooking to relationships and wine tasting.

- A networking breakfast where local businesspeople are invited to the bookstore to hear about your business book.

- An evening of spooky stories where you invite parents to bring their kids in pajamas for a story hour.

- A crafts-making session.

- A subject of perennial interest to bookstore audiences is "How to Get Published." Tailor a talk around that theme that also works in appropriate mentions of your own book.

- Would visual aids enliven your talk? Whitney Otto, bestselling author of *How to Make an American Quilt,* produced a slide show for her second novel, *The Passion Dream Book,* a book that drew inspiration from the work of great painters. The slide show and the art theme in the novel gave Whitney the opportunity to speak in art schools as well as bookstores.

- Anne Rice's tour for *The Vampire Armand* doubled as a blood donation drive at her bookstore appearances, a smart way to draw attention to the book as well as to a good cause.

THE BOOK SIGNING

You will arrive fifteen minutes or so before the event is scheduled to begin. The store manager will greet you and show you where you will be reading. Bookstores are well practiced at running these events. They provide all the necessities: Podium, microphone, or perhaps a table and chair if you are only signing books. If your appearance takes place in a city where your sales rep lives or is visiting, then the rep will probably attend the event.

If you are an unknown author, the crowd could range anywhere from a disappointing handful to a happy group of fifteen or more. For authors who have written topical works of nonfiction, the crowd can become significantly larger. For example, Susanna Kaysen's appearances for her memoir about mental illness, *Girl, Interrupted,* attracted many people who identified with her experiences. At the time Kaysen was an unknown writer, but favorable review coverage and the subject matter made her bookstore events a hit. Similarly, Mary Karr, author of a memoir called *The Liars' Club,* attracted large audiences based on the terrific review coverage and her feisty and appealing perspective on her dysfunctional family.

This should go without saying, but during the question-and-answer period, you should treat the audience with the greatest respect. Always. Even someone who asks a loopy and long-winded question. Remember: You need them so much more than they need you. I once witnessed a famous literary writer address an audience member with contempt, telling the poor man that he had obviously missed the entire point of the presentation. No one deserves that treatment. Such a bully was that author that I could feel the audience wilt and no one asked any more questions. To my mind, the author got his just reward. His nasty behavior certainly did not motivate me to read or buy his books.

Your greatest fear about your public appearances might be that no one will show up. Sometimes appearances fail to attract an audience because of competition from a local event or bad weather. Keep your chin up, keep smiling. Perhaps do what one resourceful friend of mine did. He became a volunteer bookstore clerk and helped customers. Whatever you do, do not complain to the bookstore staff. You will only alienate and embarrass them. This means that once you've left the bookstore, you've lost the support of the bookseller who might have talked to customers about your book.

An essential part of your job is to keep the bookseller feeling motivated and interested in you. After all, they booked you to appear in their bookstore because they thought your book would appeal to customers. Take this opportunity to get to know the store staff. Again, they might become your allies in a handselling campaign once you've left the store.

Let's say you tour five or six cities, and only about twelve people show up at each reading. You may come away wondering whether all your effort was worthwhile. As you see it, you're selling only a handful of books at a time. But, behind the obvious, what you are accomplishing is building an audience. With the handful of people that showed up and bought and read your book, you have created a baseline audience upon which to build for your next book. Finding an audience can be a slow growth process. Sometimes this requires long, hard work. But with persistence, you can reach the payoff.

On one occasion, a friend of mine showed up at his own reading and found that the bookstore had made little effort to promote the occasion. The store was located in a mall in Atlanta. Making the best of a bad situation, this author stood outside the store and started to drum up attention, noisily, for his book. He called people over and invited them to come inside to hear his reading. Big on personality, he soon gathered twenty or so people for the reading, and even convinced two strangers to buy copies of the book, though they never set foot in the store. He knew that if he didn't get busy to try to make some success out of the event, then his time and effort on tour would have been wasted.

You will decide for yourself if you feel comfortable with showmanship when it comes to building an audience. Remember that shyness does not sell books—unless you're able to create a Salinger-esque mystique. To thwart shyness, remind yourself that you're not promoting you. Rather, you are promoting your book and the wisdom, service, or entertainment that it offers. If it helps, you can even think of yourself as promoting reading, not just your book.

THE THIRTEEN RULES FOR AN EFFECTIVE BOOK SIGNING

1. If you are appearing on interviews that will air before your bookstore event, remember to mention the signing's date, place, and time. Alternately, before you start your interview, ask the host to mention the event.

2. Engage people who walk by your signing table by talking about your book or just being friendly.

3. Most bookstores will post signage about your appearance, but often these signs are placed around the store and not at the signing table. A simple blow up of your book jacket mounted on an easel board will help create a point of interest at your table. If your publisher doesn't make one of these for you, make one yourself. A color photocopy enlarged roughly to the size of a legal sheet of paper works just fine and, when you go on the road, it is easily portable in your suitcase.

4. Make lasting contacts of the bookstore staff by being memorable and polite. Make them into effective handsellers of your book by talking to them about the book and by taking an interest in them.

5. Practice your reading or talk ahead of time. Keep it short. Remember your job is to entertain and interest people in your book: A long speech will tire them and squelch any yearning to read the book, let alone spend money on it.

6. Cue your audience twice during your presentation that you will be happy to answer their questions at the end. Prearrange for a shill to ask a question if no one steps forward to ask the first question. Or break the ice by telling the audience that "people often ask me . . ." and asking the first question yourself. Another way of engaging with the audience is to plant your talk with some tantalizing points of interest that you don't explain in detail. Inevitably someone in the audience will ask you to elab-

orate. For example, you might say that it was essential that you publish this book before you turned forty, and then leave the somewhat mysterious comment hanging unexplained. You will most certainly be asked about why you had to publish with such urgency. You've led your audience into dialogue with you.

7. Be gracious to all customers who approach you, even if they only want directions to the bathroom.

8. Collect names and addresses of members of the audience, or better yet collect e-mail addresses for your database. If you have a seated audience, circulate a sign-up sheet, or place a collection bowl at your table for business cards to build your mailing list.

9. Thank the staff and the audience. Send thank-you notes to the staff. Or take pictures of yourself with the bookstore clerks and send the photos along with your thank-you notes.

10. With a smile on your face and a relaxed attitude, you will make the audience feel comfortable. If you show your anxiety, you will make the audience anxious.

11. Play to your audience's mood. If you sense restlessness, keep your talk engaging, lively, and short.

12. As people approach you to sign your book, engage them. Ask how they'd like the book personalized, or what else they like to read, or how they heard about the event (to learn what publicity is working). Creating a memorable event is one way to keep people talking about you. Keep the conversations brief if you happen to have a long line of people waiting for signed copies.

13. Ask the staff if you can sign any unsold copies, which will be stickered and displayed up front.

BOOKSTORE EVENTS (WITHOUT AN AUTHOR)

"Authorless" bookstore events are an alternative to bookstore appearances. These are common in children's book publishing, but less so with adult books. While children's books can be promoted with storytelling sessions (where the store's staff read to children) or with character's costumes (in which a store clerk dresses up in a costume loaned to the bookstore by the publishing house), authorless promotions for adult books are less obvious. The beauty of these events is that because they are tied to your book, the bookstores order your book for the event.

Some examples of authorless events:

- Promote a popular history book with a trivia contest. Some booksellers turn events like this into singles nights, seizing on the chance to create an interactive social event. Provide the store with a quiz with the answers on a separate sheet for the store manager to hand out.

- Booksellers will promote self-help or how-to books by working with local experts. For example, a local financial planner might talk about this year's tax changes. The bookseller sells books related to tax planning. The expert gets to promote his or her business. Propose events to booksellers that identify an expert that the bookseller could call on for an event. Offer handouts such as bookmarks or postcards—anything that reinforces the event's connection to your book. Even though the bookseller will present an array of books on the subject, your materials will help your book stand out. Another example: A staffer from a local fabrics or craft store can demonstrate easy-to-make Halloween costumes for kids, with the costume design coming from your crafts book. The kit materials that you might offer for the event are instructions, a supplies list, and an illustration or photograph of the suggested costume. Any activity-based book can be promoted in this way.

- Create attention and display for your book by creating a gift basket that a bookstore can raffle off. The basket might contain gourmet goodies and a copy of your cookbook. On a practical level, the number of stores that you can offer this promotion to is limited because the baskets will be expensive to put together. But choose your bookstores right (ask your publicist to talk to the sales reps about identifying the top upscale independent booksellers in their territories) and run the promotion during peak traffic times (holidays, Mother's Day, Father's Day) and the promotion might pay off in increased sales at those accounts. If so, then your publisher might offer the promotion in other markets.

Assembling the event kits that the bookstores will need in order to stage the event can be somewhat time-consuming and therefore a strain on an already overworked marketing or publicity group. However, if your publisher thinks the idea is a good one, then you can certainly assemble the event kits yourself. As long as you're prepared to do that legwork then your publicist and sales reps have no reason not to pitch your concept to the booksellers. (Unless of course, they think your idea is a bad one.)

Your publisher's cooperation in pitching the chain booksellers is important. The two major chains prefer to send materials to their store managers directly from the home office, and prefer to work through publishers rather than authors. If your publisher doesn't think your idea is strong enough to pitch, then your alternative is to set up events store by store. With this latter approach, you can start small and experiment with a limited number of stores. The local store managers of the chains as well as independent booksellers can set up events. When those events go well and help the booksellers sell your book, then report your success to your publisher and ask if the sales reps will now pitch the chains with your idea.

The materials that a bookseller requires to host an authorless event include:

- Text and a book jacket for the bookseller to create a promotional poster for the event

- Newsletter copy for the store newsletter

- A script for the store manager or other person who will be hosting the event

- Any other materials that are specific to your book's event

Booksellers will photocopy any materials to use as audience handouts. Last, enclose a "Dear Bookseller" cover letter that describes how the kit contents can promote your book.

Take a look at the newsletters and advice for booksellers on www.bookweb.org, the site of the American Booksellers Association. If your authorless event is a good idea, then you or your publicist could pitch the editor of the newsletter to share it with the booksellers.

SET UP SPEAKING ENGAGEMENTS AND OTHER NON-BOOKSTORE APPEARANCES

Talk to your publicist about setting up speaking engagements in your tour cities. Speaking engagements are usually sponsored by a local organization with a membership base to invite to the event. The events deliver another audience and an excellent way to anchor your visit to a local market and to appeal to local media.

For example, literary fiction writers or writers of serious nonfiction can enhance their tour schedule by contacting the heads of the applicable university departments—English or African-American studies or women's studies and so on—to set up readings and invite the relevant classes to attend. In some cases, the universities will offer a small honorarium, of, say, $250 to $500. They will often agree to display posters promoting the event, but you or your publicist may have to provide them. These are simply made from book jackets, an author photo, and information about the event pasted onto easel-backed foam core or cardboard. Meanwhile, let the university bookstore know about the talk on campus so they can order the book. Arranging university appearances can take longer than setting up bookstore events, requiring several conversations with professors, who are available only during their infrequent office hours.

Not all in-house publicists can or will book local speaking engagements. (Not all freelance publicists will book speaking engagements, either, so if this type of promotion is important to you, then clarify that before you hire someone.) Anyone can research and book his or her own speaking engagements, which should coincide with publication date or later. Because you've tied the theme of your talk to your book, you've created a ready theme for bookstores as well.

You might also speak at libraries. Throughout the United States and Canada, many libraries have active speakers programs that range from grand and formal, such as the main branch of the New York Public Library and the Cambridge Public Library, to informal though well-attended programs at local branch libraries. The booking lead time for branch libraries is four to eight weeks, longer for some of the larger library programs. You also benefit from being listed in the events' brochures or newsletters. It's all exposure for you and your book.

Some librarians will let you sell your book at the event, but ask first. While library appearances, like university talks, do not deliver significant book sales, they do deliver audiences—sometimes very large ones. These audiences can help build favorable word of mouth for your book. To find libraries in your region or in areas where you will travel, log onto www.publiclibraries.com, a portal to libraries throughout the United States, and to www.nlc-bnc.ca/canlib/epublic.htm for Canadian branch library Web sites. As previously mentioned, to get a feel for the library market, read *Library Journal* or, if you're the author of a children's book, read *School Library Journal*.

Other possible speaking venues include the Smithsonian Institution in Washington, D.C., which has a terrific year-round program called the Resident Associate Program and offers lectures on a full range of topics, and The National Archives in Washington, D.C., which also has a varied speakers program. So does your local YMCA or YMHA, the chamber of commerce, the Junior League, garden clubs, museums and historical societies, design centers, botanic gardens, and grade schools, which are particularly important for authors of children's books. Cafes and restaurants sometimes look to attract a certain kind of literary clientele and may sponsor readings. Local church groups and synagogues often welcome speakers to speak on spiritual and secular topics, and so on. Another source of ideas for places to speak is www.booktv. org. This is C-SPAN 2's site for its Book TV programming.

Speak at Libraries—One Author's Success Story

"You cannot speak at enough libraries," says novelist Laura Van Wormer. Most libraries have brown-bag lunch programs for speakers. Appearing at these events leads to an increase in demand for copies ordered at that branch and to librarians talking to colleagues at other branches, which in turn leads to increased sales and a growing readership for your work. Libraries have Web sites and are relatively easy to research and contact. "You can also create bookmarks," Van Wormer says. "The circulating staff is happy to leave them at the circulation desk as patrons check out their books."

She advises, as well, that authors get involved with their local Friends of the Library programs. Her own involvement with the restoration of the old library building in her hometown of Meriden, Connecticut, as well as her understanding of libraries has led to an invitation to give the keynote address at the annual Arizona Library Association/Mountain Plains Library Association Conference. "They wanted me to speak not because I'm an author," she says, "but because I know what they do and what they are interested in."

She knew because she made it her business to educate herself about the library marketplace. Her books appear regularly on library reading lists and account for a nice portion of sales for each new novel.

Pay particular attention to Van Wormer's last piece of advice: "Always be nice to librarians," she says. "You never know if one of them is a buyer." Meaning that the librarian may be the person selecting how many copies of your book to buy for the library system.

Still stumped for venues? To find more, just type in "author lecture" and "friends of the library" and "junior league" into your search engine and you will start to unearth hundreds of opportunities for authors, along with contact information for the organizers of the events.

Perhaps one of the most accessible organizations for authors to enter the speakers market, as well as perhaps to make a little money, is The Learning Annex. With programs in Los Angeles, New York, San Diego, San Francisco, and Toronto, The Learning Annex offers 800 inexpensive adult-education classes every month on a wide range of practical and inspirational topics. These include the arts, business, money and careers, personal growth, relationships, spirituality, sports and fitness, technology, and much more. Authors can earn a percentage of the class fee and if the course registration is more than 100 people, then The Learning Annex will sell books at the classes. (If the registration is smaller, then you are responsible for book sales.) Classes are promoted through catalogs distributed in street stands, in stores, and through direct mail. The average class length is three hours, and classes are held in hotel and conference rooms arranged by The Learning Annex.

Here are examples of some other interesting speaking forums for authors on tour:

- Frank Rich, the former theater critic for the *New York Times,* spoke at regional theaters to promote the paperback edition of *Ghost Light.*

- Bill Nye the Science Guy appeared at aquariums to promote his book, *Big Blue Ocean.*

- The American Museum of Natural History scheduled a lecture with Simon Winchester, author of *The Map That Changed the World* about the founder of modern geology.

- The Junior League of Richmond sponsors an annual Book and Author Dinner. Go to the Web site to see if you think your book qualifies for the event.

- The Friends of the Farmers' Market in Santa Fe sponsors many local events including cooking and crafts demonstrations, childrens' storytelling, chef visits, and book talks (www.farmers marketsnm.org).

- The author of *The Spirit of Butterflies*, Maraleen Manos-Jones, was invited to appear at The National Zoo to talk and to sign books.

Your speaking appearance at a local institution gives you or your publicist an additional angle to pitch in that market. Your publicist may set up a radio and newspaper interview in advance of your departure. That way the media can mention your event in advance so that interested readers can attend. The sponsor for your appearance may have its own publicity department, which can assist you with local press lists and contacts.

BOOK SALES AT EVENTS

You have options when selling books at events. At small local events that you, rather than your publisher, have arranged, you can buy books from your publisher (at your author discount rate) and sell copies at the back of the room. Better yet, the organizers of the event where you are appearing might agree to buy and sell your books. If they agree to do this, refer them to your publisher's special sales department. For much larger events, publishers will sometimes arrange for a bookseller to sell books. You are also free to contact local booksellers directly to arrange back-of-the-room sales. Remember: Keep you editor informed periodically about what you are doing so that he or she can remind the publisher of your ongoing activities to keep your book in print.

If you plan to buy upward of one thousand books for yourself—either for resale or to give away—then you might have your agent negotiate a more favorable discount in the contract. If the contract is long since executed, you might still try to negotiate a discount based on the large number of books that you intend to buy. The standard author discount is generally 40 to 50 percent. This sale is nonreturnable. Standard bookstore discounts range from 46 to 49 percent on a returnable basis. This means that the publisher's terms of sale to you are favorable to the publisher because it runs no risk of getting the books back. If the publisher refuses to give you a higher flat discount, propose a sliding scale based on the number of books you buy.

AN AUTHOR SETS UP SPEAKING ENGAGEMENTS
TO PROMOTE HER BOOKS

Katherine Wyse Goldman has written a number of books, the most recent being *Working Mothers 101*. Earlier books include *My Mother Worked and I Turned Out Okay* and *If You Can Raise Kids You Can Get a Good Job*. She is a marketer by profession and finds the "hunt" for promotional opportunities exhilarating.

To publicize one of her books, Goldman called the Greater Philadelphia Chamber of Commerce and proposed that the organization sponsor a panel discussion targeting the area's working women. The chamber agreed and found a local bank to underwrite the event—a breakfast talk called "The Distinguished Woman: Taking Charge." Joining Goldman on the panel were the president of the local United Way, the district attorney, and the general manager of a local cable channel. The chamber used the breakfast panel as a way to promote a convention it was sponsoring called The International Woman's Show: The ticket to the breakfast talk included admission to the convention and more than 500 women attended. Books were available at a 30 percent discount. To publicize the event, the chamber sent brochures to its members and ran a full-page ad in the *Philadelphia Inquirer*.

When calling a company with a book promotion idea, Goldman identifies the name of the right contact from the newspaper or magazine article where she read about their organization, or else from Internet research. Failing those leads, Goldman simply approaches the head of corporate communications. "That person usually reports to the CEO, and so is a good doorway into the company," she says. Other successful events that Goldman has set up for herself include:

■ The Women Incorporated annual conference called "Uncommon Women on Common Ground" for women entrepreneurs: After reading about the forthcoming conference in a magazine, she cold-called the organizers to ask if she could participate. Before her call, they hadn't considered including a session on work/life balance issues. They sold books, paid half of her expenses to California, and Goldman convinced her publisher to pay the balance.

■ *MetroKids,* the parenting newspaper in Philadelphia: Goldman simply called the editor of the paper and asked if it ever sponsored any conferences. When the editor later had an idea for a conference, she called Goldman to participate as the keynote speaker on the subject "Family Focus: Resources for Today's Families."

■ Delaware County Community College: Goldman called the college after reading an article about its program for older women who want to get a college degree. She interviewed the head of the program for her book, who later invited Goldman to be the graduation speaker.

■ Goldman also set up and participated in The Nordstrom's Grandmother Club breakfast, the Child Abuse Council annual fundraising breakfast, the Lakeshore Health System's Annual Women's Symposium, and the Women's Division of the Jewish Welfare Fund for a fund-raising dinner where she spoke on "Working Women as Role Models for the Family and the Community." She also successfully pitched the Cleveland Bar Association's program on "Making Mentoring Part of Law Firms" and Case Western Reserve University's "Women's Voices Lecture." In her appearances, Goldman often delivered the keynote address to audiences ranging from 50 to 800 people. At all events, the sponsors sold copies of her books, which is her prerequisite for appearing at an event. She also suggests that instead of selling the book to attendees, the host organizations buy copies of the books to give away as table gifts.

Another idea that Goldman had that did not pan out, but is nonetheless a good example of how to think like a marketer, involves

Ford Motors. When Goldman read that an all-woman team designed the Ford Windstar, she figured why not ask the company to offer her book as an incentive for potential customers to test-drive the vehicle. After all, their customers and her customers are the same people. Though the idea fell through, it was a good one: Car companies often use books as test-drive incentives.

Goldman advises that when you talk to companies you should pitch to their goals. Corporations have deeper pockets for promotion than book publishers do. But they will support your book only if the program you pitch furthers the marketing goals for their own products or services.

A SELF-PUBLISHED AUTHOR CREATES HER OWN GRASSROOTS PUBLICITY CAMPAIGN

Nelvia Brady is a self-published author who planned all her own promotions and publicity for her book, *This Mother's Daughter*. Through interviews with women about their mothers, the book addresses the nature of the mother-daughter bond. The author's promotional efforts resulted in good publicity and sales, enough so that the publishing house, St. Martins, later bought the paperback rights.

To promote her book, Brady appeared at churches and private parties, set up by friends in many cities. She says, "The events where I can speak to the substance of the book are more successful than just a book signing." She planned the events carefully. Her approach was to begin with interactive games that drew the audience into her subject matter and made them feel comfortable. Then she addressed the serious aspects of relationships between mothers and daughters. An educator by training, Brady drew on her expertise to engage her audience. She also shared stories about her own mother, and so created an atmosphere in which people felt free to open up. At her events, she sold copies to most people in the room.

To tap into her network of friends, Brady simply called them and asked for help in their community. Some friends belonged to professional organizations or clubs that sponsored events. Others hosted events for their friends in their homes or at bookstores. At every event, attendees were impressed about meeting a genuine author. This took Brady by surprise: She had hardly begun to see herself in such terms.

Having her friends set up and host bookstore signings worked particularly well. Her contacts called bookstores to offer to host events in the store. They'd send postcard invitations, supplied by Brady, to friends and associates. They even supplied refreshments.

"Bookstores like it because it ensures a turnout," says Brady. "It also takes the pressure off a hostess because she doesn't have to worry about using her home or finding a site. There is always parking and the locations are usually pretty convenient. I have also had organizations host their events in the bookstore. Most recently I did a book signing event for a suburban YWCA that was held in a Borders bookstore."

What Brady had not anticipated was the financial cost. She had travel expenses that, with some early planning, could have been reduced. Also, because she preferred not to handle cash transactions herself at her events, she hired someone to travel with her to manage that.

However, her commitment continues to pay off: For the Today's Black Woman Expo in Chicago she set up a game show, based loosely on television's old show *The Newlywed Game,* staged, instead, with mothers and daughters. She also has some leads into *The Oprah Winfrey Show,* and is cautiously hopeful about the possibility of an appearance. She has also retained Vanesse Lloyd-Sgambati, a publicist based in Philadelphia who specializes in African-American books.

Brady says that setting up promotions and publicity requires total commitment, which gave her the impetus to accomplish as much as she did. She is now working on a new book about fathers and daughters.

JOIN THE SPEAKING CIRCUIT—BECOMING A PROFESSIONAL SPEAKER

If you are an effective speaker and your subject matter is topical, consider building up your credentials and signing up with a speaker's bureau, an agency that will set up paid speaking engagements on your behalf. The agency's desire to sign you will depend on several factors:

- How well you deliver a speech

- How well your speech is put together (there is an art to this, and you may need to work with a speech coach on both delivery and content)

- The extent to which your speech is marketable to potential audiences

Speaker's bureaus will want to see a videotape of you giving a speech, as well as a complete press kit about you and your book. You will need to market yourself to them much in the same way that you might have done when you were first looking for a literary agent. (For hundreds of tips on giving effective speeches, basic presentation skills, understanding your audience, getting over stage fright, and other advice related to public speaking, check out www.antion.com.) If you manage to get signed on with a speaker's bureau to set up regular speaking engagements, you will benefit from supplemental income as well as exposure for your book. Your hosts will arrange to sell the book at the back of the room. Speaker's bureaus take a commission of 15 to 30 percent of your fees.

If you're not proficient enough to command a speaker's bureau interest, start small and work your way up. This could mean taking speaking engagements for little or no fee, but you get to polish your skills and keep your book's audience growing. To find a list of speaker's bureaus (or lecture agents), go to www.literarymarketplace.com. You will need to register, and then you will have free access to several useful publishing databases including lecture agents and publicity firms.

When starting out on the speaker's circuit, it will be difficult, at first, to get paid for your appearances. In the beginning, however, generating an income should not be your goal. More important is improving your credentials by starting with local chapters of national organizations. Increase your exposure. Ask your hosts to recommend you to the groups' national chapters. Gradually you will sharpen your speaking skills, create exposure for your book, and possibly attract interest from speaker's bureaus.

How do you find these organizations? You will need to invest some time to research and contact leads. You will need to create a professional-looking packet of information about yourself: A one-sheeter about your proposed topic; a press release about your book; a biography of yourself; a photocopy of the cover of your book; and a copy of the page from your publisher's catalog. A Web site can come in handy to display appropriate information to the people you are pitching.

If you are at all serious about speaking, take the time to prepare a professional-looking presentation kit. The speaker's market is a competitive one. You will market yourself to speaker's bureaus and to organizations with the same assiduousness and smart thinking that you will bring to the marketing of your book to your various target audiences.

BOOKSTORE APPEARANCES AND SPEAKING ENGAGEMENTS— A SUMMARY

Like your media appearances, your bookstore and speaking appearances should entertain your audience to motivate them to buy your book. The opportunities for public appearances are limitless, if you can come up with an interesting and effective presentation and are willing to pitch yourself. To do this:

- Create a talk about your book and practice it before you unleash it on the public.

- Research venues to speak in your community by paying attention to events and businesses that might take an interest in your book. You can pitch yourself to speak to the organization, or for the company to cosponsor your bookstore events so that you can attract a larger, targeted audience.

- Be bold and cold-call individuals at organizations that might host you—the payoff could be big.

- Have your press materials at the ready so that you can respond quickly to a potential host's interest.

- Set yourself a reasonable goal for continual exposure—perhaps one appearance a month.

11

INTERNET MARKETING

SELLING your book successfully is an impressive achievement—for you and your publisher. The plain truth is that competition in the marketplace is fierce. Consumers enjoy so many choices of entertainment and news media, your product has to stand out sharp in order to survive. According to Seth Godin's book *Permission Marketing*, consumers see an estimated 3,000 marketing messages every day. Your challenge is to raise your book above the media clutter.

The good news is the Internet. Harnessed properly, the Internet's power as a marketing tool can be awesome in creating attention for your book. It can connect you to the right communities of readers for your book. You can use it to build relationships with potential readers and perhaps even parlay those relationships into book sales. A word of caution, though. Improperly handled, the Internet can be a waste of your time and money. You can be misled into overspending on a fancy-looking Web site that is undermarketed and useless.

The Internet has made significant contributions to book publishing by providing sales venues through online retailers, by increasing promotional opportunities, and by offering an amazingly fast and efficient research capability. Through readily available online resources, you can find out about competing titles, the names and addresses of reporters, articles in out-of-town papers, freelance publicists, writer's groups, speaker's bureaus, and so on. No doubt about it, the Internet has vastly improved certain aspects of the publicist's (and the author's) job.

Online booksellers range from the big guns like Amazon or Barnes & Noble to the independent bookseller site www.booksense.com to special-interest sites run by individuals with a "buy this book" affiliate link to one of the e-tailers. The proliferation of online retailers is good news. They serve customers who can't find a book at the local bookstore, but who can access virtually any book through the Web. (My favorite book search site is www.bookfinder.com, which tracks down sources to buy new and used copies of most any book.) The e-tailers also offer a way to capture consumers who might not have heard about your book from other sources.

Your publisher's sales reps call on the larger accounts, but the reps do not have time to scout out all online bookselling opportunities. If you want to reach this medium, you must build relationships yourself with the sites that might be interested in either selling or promoting your book.

Then of course you might build your own Web site. According to author and business consultant Michael Schrage, you are cheating yourself if you do not figure out how to represent yourself and your work on the Web. A Web site of your own provides many opportunities to create a presence among active online communities that share your interest. Schrage argues that since the Internet is a medium that requires its participants to read, you know you're reaching an audience that chooses to read in its leisure time. Because the link between an online promotion and a purchase is only a few clicks away, an enormous sales potential for books exists on the Web. He believes that this resource is still relatively untapped.

As you set out to find your audience on the Internet, keep in mind that you should find your specific audience and market particularly to them. Do not try to sell to everyone—you'll end up missing your core audience with a scattershot message. The Internet is a tool that allows you to pinpoint the individuals who are most likely to care about your book.

INTERNET BOOK MARKETING BASICS

Whether or not you have your own Web site, you can market your book on the Internet in many ways:

- Check the major e-tailer sites to see if your publisher has uploaded your book jacket and other pertinent information. If the information about your book is missing, then track down the person at the publishing house whose job this is. If you end up having to submit the information yourself, then check each e-tailer's site for its submission guidelines. You will need to provide a JPEG file of your book jacket. You should be able to get this from your art director if not your publicist. If necessary, scan your book jacket at Kinko's.

- Log onto your book's listing on the e-tailers' sites and fill in the author's comments section. Any good reviews? Submit them to the e-tailers' sites.

- Use a search engine to locate online newsletters and sites that pertain to your book topic. Contact the sites and offer a free column or excerpt from your book. In exchange, ask if the site is willing to link to yours.

- Log onto www.about.com's publishing chat rooms and join any appropriate discussions and ask for ideas about promoting your book. The publishing area has a bulletin board where you can post your queries about book publishing.

- Join chat groups in subject areas that you are genuinely interested in—perhaps sites with other authors talking about publishing. Log on and start talking. By contacting special interest sites that would have a natural interest in your book, you can build an interested audience.

- Set up an electronic signature that includes information about your book (and your Web site's address). The information in your signature will appear at the bottom of every e-mail that you send. If you do not know how to set up a signature, use your software help function, which will direct you to your toolbar.

- Set up and participate in online interviews or chats, such as the ones found on Talk City or on America Online (AOL), by exploring the sites and finding the right contacts.

- Collect e-mail addresses of friends, family, business associates, and anyone potentially interested in you and your book topic. Organize them into an address group, to which you will send periodic e-mails about your upcoming book events.

- Booksellers (both e-tailers and brick-and-mortar stores) often send special e-mailings to their customers. Ask your publisher about offering an excerpt or a specially written article for the booksellers to use.

- Offer to write for relevant industry e-newsletters. Many welcome relevant content. For example, novelist Sarah Bird wrote an article for the *Publishers Weekly* daily e-mail newsletter about the military brats of all ages who showed up at her bookstore events for *The Yokota Officers Club*.

- If you already have an active and growing database of fans, offer them a sneak online or e-mail preview of your work, perhaps the first chapter, just before the book is shipped to bookstores.

E-MAIL LISTS AND NEWSGROUPS

Another way to market online is to participate in e-mail lists and newsgroups, which are forms of electronic discussion groups.

E-mail lists are essentially e-mail clubs for people who share the same interests. Sign up with a list on a topic that's of interest to you, and you will start to receive e-mails from other list members. Some groups are more active than others and produce a flood of e-mails. If the list is a reading group, then the e-mails will be about the current book under discussion. If the list is about self-publishing, then you will read e-mails from people asking for advice for anything from finding a book jacket designer to working with distributors.

To find e-mail lists on your area of interest, type "e-mail lists" or "Listservs" into your search engine and start searching around for lists that interest you. (E-mail lists are often referred to as Listservs, though Listserv is actually the name of the software program that manages the lists.) Joining a list is free, the instructions for signing up are clearly explained, and you can unsubscribe at any time. You need to stay within the appropriate boundaries established by the operator of the list. The rules are clear when you sign up. You can't use the list to promote your book aggressively, especially if the book's topic has little to do with the subject of the list. If you try to promote the book in an obvious or inappropriate way, you will receive a flurry of harsh comments objecting to your efforts. If you abuse the privilege again, then the list operator might eject you from the list. However, once the members of the list become familiar with you, you can mention your book. You will understand what level of promotion is acceptable once you spend a little time with newsgroups and e-mail lists.

One way to gain exposure on e-mail lists without breaching protocol is to e-mail the list host and offer a free chapter of your book to list members. You can suggest to the host that interested readers can e-mail you directly for the excerpt. If the host is interested in sharing your work with list members, then he or she will e-mail the information to the list.

If you have a Web site, promoting your book is much easier. You can simply include your Web site's address in your signature (see page 222 on electronic signatures) so that list members can click to your site if they are interested.

Whereas members of lists e-mail one another, members of newsgroups instead post messages on the newsgroup's Web site. Once you join a newsgroup—usually you must register before you can interact with other members—you must revisit the site to read any new messages. To find newsgroups, use the Google search engine and click on Groups. Search for a newsgroup by topic or by keywords, which will show you links to relevant messages in all newsgroups.

ONLINE READING GROUPS

Reading groups use the Internet in several ways. Some groups post their booklists on a Web site as a service to their members and then meet in person. The group called Mostly, We Eat has a Web site that welcomes nonmembers and a free e-mail newsletter (www.mostly-weeat.org). Some reading groups are run entirely as e-mail lists, meaning that members never meet in person. Instead, the members e-mail one another and the dialogue takes place entirely online through the ongoing replies. Or else an online reading group might host live-time newsgroup chats where the dialogue appears on its Web site. An example of this, on a grand scale, is the *USA Today* reading group, which posts questions for readers on its Web site (www.usatoday.com, go to the Life section and then to Books) and hosts online chats with the author of the featured book.

As reported in the *Atlanta Journal-Constitution,* Walter Mosley's publicist, Sally McCartin, contacted more than 250 online reading clubs by e-mail and sent them advance copies of Mosley's new novel. Some of the clubs interviewed Mosley. Others added his new book to their reading lists. The *New York Times* reported on how Donna Woolfolk Cross built an audience for her historical novel by marketing to reading groups. Her book, *Pope Joan,* has more than 100,000 copies in print in its paperback edition. Her site, www.popejoan.com, offers a section dedicated to reading groups, encouraging the groups to contact her to set up an "appearance" by speakerphone. She offers a discount to reading groups if they purchase the book online through the site. Smart. In fact Cross's efforts are credited with prompting booksellers to offer speakerphone author events to reading groups that meet in their bookstores.

Several reading groups gained national prominence after being featured on some of the televised book clubs. Search for these groups online and you will come up with hundreds of articles. Some of the prominent groups include The Pulpwood Queens (East Texas), the Sweet Potato Queens Eating and Reading Club (Jackson, Mississippi), and the Urban Pages (Cleveland, Ohio). Try the books section of Yahoo! clubs at groups.yahoo.com. When you find groups that seem appropriate to the subject matter of your book, simply e-mail the group's host or Web site manager to ask if you can send a complimentary copy of your book for consideration. Let the host know that if the group selects your book, you would happily make yourself available by phone or in person for an upcoming meeting, depending on your location.

AUTHOR WEB SITES

A Web site can have multiple uses, and you may not even realize its full potential until you have one up and running. Author sites range from a few pages of basic biographical information to full-fledged interactive hangouts. The two key decision points that you'll need to consider before creating a Web site are what you want to offer readers and how you will market the site.

Most publishing houses lack the resources to set up a site for every author. In any case, it's more desirable that you set up the site yourself so that you can control its content. Do not design a Web site until you understand what you want it to accomplish and how you will attract visitors. Educate yourself before you start the process. Check out the sites of other authors to see what features you would like to incorporate into your own. Which ones make you curious about the author or to buy their books? If you really like a particular author's site, send the author an e-mail to ask for contact information for the site's designer.

A great site is www.lemonysnicket.com, which displays Lemony Snicket's kids' books perfectly and provides fun (and creepy) interactive content. The home page welcomes you with a warning to leave the site saying, "You have undoubtedly reached this Web site by mistake." Snicket's droll and faintly sick humor is consistent through the site: Never does he drop his authorial voice. He also provides a printable poster, games, and a screensaver as well as an author biography and list of books. The site strikes exactly the right tone: It engages without overhyping and provides real content.

Another children's author who has created a content-rich site is Jan Brett, www.janbrett.com. She offers an impressively high level of interactivity for users, including contests for schools and libraries to win copies of her books and an author visit, e-mail postcards, printable notecards and envelopes, coloring pages, and more. See also Kevin Henkes's, site, www.kevinhenkes.com, where he has games for kids, recipes for dishes mentioned in his books, and a mouse maze. Beverly Cleary's site, www.beverlycleary.com, has trivia quizzes based on her many books, and also an interactive neighborhood map where her characters live. Perhaps children's authors have a leg up when it comes to creating a playful site, as their books are inherently about learning as play. Although authors of adult books could certainly adapt some of the features of children's book sites.

Look at mystery writer Laura Lippman's site, www.lauralippman. com. While simple in design, it is also attractive and hugely informative. The site makes great use of hyperlinks—links embedded in the text—so that you can find out more information about the people or places that Lippman talks about. Ray Bradbury's site is not overly embellished, but it covers the breadth and depth of this prolific writer's career, at www.raybradbury.com. Isabel Allende has created a very personal site at www.isabelallende.com. Naturally there is information about all of her books here, but there is also a photo gallery of Allende with her family, and a page of frequently asked questions based on her fan mail. The home page is beautiful.

Nelvia Brady says that her site, www.thismothersdaughter.com, has performed well. The site is a clean, professional, and good-looking one, and has saved her time and money on mailings. For friends hosting book signing parties, the site provides ready-made information in the form of downloadable photos and book cover. She's also found that sites that post online reviews often link to hers. Brady is uncertain whether the site has led to any sales because it lacks a commerce function, but says that it has definitely generated many leads. The Web site's address is displayed on the jacket of her book, *This Mother's Daughter,* as well as on promotional materials including bookmarks and postcards.

Another approach to take when developing a site is to try to "own" the topic you have written about. In other words, you can make your site the destination for people interested in your topic. One example of this is Michael Webb's site for his book *The Romantic's Guide,* www. theromantic.com, which is jam-packed with ideas for a romantic date, quizzes, love songs, love poetry, links to a lingerie store and a store that sells romantic gifts and games, and more.

For a top-of-the-line example of a customized site, from an author who also positioned his site as a destination for users interested in his subject, go to www.sonsofheaven.com. Admittedly, author Terrence Cheng had a leg up in planning the site for his first novel, as he runs the Internet division for a major publisher. But his site—even though it's full of multimedia attractions—provides a good case study. Cheng intended to make his site a resource for anyone who is interested in Chinese fiction, politics, and society, and particularly in the events that took place in Tiananman Square in 1989, the starting point for his novel *Sons of Heaven*. The site includes a discussion forum, information about current events, books, and writers related to China, as well as background about the book.

Cheng started planning the site's design a full year before his book was published. He showed a designer twenty Web sites that he liked, not restricting himself to author sites. Then he and the designer focused on the elements that he would incorporate into his site. He gave the designer a flow chart on paper showing the content that he intended to include. Then the designer submitted his first screen, and the two worked together to refine the site. (If you'd like your site to have high-tech audio and visual components such as those found at Cheng's site, contact designer Asaf Shakham at www.milo-18.com.)

As you hone in on what you like, you will find that you have many options to choose from. First of all, what degree of interactivity do you desire with users? Some sites merely post biographical data; others are more interactive and kept continually up to date. Will you post original content, as well as an electronic press kit? Do you want to track downloads from your site and collect e-mail addresses of visitors? What audiences will you market your site to? Your readers, the press, speaking bureaus, bookstores, all of the above?

These are just some of the specific features that your Web site might offer:

- A book jacket image and descriptive paragraph that booksellers can download for store newsletters. Also an author biography and photo, and press release about your book. Note that a book jacket on your home page will help make it instantly clear to readers that you are an author of books. Surprisingly, some author sites manage to keep that fact buried.

- A reading group guide to your book for bookstores and reading groups. For sample downloadable guides, go to www.readinggroup guides.com and www.readinggroupchoices.com.

- A book excerpt. E-mail your Web site link to reporters along with a pithy reason why they should care—a relatively efficient way to get reporters to check out your site and your book.

- Free content. Invite users to download and use original article(s) providing that they credit you and your book. You will specify the credit line that they must run if they reprint your content. You may get some terrific pickup in small newspapers and journals. (Under no circumstances should you reach out to a reporter at a large metro-politan newspaper to run your articles for free: It will be a turnoff.)

- Your speech-making credentials. Pages aimed at organizations for which you might give speeches should include the topics that you can address, any endorsements from organizations that have already hosted you, and a resume of your speaking experience.

- A link to buy your book. Set yourself up as an affiliate or associ-ate with one of the online booksellers so that you get a percentage of sales when readers click through from your site to the retailer's site. Go to www.amazon.com, www.bn.com, or www.booksense.com to read the guidelines for affiliates.

- Contests. Give out free copies of your book or galley on a limited, while-supplies-last basis. You can offer the copies to, say, the first twenty-five users to register for the prize. This way you can capture all the contestant's names in your growing database. Promote the giveaway to other sites to encourage linkage to yours.

▪ E-mail newsletters. Check out the site www.carsecrets.com. Author Corey Rudl offers a free periodic e-mail newsletter, which reveals tips about getting a better deal and, of course, always promotes his book, *Car Secrets Revealed*. This site is heavily oriented toward commerce and sells much harder than most author sites, but the information Rudl provides is nonetheless useful for his target audience.

▪ A media center or press room with your press materials.

▪ Links to other sites where you have contributed articles or where there is press coverage for your book(s).

▪ Links to related sites, making your site a resource and destination that users will bookmark.

▪ An e-mail link so that readers of your site can reach you in one click.

▪ A way for users to forward your Web site pages to a friend via e-mail. Otherwise recommending your site becomes a copy-and-paste process for the user and unless prompted, the user might not even think about passing it along.

▪ Ongoing fresh content, such as press articles about your book or links to them, a schedule of upcoming appearances (and don't forget to take the schedule down when it's finished), or even a book tour diary.

CREATE YOUR SITE

Creating a site involves a few steps:

▪ Registering for a domain name (or URL)

▪ Designing the site

▪ Finding a host server (i.e., once the site is built, it needs a place to sit)

Some companies offer domain registration, design, and hosting all in one package, with prices ranging from rock-bottom all the way to luxury class. You have an array of choices:

- Build the site yourself for free. Use the Web page templates of a service that, in exchange, requires you to use its server. The downside: The service will run advertisements on your site, and some people find the advertisements intrusive. In some cases the advertising presence may be extreme, slowing your site's download time, while in others the ad presence will be more discreet. Also, the free sites sometimes encumber you with a clunky and hard-to-remember URL. Then later on, if you want to switch your site to another host server, you will have to build a new site all over again. Two options are www.homestead.com and www.tripod.com.

- Build the site yourself for a reasonable monthly fee. Use the Web page templates of a do-it-yourself design and hosting service such as www.authorsguild.net, www.geocities.com, www.register.com, www.planetnet.com, and www.verisign.com. Authorguild.net offers a straightforward and easy-to-use template and very reasonable monthly hosting fees, as low as three dollars a month for a single page, or nine dollars a month for as much as fifty pages of content. VeriSign offers a five-page Web site for less than one hundred dollars a year. The package includes hosting, and the templates are smartly businesslike. Register.com offers a free three-page Web site along with your domain registration and offers a funkier range of looks for your site. PlanetNet offers a sleekly professional-looking package at slightly higher prices. Geocities also offers a full range of services and packages to suit a range of budgets.

- Build *and* design the site yourself. Use downloadable software to design the site to suit your tastes. The process is a little more challenging than using the template-based services, and you will need to find a host server. Dreamweaver is one popular program, complete with layout tools and text editing capabilities. (See www.macromedia.com/software/dreamweaver. For hosting options go to www.tophostreview.com which rates and reviews various host servers.)

■ Hire a designer to create your site. Fees range from a few hundred dollars to a few thousand. At the far end of the pricing extreme, for a highly customized and high-tech site with audio and video components, you might pay a designer as much as $5,000 to $10,000. You will still need to find a host server, though a designer can find or recommend one.

■ Hire a service that specializes in author Web sites. Authors on the Web, www.authorsontheweb.com, offers the choice of templates as well as a customized design service, and will also host the site. The service's e-mail newsletter, the *Book Reporter,* draws readers to its own site, which is crammed with information, reviews, contests about books and publishing, and links to author Web sites. Therefore your own site benefits from a continual marketing effort to potential readers. Because Authors on the Web is a reader's environment, you are reaching a targeted audience—readers of quality fiction and nonfiction. Rates are higher than the do-it-yourself options, but still reasonably priced. Other services that specialize in developing author sites are www.bookzone.com, www.literati.net, and www.previewport.com. Again, look at the environment that these sites offer and how they promote themselves. The ones that are more active in promoting their services and offer ongoing programming for readers are more likely to attract the audience that you're seeking as an ancillary benefit to having them build your site.

You'll find some of these services to be intuitive and simple to work with. Others, because of their confusing array of choices or cumbersome editing programs, will drive you crazy. Some will offer you only a few pages and restricted add-on options. Others will offer an abundance of add-on features like a commerce capability (to sell your own books), games, and other interactive features. Compare the sites to see what appeals to your taste and budget. At this stage, remember, you are simply exploring. No matter who designs your site, it should accommodate future edits and add-ons. Updating your site is a must. There's nothing more frustrating for the user than connecting to sites that are clearly out of date.

WORKING WITH WEB DESIGNERS

Web site designers have a strong Web presence, as you might expect. You can find them easily through your search engine, and their sites display their portfolios and, sometimes, their prices. The designer does not need to specialize in author sites to be able to produce a good one for you.

If you're planning to hire a designer to create a customized site, do not overspend on bells and whistles that do not serve your needs. Before you sign up with any designer, ask for references and call them. Try to find one in your area so that you can meet in person. As your site evolves from the initial design, you and your designer might show one another your ideas on paper. Keep your design clean and the content accessible. The more graphics you have, the slower it will be to download and the less likely users will stick around before clicking to another site.

One reasonably priced designer is Anne Gerdes of Anne Gerdes Web Design (http://gerdesdesign.com). She will design a basic six-page site for $400, which includes client training so that you can continue to update the site. Her client questionnaire is very useful, as it prompts you to think about what you want on your site: She asks your goals for the site over a two-year period, your target market, and the addresses of sites that you like and sites that you perceive as your competition.

Kristen Powers (kristenpowers@yahoo.com), who designed novelist Jane Heller's Web site (www.janeheller.com), favors a straightforward and simple approach to Web design. She explains that Web site designers provide more than just design. They also provide technology and marketing assistance. Because your site should work for any user, your designer should test how well the site will download at various modem speeds, for users of either the Internet Explorer or Netscape browser, as well as those who are coming from the AOL environment.

Web site designers may also register your domain, shop around for the best host server, and register your site on search engines. Some designers offer ongoing service in the form of periodic site updates and expansion: Their work isn't necessarily a finite project that ends the moment your site is loaded onto the host server, so select someone you like and trust.

If you want a designer to set up a basic customized site with several pages of text and handle all the technical aspects of your site as well as some ongoing services, you can expect to pay between $1,000 and $1,500. The more bells and whistles you add, and the more time-intensive your site is to maintain, the more expensive the designer will be.

REGISTER YOUR DOMAIN NAME, LIST IT ON SEARCH ENGINES

Your Web site designer or service can register your domain name or URL for you. Or you can register the site yourself through VeriSign for thirty-five dollars a year. (The site does not have to exist yet in order for you to register the name.) Select an address that makes your site easy to find. Most likely your book publicity will center on the title of your book so you might use that as your address. If you are building ongoing visibility through your own name or if you've written more than one book, then consider using your name in the domain. Like the title of your book, choose your domain name carefully. A long or complicated name will be hard for users to remember: The name should help drive people to your site once you start marketing it.

No matter who designs and builds your site, you will need to work with them to come up with descriptive words and phrases that summarize what your site's about. This is because you will register your site on search engines. Make the description short and truly descriptive, rather than promotional, to increase the likelihood that the search engines will use your copy rather than their own edited version. Pay attention to how other sites are described in the various search engines to get a feel for how to write your copy.

Another consideration: You want your site to appear in a search engine's top ten list after a relevant search. For example, if you've written a book on dog grooming, you want a user to find your site quickly through a search engine when they type in "pet care" or similar phrases. The description and keywords that identify your site to search engines determine your site's ranking.

Karyn Zoldan of Bridge Marketing, a company that provides content, copy, and Web site consulting, recommends that you involve yourself in the choices of keywords and not abdicate them to the designer. To come up with the right keywords for your site, think about the words that a consumer is likely to use when searching for information about your topic. Go to www.bridgemarketing.com for more good ideas about creating an effective Web site. See also the site www.rankwrite.com for excellent free articles on key words and search engines, by Internet writing specialists Jill Whalen and Heather Lloyd-Martin. They have lots of advice about optimizing your site for search engines and emphasize the importance of choosing your site's keywords and description carefully, because once your site is submitted to search engines, the listings are hard to change.

Listing your site on search engines, directories, and Internet yellow pages will be an ongoing periodic task, as the engines constantly change the way they rank sites within a search. Several paid services will register your site on search engines, but with varying degrees of success. In *How to Publish and Promote Online*, by M. J. Rose and Angela Adair-Hoy, the authors recommend a service called Submit Plus, which will list your site on key search engines. Submit Plus (www.submit411.com) offers an array of free and paid services. These include free submission to a limited number of search engines and paid submission to more than 1,000 search engines and directories, and optimization of your site to ensure that search engines list it in the top ten results after a search on your key words. Submit Plus has tools that allow you to test your site's optimization for search engines, and also displays some examples of "bad" and "ugly" amateurish sites that would never get listed on search engines. (Learn from them: They are quite funny.)

If you do not want to use a paid service, list your site for free, which will require some time and patience, but is quite doable. Check out a site called www.searchengines.com. There you will find excellent information about registering your site including hot links to the important search engines and directories, as well as charts that explain the registration information required by each search engine. A useful article on this site talks about how the placement of your keywords throughout your site affects its ranking on search engines. The submission process can take several weeks before your site will appear on a search engine. You will need to reregister your site periodically.

SOME WORDS OF ADVICE FROM A WEB SITE CONSULTANT

Zoldan offers the following ten dos and don'ts to consider before getting a Web site:

1. Do shop around. Start surfing and write down the URLs (Web site addresses) of sites you like and don't like and why. A good Web designer should ask for this information just to get a clue about your expectations.

2. Do register your own domain name (yourbusiness.com) or if the Web designer does, be sure you or your company is listed as "administrator." It's similar to owning a car and having your name on the pink slip. You don't want anyone else to own your Web site.

3. Do request that the Web host or Web designer provide you with the FTP host name, login, and password. If you don't have this information and the host or designer dies or runs off to Hollywood, you have no way of ever accessing your site again.

4. Do read the contract carefully and know up front how much it costs to add additional pages and to update information. Are you paying a maintenance fee and if so, what does it include? Be sure you understand the procedure (and get it in writing) if you

decide to change hosts or designers. How is it handled and how long does the process take?

5. Do focus on content. Web users want immediate gratification without sensationalism.

6. Don't get carried away by graphics. Most people use a 28.8 modem and unless the graphic is well, graphic, they don't care to wait around for the suspense. Remember less is more with graphics.

7. Don't believe it if you're offered a free Web site, the deal of a lifetime, or that a Web site will get a million "hits" tomorrow. Realize that a Web site is another form of marketing with the best reach for the money.

8. Don't hire your neighbor's son to design your Web site. He may be a Web wiz but can he design a site that's appropriate for your target audience?

9. Don't be held captive by cyber-babble gibberish. Ask questions and if your host or designer doesn't communicate in terminology you understand, find one who will.

10. Do update your site often. If you posted an event that happened in April and it's now May, your information is stale. Lack of updating content sends a message to customers that you don't care.

To Zoldan's ten points, I add the following seven:

11. Does the service or designer optimize the site for search engines?

12. Will the service regularly submit your site to search engines or will you do that yourself? If you're hiring a designer, will they explain to you how to submit your site to search engines or will they do that for you on an ongoing basis?

13. Once the site is built, can you easily edit content yourself or will the designer do that for you? If the designer will do that then how quickly can they make changes for you?

14. Do other sites built by the service look good? Can you find them on search engines?

15. Has the service/designer created sites for other authors? Have you contacted those authors for references?

16. If you "outgrow" your site, and need to offer more pages of content, does the service offer "add-on" features, like a commerce capability or linking, for a reasonable price? Or can you add these embellishments yourself?

17. Is the designer willing to work with you for a two-week trial period or to give you mock designs before you commit to the entire project?

LINK TO OTHER SITES

Once you've set up your site, one way to drive traffic there is to cross-link with other sites. To do this, you will approach the sites directly. "If you sell bananas, you'd want to link to pages like Banana Importers Trade Association, 1001 Banana Pie Recipes, or Healthy Eating," says Mark Gebbie, publisher of the *All-In-One Directory*, www.gebbieinc. com. "The idea is not to hook up with others who sell bananas, but others who are in some way related to bananas. People who eat them, research them, cook with them, promote them ('Banana Promotion Council'), paint them, whatever. When requesting cross-links, be polite and friendly. Perhaps begin by saying, 'Saw your site, and I'm very impressed with the work you have put into it.' Explain who you are, and why you would consider their link to be 'a fine addition' to your page. Suggest why your link may be of import to them, even if it is obvious. . . . Send your URL and a few lines of text to go with it so they can link to you if they agree. As your page becomes more of a resource rather than an ad, it becomes a more attractive place for everyone concerned.

"To promote the Gebbie Press *All-In-One Directory*, I contacted public relations firms, advertising, marketing, promotion firms, free-lance writers, photographers, journalists, and the like. As it is a media reference work, I've approached hundreds of newspapers, magazines, radio and television stations, and so on. You will have to come up with your own ideas as to who to cross-link with, depending on your product or services offered."

Mark Gebbie came up with another smart way to get his site linked to others. He started an award program. Because his site includes hot links to media outlets, he created a Station of the Month logo, which a number of the radio stations agreed to post on their sites, creating another link to Gebbie's site.

WHATEVER HAPPENED TO E-BOOKS?

E-books were for one brief shining moment, the new Internet-based vision of book publishing: Readers would embrace an electronic form of books and revolutionize the business of reading. While this has not happened, electronic books—which can be downloaded onto your personal computer from any online bookseller—have turned into a significant promotional opportunity for the printed form of books. Erase from your mind the notion of the e-book as a potential revenue stream, at least for now. The market is immature. The e-book's value is greater as a promotional tool rather than as a source of income.

Three very different writers have led the market for e-books. Through their experiences, you can see how an electronic edition of your own book might benefit you.

Go to horror novelist Douglas Clegg's site at www.douglasclegg. com. The site works beautifully to introduce new readers to Clegg's work as well as to provide fans with news about his new books and other activities. Clegg credits his Web site with rebuilding an audience for his work. When his book sales were dropping, Clegg began offering free electronic versions of his new work at the site. Readers who down-loaded the free editions started going into bookstores to look for titles on his backlist. The downward trend in sales was reversed over the course of about eighteen months, and his publishers began to reissue titles that had gone out of print.

Another writer who has shown that e-books can create a market for the printed editions of the work is Seth Godin. His book, *Unleashing the Ideavirus,* talks about how to turn your customers or clients into marketers for your business or product through powerful word of mouth (www.ideavirus.com). Before the printed edition of the book was available, he offered the book as a free download. The freebie created such enthusiasm and positive word of mouth that on the first day of the book's release in hardcover, it went straight to number five on Amazon. The first hardcover printing was 26,500 copies priced at forty dollars and at this writing, according to Godin, one million downloads were reported. Despite the fact that Godin had offered the content for free online, he created the market for the successful publishing of the hardcover edition of the book, and subsequently for the paperback. Godin says that he made *Unleashing the Ideavirus* available electronically to see if free online content might enhance rather than harm book sales, and help create a market of readers. He gave the book away in order to sell it.

Author M. J. Rose couldn't find a publisher for her first novel, *Lip Service.* So she self-published an e-book edition and then spent considerable time on marketing it to all the female-friendly sites she could find on the Internet. Her efforts caught the attention of Doubleday Book Club, which offered a print edition to its members. After that, Pocket Books offered her a contract for the book publishing rights. Go to www.mjrose.com for the full story.

INTERNET MARKETING—A SUMMARY

The Internet is your powerful and efficient research tool, and provides you with opportunities to build an audience for your book. You can:

- Join e-mail lists and newsgroups about subjects related to your book.

- Participate in online discussions.

- Make sure the online retailers have posted the appropriate marketing information about your book.

- Build an e-mail database to market to.

- Offer content to Web sites in exchange for mentioning your book.

If you create and market your Web site, keep the following points in mind:

- Look at other author's Web sites to pick and choose the elements you like.

- Before you build the site, plan on how you will use and market it, both in the short and long run.

- Take a couple of hours to learn about Web building basics so that you can work constructively with your designer.

- Continually update your site so that your content appears fresh and relevant.

- Get your publisher to mention the site on all written materials, including the catalog page, press releases, and your book jacket.

- Periodically, reregister your site with search engines.

- Market the site to your target audiences, reading groups, e-mail lists, newsgroups, other related sites, organizations that might host you as a speaker, booksellers, and the media.

12

SET UP YOUR OWN PUBLICITY

IN any number of scenarios you will become your own publicist to a greater or lesser extent. Perhaps your publisher is doing nothing to promote your book. Perhaps you want to supplement your publisher's national media efforts by targeting local media in certain markets. Or perhaps your book was published last season—or even last year—and your publicist is working on new projects, while you want to continue the media effort. If you have hired your own publicist, you may even assist her efforts. There is no rule book that says an author can't call the media. If your overextended publicist makes anxious noises when you propose a go at your own publicity, do not be disheartened. Do what you need to do. It's your book, not hers.

This is your action-plan checklist, some of which you may have already accomplished in the months leading up to your book's publication:

- Find out what your in-house publicist is covering. Though her efforts may be limited, it is nonetheless foolish to duplicate or to get in the way of her work. Remember: Throughout the campaign her support, however nominal, is essential.

- Set your budget—just as if you were hiring a freelancer, your budget will be driven by the extent of the campaign that you desire.

How much are you willing to spend on expenses like mailings, phone calls, photocopying, and travel? (See Chapter Four on page 103 for a list of campaign costs.) Your expenses will be affected, naturally, by your access to resources like photocopying and fax machines, so factor those in accordingly.

- Formulate how you will position the book for the media and write a press release and/or pitch letter. (See Chapter Five, page 118 for the rules on writing press releases, See Chapter Two starting on page 31 for coming up with angles to pitch your book to the media.)

- Create a list of media targets with contact information.

- Develop customized pitch letters for the most important press contacts.

- Send copies of your book and press release to the media.

- Make follow-up calls.

When you're accomplishing publicity hits, report them to your editor and in-house publicist. This allows them to track your book's sales. If the publicity bookings are significant, such as a major national television show, then your publisher will ask the sales reps to call their accounts and get more copies into the stores before the appearance airs. If the publicity seems to be triggering reorders then you can certainly ask your publicist or editor for reimbursement for reasonable out-of-pocket expenses. Hard for them to say no when the book goes back to press as a result of your work.

WHAT YOU MIGHT GET FROM YOUR PUBLISHER FOR FREE

Chances are that you can persuade your publicist or editor to provide you with the following items, which will help offset your promotional costs:

- Reams of stationery or copy paper.

- Photocopying. Offer to provide the publicist with your press materials to have copied at the publisher's copy center. Provide them several weeks ahead of the date that you will need them: The centers are sometimes slow. If you live in the same city as your publisher, ask if you can come in to use the photocopier.

- Access to an empty office and a phone to make long-distance calls, if you live in the same city as your publisher.

- Editing consultation. Ask your editor and publicist if they are willing to review any press materials that you write.

- Facilities to mail review copies and postage. Your publicist might agree to stuff and send your mailing packets, or that you come into the office and stuff them yourself. The publishing house may cover the postal expense for you.

- Reimbursement for travel expenses. If you book yourself on a major national television show, your publisher will likely pay your expenses.

- Mailing lists. Your publicist can print out media lists for you, both in the form of "call lists" or "call sheets" and mailing labels. Call sheets are the pages you will use to track your follow-up calls to the media. They include complete information about the media contacts: names and addresses, some notes about the show's ranking in the market and booking preferences, phone numbers, and sometimes e-mail addresses. Call sheets are used as a checklist and a place to take notes about your conversations with reporters and producers. (Note that some publicists will not share their mailing lists, as they actively discourage authors from contacting the media. This is not a thoughtless decision on their part. Some authors are loose cannons and should be kept from doing any damage! You can discuss with your publicist how you've thought out your pitch and won't say anything to producers that is potentially foolish. Point out that you can research the information anyway, so they may as well make it easier for you to help market the book. If they still won't give you media lists, you can try talking to the publicity director or your editor for help. Failing that, you're on your own.)

- Free advice. Ask your publicist and editor what they think of your media strategy. See if your publicist has any advice or criticism about your approach.

- Invitations to the book party you are throwing for yourself. Publishers will sometimes pay for these, as well as a little wine and cheese. You can probably persuade your publicist to send party invitations to the local media, or at least identify the right media to invite.

- Books. Tell your publicist that you are using them for publicity purposes and not giving them away to your friends. As long as your publisher sees your publicity efforts paying off, they will probably continue to supply you with promotional copies.

- Jiffy mailers and envelopes. Some publicists and editors and editorial assistants might provide you with these for your book mailing.

- Extra copies of your book jacket. If you will be doing a lot of publicity work, you will need a fair quantity of these, say twenty-five to fifty. You will send one or two to every event venue that you set up so plan accordingly. Your publicist can dig some up from the publicity and art departments.

Bear in mind that your publisher will not give you these goodies for an unlimited time. Unless your book has become newsworthy or unless the sales are still strong, you will likely wear out your welcome after about three months following publication date.

DEFINE THE EXTENT OF YOUR CAMPAIGN

If you have limited time but a lot of confidence and/or media experience, focus your effort on a few targeted press opportunities with the biggest potential payoff. These would include national radio and television shows, nationally syndicated columnists, leading metropolitan newspapers, especially those affiliated with syndicates, and top local radio and television shows.

For media novices, starting out small makes sense, and the easiest path of entry into the world of media is radio. Radio producers are fairly accessible people, and even when rushed, they will usually hear out your pitch and give you a quick yes or no. Start by pitching talk show producers at top radio stations (100,000-plus listeners) in major markets and to syndicated radio programs. Start by mailing or faxing your release to a group of twenty-five stations to start practicing your pitch and your follow-up technique. Do these interviews from your home or office or in studio if you're in the same city. Keep this effort alive as long as you like: The pool of media is virtually endless. According to *Talkers Magazine*, there are 4,300 radio talk show hosts in the United States. If you prove to be a good guest, some radio stations will have you back on air again within a few months. Also pitch your local print and television shows, and then branch out into pitching the national television programs as you gain more confidence.

Before you pitch the big-time TV shows, get some television experience under your belt by pitching local cable shows. With regard to the performance quality of guests, cable is less demanding than the national network shows. When you appear at the station, give the producer a blank videocassette to make a tape for you. Or ask if the producer will kindly send you a copy of the show once it airs. Providing that your appearance was a decent one, this tape will help you book yourself on other shows. Do not send your only copy to other stations—they will certainly misplace it. Make duplicates. As you gain experience in booking yourself, you can approach the larger media with confidence.

If you send your pitch mailings out in small batches, you can limit the project to manageable blocks of time. You will fine-tune your pitch in the follow-up calls from your first mailing before you commit time and money on a mass mailing.

If you're uncomfortable with the idea of radio or television interviews, but your pitch is nonetheless a topical one, you might conduct a print campaign to feature reporters and syndicated columnists nationwide. You might start by targeting, say, the top fifty newspapers in the United States and Canada, and then branch out from there as your time allows.

Be aware that some reporters are loath to entertain calls directly from authors. They can be downright rude if they perceive you as amateurish or a waste of their time, particularly if you are a self-published author. You can help overcome the media resistance by presenting yourself in a professional manner, and by understanding the media before you pitch them. Sometimes there is a plus side to doing your own publicity. Preferring to talk to an author than to a "flack" (the journalist's derogatory nickname for a publicist), other reporters will be open to hearing from you. Your naturalness may seem endearing and your amateurism will work to your advantage.

GET THE CONTACT INFORMATION FOR YOUR MEDIA TARGETS

Names and addresses of the media can be found online and from media directories such as Bacon's, Burrelle's, and Gebbie's *All-In-One Directory,* which are often available at your local library. You might obtain these also by persuading your publicist (or publicity or editorial assistant) to photocopy the pages from the publisher's media directories, as well as to print out a call list and labels from the publicity department's media database. Media lists are also available through www.literarymarketplace.com in the public relations services section.

To find print contacts, use the newspaper Web sites listed in Chapter Six on page 133. In addition, a great site for locating radio stations is www.radio-locator.com to search stations by zip code, city, state or province, format, and call letters. Click to www.npr.org for a link to all the National Public Radio stations nationwide, and many of the sites will give you information about the shows' producers. Get a feel for commercial talk radio from the industry's trade magazine at www.talkers.com. Click onto the Heavy 100 section of the archives to find an annotated list of the top 100 talk radio hosts, and a brief description of their shows and contact information. The site also sells a radio media directory.

The Web site www.radiopublicity.com sells a radio media list database for the top 1,364 radio shows in the United States for just under $400. The site and database is run by Alex Carroll, an author who over the years has booked himself on hundreds of radio programs to promote his book, *Beat the Cops: The Guide to Fighting Your Traffic Ticket and Winning.* (His book site is www.copouts.com.) His experience in the media led to the sideline of selling his publicity expertise and radio databases. If you are planning to concentrate on booking many radio interviews for yourself, and if you've already done a few radio interviews and know that you are effective on air, then this radio database is a worthy purchase. Talk to your publicist to see what she thinks of her department's radio media list. If she thinks it could use some help, see if she will arrange to have your publisher pay for the cost of the list so that they can adapt it for their own use as well as give you a copy.

I also like another resource offered at the same site. If you are booking interviews yourself, you will probably find Carroll's downloadable book, *The Radio Publicity Manual,* to be very helpful. The book reveals hundreds of terrific tips to setting up an effective interview: the worst day and time of the week to do interviews (Friday afternoons, because you lose the audience that would have spread word of mouth about your book in the workplace), how to present yourself in the best possible way to get a radio booking, and tips on selling your books to listeners through a toll-free number. The book is particularly helpful if you have an interest in selling your book directly to consumers.

FOLLOW-UP CALLS AND THE PROTOCOLS OF DEALING
WITH THE PRESS

Once you've done a mailing, do not sit back waiting for the phone to ring off the hook with many anxious producers calling to book you as a guest. This will not happen. These people get hundreds of press releases every day. They have scant time to sort out which among the pile might offer a promising guest. For a recent mailing from my office to 150 radio stations, only four producers called to book the guest. For the dozens of other interviews, we initiated the calls ourselves. (In many cases, you can call the radio station without having sent any material. Pitch the idea on the phone and the producer will know right away if the topic is right for the show's audience and if you could be a good guest.)

Start to make follow-up calls within a day or so of when you think your press release has landed on producer's desks. To get through the list of producers fairly quickly, plan on setting aside an hour or two a day for a few days to work through the list. If your calls are met with instant rejections, then reconsider your pitch or your approach. Ask the producer or reporter why he or she is not interested in your idea: The answer can help you refine your pitch or your strategy. Are you calling in midafternoon when daily print reporters may be on deadline and less tolerant of interruptions? Or are you calling radio producers while the show they produce is on air? Have you targeted the right reporter or show? Are you presenting your ideas in a long-winded way and not getting to the point fast enough? Is your pitch off base? Fine-tune and practice your pitch, then try again. If you're still meeting resistance, you might try talking to a publicity firm about a couple of hours of consultation to help you get on the right track.

Tami DePalma and Kim Dushinski, partners of MarketAbility, a public relations firm that handles book campaigns, say, "In making follow-up calls, your goal is to be pleasantly persistent. Realize that each media contact needs good stories, solid information, and credible experts just as badly as you need media coverage. Every reporter, producer, and editor has a certain number of column inches or airtime to fill. You just might be the solution—if you know how to present yourself." On their site, www.marketability.com, they offer the following excellent advice for people who are making their first publicity follow-up calls:

- Sometimes you have to force yourself to get started on follow-up calls. Once you get started, if you just are not communicating effectively after five to seven calls, consider starting over later in the day or tomorrow.

- If you are nervous or hesitant, make a practice call to someone you know but pretend they are a media contact. Start speaking exactly as you will on a real follow-up call. After all, you won't get a chance to say, 'Can I try out my script on you?' to a media contact.

- At the beginning of every call, always ask if you have reached them at a good time. If not, *do not try to sell your story anyway!* Just because you have them on the phone right now does not mean you need to grab them while you can. Ask them what day and what time would be better. And *let them go!*

- *Call back when you say you will!* The media is amazed by how often people say they will call back, never to be heard from again. This is a big lost opportunity. You've sparked an interest. Do not let the fire go out now.

- At one time, voice mail was used to screen people out. Not anymore. It is absolutely necessary and often used to screen the good stories in! Do not be afraid to leave voice mail messages. When you do, leave your name, company name, and phone number at the beginning and the end of the message so they don't have to rewind to get your contact information.

- On voice mail, mention that if you don't hear from them in a given time period—at least a week from original call date when time permits—you will probably try them again later. Then, rather than pestering them you are simply fulfilling an obligation. Keep voice mail messages short.

■ When you reach them in person, but they have not made a decision for whatever reason, ask them, 'Would it be appropriate to call you back in about two weeks?' Then ask what a good day and a good time to call are. Keep track of this information.

■ Smile with every phone call. Yes, you are bound to get cranky people who are on strict deadline. It will happen. Smile even bigger and ask them when a better time would be to call, then call them precisely at that moment! You may be surprised what a difference a deadline can make. They will probably be a whole new person.

■ Never belittle the person who answers the phone. Get them interested in your story as well. They just may be the managing editor or the executive producer.

■ Rejection is the best way to sell your next contact on your story. What about your story didn't they like? Was it too visual? Not visual enough? Too much or too little content for the length of their show? Do they like the story but just need an opposite opinion to balance yours? Would it fit the format of any other columns or shows?

■ Don't take any one opinion as gold. Evaluate your rejections. What valid information have you received? Was the reviewer just having a bad day, a bad year, and a bad life? Was he or she simply on deadline? How can they help you improve your pitch?

■ Remember, publicity is about making the news. Do not limit yourself to pursuing a book review. Your book might represent a bigger story or a trend developing.

The callback scripts below are adapted from MarketAbility, and you might use them in your own follow-up calls. DePalma and Dushinski suggest that you start by calling any media contacts that you may already know, or else those who are obvious matches for your story idea first. These are easier calls to make and they will get you on a roll. Adapt these scripts for your own book pitch and work from them while you make your calls until you feel comfortable enough to work without them.

Pre-calling helps you identify the right media targets to send your materials to. Do this to save time and money on mailings that might otherwise reach inappropriate contacts.

> "Hi. This is [your name], author of [your book]. I have an idea for a feature/news story that will interest your audience. [Briefly state your idea.] Have I reached you at a good time? Would you be interested in receiving specific information that makes it a story?
>
> "Great! What's the best way for me to get it to you, mail or fax? What's your current address/fax number? Could I call you back [in a few hours if you're faxing, in a few days if you're mailing]? What will be the best time on that day?"

Follow-up calls should be made very shortly after you expect that your mailing or fax has arrived at the office of your media target.

> "Hi. This is [your name], author of [your book.] [Give new information or a new angle to the story you talked about earlier.] You probably received this information via mail/fax a few days/hours ago. Does it sound like something that will work for your show/publication?"

If you get a reporter's voice mail, leave a message. Many times reporters screen their calls so if you leave your pitch on their voice mail, you may get a call back.

> "Hi. This is [your name], author of [your book] at [your phone number]. I have an idea for a feature/news story that will interest your audience. [Briefly state your idea.] I will be mailing/faxing you specific information that makes it a story to address/fax number. I will call you back [in a few hours if you're faxing, in a few days if you're mailing] to see what you think of the idea and answer any questions you

may have. If you'd like to reach me first, please call [your name] at [your phone number].

WHEN A PRODUCER OR REPORTER SAYS YES

Once you've got the reporter or producer's interest, you're nearly home free. But some people make crucial mistakes at this stage and lose the media opportunity. Follow these simple guidelines to complete the transaction and get the coverage you've been planning for.

- When a producer or reporter returns your call and leaves a voice-mail message, call back as soon as possible. If you postpone calling, the reporter may lose interest and move on to another story. Or you might miss the reporter's deadline and fail to get into their story. The media moves quickly.

- When you connect with the reporter, ask for the deadline. Send any follow-up material that the reporter needs well in advance of deadline.

- Ask what the article is about. The reporter will not have read your book and may be calling you for a quick comment. In other words, the reporter is probably not writing an article about your book alone. It is up to you to contribute a point of view that helps the reporter flesh out his or her article.

- After your interview, ask the reporter to identify you as the author of your book. Although your book may not be the focus, the title is mentioned in the piece. Spell your name and your book's title for the reporter.

- If the reporter wants to interview you immediately but you do not feel sufficiently prepared, schedule the interview for later in the day or on another day, if the reporter's deadline permits. The exception is when you've positioned yourself as an expert on events in the news: In that case you are obliged to make yourself available at a moment's notice.

■ When arranging an interview, get the reporter's phone number and e-mail address in case you need to call back to reschedule or cancel for any reason.

■ If you're concerned about how you are quoted, do not ask a reporter for a copy of the article before it has appeared in print. Reporters can't do that, as stories can be killed or delayed at the last moment to make place for other articles or breaking news coverage. Sending you a copy of the article before it runs is considered a breach of ethics. However, you may ask the reporter to read your quotes back to you before the piece is filed. But don't exercise this option unless your subject matter is sensitive or complex. Otherwise, you've earned the reputation as a cumbersome source and not one that the reporter is likely to turn to again, unless you are the leading expert in your field.

■ After you've given an interview to a print reporter, ask when the article is expected to run and if the reporter will send you a copy of the article. On the day the article is supposed to appear, check the paper's Web site to see if it ran. If not, drop an e-mail to the reporter or call to ask when it might appear.

■ Keep track of your forthcoming interviews in an organized format, so that you don't accidentally forget them.

■ When you arrange to set up a radio interview that will take place by phone, take down all the following information: name of host, name of producer, live studio phone number, producer's phone number, the city or town the station is located, the time of the interview in the station's time zone and in yours, whether the station is to call you or if you are to call the station (in which case ask for their 800 number), whether the interview is live or taped, how long the interview will last. Ask the producer about the host's manner with guests. Is it an irreverent approach, a conservative, humorous, or intellectual spin? Will the host mention your publisher's 800 number so that listeners can order the book? If so, note that on your schedule and write the number down, too. A day before the interview, you will call the producer to reconfirm the interview and all the pertinent information. If you're scheduling multiple interviews for yourself, then keep an interview itinerary similar to that of a tour itinerary. (See the appendix on page 301 for an example.)

Clipping Services

Do not waste your money on a clipping service. These are companies that will send you press clippings about your book for free. The volume of press clippings for one book is too small to make the service worthwhile, and the press clips are readily available directly from the newspaper Web sites. Find articles also by typing your book title into search engines.

THE E-MAIL PITCH

Many reporters prefer to be contacted by e-mail, and pitching them this way is acceptable if you follow certain protocols. If you do not have a relationship with the reporter, send a quick query asking if they'd like further information about your book. Make the query's subject line succinct and informative, such as: New Book Says Pets Improve Their Owner's Health. (Note that the subject line should probably be the same as your press release's headline.) In the body of the e-mail, mention the highlights of your book—and this could be the first paragraph of your press release—and invite the reporter to e-mail you if they want further information.

Keep the body of the e-mail short, confined to one screen view. Do not cut and paste your two-page press release into the e-mail screen. And *never* send an attached file unless invited. With sensitivity to viruses, most reporters will not download your files unless they've specifically asked for them. If they want more information they will let you know.

Do not send mass e-mailings in which you have copied other reporters' names into the address field or the cc field. This is a serious breach of media etiquette. Target the right reporter: Do not do a blanket e-mailing just because the technology is capable of doing so. Make your releases or letters targeted and to the point. Your contact information should include your phone number, as your e-mail address alone is not sufficient. When reporters pursue a subject, many prefer to call.

Be cautious of press release distribution services that e-mail press releases to media lists. The service may tell you that the mailing list recipients have opted to receive the e-mails. Well, I would question the kind of reporters who opt to receive e-mail press releases. Serious reporters at most newspapers don't need them—they already get so much mail.

IDENTIFY ONGOING MARKETING OPPORTUNITIES

Political and cultural events continually propel certain books and authors into the limelight. Backlist titles bubble up in the popular press all the time. Definitions vary but essentially a book becomes backlist about a year following publication. As long as the information in the book is of perennial or renewed interest, there is a continued market for it. For instance, when George W. Bush became president, Paul C. Nagel, the author of *John Quincy Adams: A Public Life, a Private Life*, was invited to appear on interviews even though his book had been published four years earlier. Why? Because Adams was the only other son of a former president to become president.

Periodically, a film or television program will refer to a book, suddenly bringing it back into vogue for a time. The television drama *The Sopranos* mentioned *The Art of War*, the ancient text on strategy by Sun Tzu, bringing that book into the fore again with a sudden flurry of attention. And the film *Shakespeare in Love* brought attention to all things Shakespeare for a while. President Clinton's reading list one summer included a novel by Walter Mosley, as reported prominently in the *New York Times*. If you're the beneficiary of one of these chancy and unexpected events, then good for you. But you can also deliberately create some momentum around your backlist book, to keep the book alive in the market and in print. Although the world likes "new," as long as you are presenting ideas and information that fit the media's needs, you can continue to publicize your book no matter how long it has been in print. Here are some ideas to do so:

- If you are visiting cities on business or for pleasure, make time for a book signing as part of your visit. (Call the bookstore six to eight weeks or more in advance of your visit so your event can get on the store calendar.) If you have the time, create a full market push for the book in that city. Do this by contacting the local media and sending out press releases four to six weeks before you arrive in town. If you have less advance notice before your trip, you may have to forego the bookstore event but you can book some media for yourself.

- Look for articles about individuals who might take an interest in your book. For example, say you've written a book on early child development and you come across an interview with someone who believes in the charter movement for elementary school kids. Write to that person expressing support for his or her point of view and enclose a complimentary copy of your book. Depending on the individual's status within their own organization, you may suggest that they invite you to speak at a forthcoming meeting. Thus, you are building the circle of people who are aware of your book as well as building your professional credentials. The book becomes a way to network. You can also contact the reporter of the article to say that you enjoyed the article and to express your own point of view on the subject. In your correspondence, include your contact information and credentials so that the reporter can get in touch with you for a follow-up story, which you can even suggest.

- Send out periodic topical releases about your book.

■ Certain titles lend themselves to evergreen promotion. Cookbooks are one example of this, and well-timed press releases (summer grilling recipes, ideas for Halloween treats, holiday recipes, leftover turkey recipes) can help keep the book alive in the print media.

■ Pitch yourself for seasonal stories related to the subject of your book. For example, if you are an author of a book on dating or relationships, then pitch the idea that the holidays are the loneliest time for singles. Support the pitch with a statistic from, say, the American Psychiatric Association revealing that singles seek therapy more frequently in November and December. Then describe your prescription for singles to cope with the holiday blues and mention your book.

■ Radio interviews conducted by phone are a cost-effective and time-efficient way of maintaining a public profile. They are relatively easy to set up. Give yourself a reasonable goal, say, five to ten interviews a week to keep the momentum going.

■ Let your editor and publicist know immediately if breaking news happens that connects with the subject of your book. Don't assume that they'll make the connection themselves between events and your book. You or your publicist should write a press release or media alert to advise the press about your expertise. Depending on the circumstances, your publicist may even contact the national media to arrange interviews.

■ Ongoing media and bookstore signings and other appearances keep you visible to your publisher. Some publishers—particularly small ones—will keep a book in print even at low annual sales volume if they know that the author is an active promoter.

■ The Internet offers infinite opportunities to reach your target audience. Finding appropriate sites, links, and discussion groups can be time-consuming, but set aside half an hour a day and you may find that your efforts pay off.

- Position yourself as an expert in your field. Drop a note to newspaper and magazine reporters who cover your beat and explain your credentials. Even if they end up contacting you for an interview that's not directly connected to your book's topic, your book's title will almost certainly be mentioned in connection with the piece.

SET UP YOUR OWN PUBLICITY—A SUMMARY

If you will be doing your own publicity bookings, you are limited only by the time available to you. You can conduct an ongoing campaign indefinitely—there are thousands of radio stations and newspapers to pitch. As you get comfortable with the mechanics of doing publicity, you might find a rhythm that blends into your normal schedule where you are pitching and conducting several interviews a week. As you gain confidence, you can graduate yourself to pitching the national television media.

If you are doing your own publicity you will:

- Set a budget

- Define the extent of your campaign

- Refine your pitch

- Research the media to contact

- Pitch the media in batches to keep the project manageable on an ongoing basis

- Report any positive results to your publisher

With publicity, there are no guarantees about the kind of exposure you will get. But certainly you are creating opportunities for yourself that can deliver significant rewards.

13

PARTING THOUGHTS

BEING an active and smart participant in your own marketing and publicity campaign will help cut paths to your own success. By continually promoting your book to the media, you may stimulate ongoing sales and keep your book in print. Your efforts, though they may not seem to deliver immediate benefits, will pay off in other ways that you might not anticipate.

- You will improve your book's sell-through, creating a success of your book in the mind of booksellers even if they didn't order many copies. Booksellers view a book as a success if they sell all the copies they bought whether they ordered two or ten of them. This helps your publisher advance higher numbers of your next book.

- Your efforts for the hardcover edition of your book might provoke a significant increase in sales for your book's paperback edition.

- Your interviews might lead to a large corporate bulk purchase because someone at the company heard you on a radio interview. Or you might receive invitations to speak at events or to be interviewed by other media.

- You will create a track record with book reviewers, which gives you ammunition to sell your next book to a publisher.

- You will find readers entirely as a result of your own efforts.

- You will develop a way of thinking about marketing your work that will be helpful to you in many other areas of your life.

In some ways, being a first-time author is like being a stranger in a strange land, an immigrant venturing beyond the familiarity of home. You've arrived at the golden mountain and to your eyes, every new experience is an opportunity. You are like an entrepreneur, who is willing to take risks, explore possibilities, and be bold about it. With this drive and attitude, success is bound to follow.

Good luck!

RESOURCES: A DIRECTORY OF SERVICES FOR AUTHORS AND PUBLICISTS

AUTHOR WEB SITES FOR AUTHORS MENTIONED IN THIS BOOK

Angela Adair-Hoy
www.writersweekly.com

Isabel Allende
www.isabelallende.com

Clive Barker
www.clivebarker.com

James Barron
www.jamesbarronbooks.com

T. C. Boyle
www.tcboyle.com

Ray Bradbury
www.raybradbury.com

Nelvia Brady
www.thismothersdaughter.com

Jan Brett
www.janbrett.com

Alex Carroll
www.copouts.com
www.radiopublicity.com

Terrence Cheng
www.sonsofheaven.com

Beverly Cleary
www.beverlycleary.com

Douglas Clegg
www.douglasclegg.com

Lawrence Cohen
www.playfulparenting.com

Donna Woolfolk Cross
www.popejoan.com

Barbara D'Amato
www.barbaradamato.com

Kenneth Davis
www.dontknowmuch.com

Neil Gaiman
www.americangods.com

Seth Godin
www.ideavirus.com

Lee Harris, Jonnie Jacobs, Lora Roberts,
and Valerie Wolzien
www.nmomysteries.com

Jane Heller
www.janeheller.com

Kevin Henkes
www.kevinhenkes.com

Kelvin Christopher James
www.kelvinchristopherjames.com

Clarence Jones
www.winning-newsmedia.com

Laurie Beth Jones
www.lauriebethjones.com

Sebastian Junger
www.literati.net/Junger

Dennis Lehane
www.dennislehane.com

Jay Conrad Levinson
www.jayconradlevinson.com

Laura Lippman
www.lauralippman.com

Diane McKinney-Whetstone
www.mckinney-whetstone.com

Brad Meltzer
www.bradmeltzer.com

Steve O'Keefe
www.ideasiteforbusiness.com/
steve.htm

Ellen Phillips
www.ellenphillips.net

Monty Roberts
www.montyroberts.com

M. J. Rose
www.mjrose.com

Corey Rudl
www.carsecrets.com

Lemony Snicket
www.lemonysnicket.com

Andrew Sobel
www.andrewsobel.com

Mariah Stewart
www.geocities.com/mariahstewart

Laura Van Wormer
www.lauravanwormer.com

Michael Webb
www.theromantic.com

BOOK FAIRS AND FESTIVALS, BOOK AND AUTHOR LUNCHEONS

Go to www.booktv.org, the online complement to C-SPAN 2 Book TV programming. The site includes a full listing of book fairs as well as other useful information about author venues.

Go to Writers Festival for a directory of fairs around the world. www.mwf.com.au/litlinks2.html

Arizona Book Festival
Phoenix, Arizona, Spring
(602) 712-1256, www.azbookfestival.org
Celebrates the Southwest. Events with authors and activities for children.

Austin Poetry Festival
Austin, Texas, Spring
www.aipf.org
Poets, performances, and slams.

Baltimore Book Festival
Baltimore, Maryland, Fall
(410) 837-4636, www.bop.org
Readings and talks by authors, and cooking demonstrations.

Banff Mountain Book Festival
Banff, Alberta, Canada, Fall
(403) 762-6406, www.banffcentre.ab.ca/mountainculture
Specializes in the literature of the outdoors, and includes seminars and readings.

Black Expo
Search for "Black Expo" online to find sites for expos nationwide, including Dallas, Indiana, Los Angeles, Missouri, New York, and Philadelphia. The expos offer entertainment, author seminars and signings, career seminars, and vendor booths.

Border Book Festival
Las Cruces, New Mexico, Spring
(505) 524-1499, www.zianet.com/bbf
A weeklong festival. Includes writers, artists and storytellers, vendors, panels and workshops for adults and children, and readings and performances.

Boston Globe **Book Festival**
Boston, Massachusetts, Fall
(617) 929-2641
A series of readings and literary luncheons staged at various locations throughout the city.

Buckeye State Book Festival
Wooster, Ohio, Fall
(330) 287-1617
Features many author appearances.

Bumbershoot Literary Arts Festival
Seattle, Washington, End of summer
(206) 281-7788, www.bumbershoot.org
Part of Seattle's biggest public arts and music celebration. Includes author appearances.

Detroit News Book and Author Luncheon
Detroit, Michigan, Spring
(313) 222-2492
Invites five authors annually. Audience members pay in advance for tickets.

Fall for the Book Literary Festival
Fairfax, Virginia, Fall
(703) 993-3986, fallforthebook.org
Sponsored by the *Washington Post,* George Mason University, and the Fairfax
County Public Library, this street festival includes storytelling, author talks
and panels, poetry slams, events for children, and cooking demonstrations.
The events are held in the city of Fairfax and at the George Mason University
campus.

Great Basin Book Festival
Reno, Nevada, Fall
(775) 784-6587; www.unr.edu/nhc/book_festival.com
Includes a book fair, author readings and discussions.

Great Salt Lake Book Festival
Salt Lake City, Utah, Fall
(801) 359-9670, www.utahhumanities.org
Includes author appearances and seminars on papermaking and other book
arts.

Hampton Roads African Heritage Book Expo
Norfolk, Virginia, Fall
(757) 547 5542, www.melanet.com/eca
Showcases multicultural booksellers, publishers, and authors.

Harbourfront
Toronto, Ontario, Canada, Fall
www.readings.org
If you are lucky enough to get yourself invited to Harbourfront's annual
reading festival in October, then you should be very happy. The Book Festival
is the dream event for authors, with packed audiences, long lines of people
buying books, a liberal entertainment budget, and lots of opportunities to
meet your fellow writers. The focus of the festival is literary, and audience
members buy tickets to attend up to one year in advance. Sign up on the site to
get a free reading schedule newsletter by e-mail. The Harbourfront Web site
includes contact names and numbers, as well as links to other reading venues
and writers' festivals in Canada. Also includes information about Canadian
awards and prizes and links to literary journals.

Harlem Book Fair
New York, New York, Summer
www.qbr.com/hbf2001.html
Panel discussions, readings, storytellers, musicians, and other entertainment.

High Plains Book Festival
Amarillo, Texas, Fall
(806) 378-4228, bookfestival.arn.net
Book fair and poetry corner.

Kentucky Book Fair
Frankfort, Kentucky, Fall
(606) 873-8989, www.kybookfair.com
Kentucky's primary literary event raises money for public libraries and hosts as many as 150 authors.

The Latino Book & Family Festival
Spring and Fall depending on the city
www.latinofestivals.com
The festival is produced by actor Edward James Olmos and is a weekend-long event held in Hispanic markets including Chicago, Houston, Inland Empire (southern California), Los Angeles, New York, Phoenix, and San Diego. Features author appearances and educational and family programs.

Los Angeles *Times* Festival of Books
Los Angeles, California, Spring
(800) LATIMES, www.latimes.com/festivalofbooks
A large and well-attended fair that includes more than seventy-five panel discussions with authors and about 300 authors. The fair helps to raise money and awareness for literacy.

Miami Book Fair International
Miami, Florida, Fall
(305) 237-3258; www.miamibookfair.com
A very well-organized and vastly enjoyable weeklong fair of author events, cooking demonstrations, and children's activities.

New York Is Book Country
New York, New York, Fall
(212) 207-7242, www.nyisbookcountry.com

Citywide author events for adults and children. Includes several formal book and author luncheons sponsored by the *New York Times* and other organizations.

Northwest Bookfest
Seattle, Washington, Fall
(206) 378-1883, www.nwbookfest.org
More than 250 authors participate in a range of events, including a cooking stage and events for children. Attracts 25,000 visitors.

Novello Festival of Reading
Charlotte, North Carolina, Fall
(704) 336-2801, www.novellofestival.net
Readings, lectures, and a book fair. North Carolina's largest annual book event.

Printer's Row Book Fair
Chicago, Illinois, Summer
(312) 987-9896, www.printersrowbookfair.org
The largest outdoor literary event in the Midwest, this fair offers literary programs and vendors of new, used, antiquarian, and specialty books. Events include music, storytellers, and children's storybook characters in costume.

Rocky Mountain Book Festival
Denver, Colorado, Fall
(303) 839-8320, www.aclin.org/~ccftb
Author events and activities and events for children.

Sacramento Reads
Sacramento, California, Fall
(916) 443-6223
Author events for adults and children.

San Francisco Bay Area Book Festival
San Francisco, California, Fall
(415) 487-4550
Readings, lectures, and vendors, including children's events.

Santa Fe Festival of the Book
Santa Fe, Fall
(505) 955-6780, www.ci.santa-fe.nm.us/sfpl/festival.html
Readings and talks by authors, and cooking demonstrations.

Sarasota Reading Festival
Sarasota, Florida, Fall
Contact information varies annually. Find the festival through a search engine
and e-mail the current contact that is listed in the fair's link.
Up to 250 events with authors, including readings and panel discussions,
sponsored by the *Herald-Tribune*.

Small Press Book Fair
New York, New York, Spring
(212) 764-7021, www.smallpress.org
Includes bookmaking and printing demonstrations, readings, and workshops
featuring panels of authors and their publishers.

Southern Festival of Books
Nashville, Tennessee, Fall
(615) 320-7001, www.tn-humanities.org/sfbmain.htm
Includes both southern and national writers, with exhibits and author panels.

St. Petersburg *Times* Festival of Reading
St. Petersburg, Florida, Fall
(727) 893-8481; www.festivalofreading.com
Author events and events for children.

Tennessee Williams/New Orleans Literary Festival
New Orleans, Louisiana, Spring
(800) 965-4827, (504) 581-1144, www.tennesseewilliams.net
Includes readings, workshops, panel discussions, and a book fair.

Texas Book Festival
Austin, Texas, Fall
(512) 477-4055, www.texasbookfestival.org
Features many authors in lectures and readings, as well as cookbook author
events.

The Book and Author Luncheon
San Antonio, Texas, Fall
(210) 735-9009, www.baptisthealthsystem.org/foundation/book.asp
Sponsored by the *San Antonio Express-News,* Baptist Health System, and the Cancer Therapy & Research Center. The luncheon invites six authors, including those who may be of strong local interest.

Vegas Valley Book Festival
Henderson, Nevada, Fall
www.vegasvalleybookfest.org
Author events and events for children.

Virginia Festival of the Book
Charlottesville, Virginia, Spring
(804) 924-6890, www.vabook.org
Features writers in panel discussions and talks, and a vendor's fair.

BOOKS AND RELATED READING

How to Get Happily Published, 5th edition
Judith Applebaum
HarperCollins
This book explains the full publishing process and what the author should do to get involved.

Unleashing the Ideavirus
Seth Godin
Hyperion
Download this great book about viral marketing at www.ideavirus.com. It will inspire you to think creatively about marketing your own work.

1001 Ways to Market Your Books, 5th Edition
John Kremer
Open Horizons
Packed with many great ideas for authors and examples of what other authors have done to market their books.

Trash Proof News Releases
Paul Krupin
Direct Contact Publishing

Downloadable e-book available from www.imediafax.com that shares many examples of well-written press releases and discusses successful press release writing techniques.

Guerrilla Marketing for Writers
Jay Conrad Levinson, Rick Frishman, and Michael Larsen
Writers Digest Books
Great advice for writers, with many ideas for how to market your book. I like the authors' get-with-it, no-nonsense approach.

Complete Guide to Internet Publicity
Steve O'Keefe
John Wiley & Sons
The follow-up book to O'Keefe's excellent *Publicity on the Internet*, this book lays out everything the novice needs to know about promoting his or her book online.

Grants and Awards Available to American Writers
This book lists more than 1,000 grants and contact information. Available through PEN (www.pen.org) and other book retailers.

How to Publish and Promote Online
M. J. Rose and Angela Adair-Hoy
St. Martin's Press
A rich resource for all aspects of online promotion with many references to useful links and services.

Buzz Your Book
M. J. Rose and Douglas Clegg
Available as a downloadable e-book. Filled with strategies for coming up with a marketing plan for your book and how to implement it. See www.BuzzYour.com, Amazon, or www.Pigeonholepress.com

Jump Start Your Book Sales
Marilyn and Tom Ross
Writers Digest Books
Full of great ideas for sales and promotion. Aimed at the self-published author but filled with plenty of advice that's pertinent to the author with a publishing house.

BOOKSTORE DIRECTORIES

Barnes & Noble
www.bn.com
Locate any store in the chain here.

Books-A-Million
www.booksamillion.com
Locate any store in the chain here.

Borders
www.borders.com
Locate any store in the chain here.

New England Booksellers Association
www.newenglandbooks.org
Offers regional bookseller news as well as a good store locator for the region.

www.booksense.com
The site for independent booksellers. Use the zip code locator there to find stores in any town you will be visiting. (The list will include independents only, not chains.)

www.bookweb.org
Lists members of the American Booksellers Association. The site includes addresses and bookstore Web sites.

ESCORTS

Shirley Carp
Dayton, Ohio
(248) 851-1319

Kate Clark
Austin, Texas
(512) 478-7127

Joy Delf Media Services
Seattle, Washington
(425) 562-0107
jdms@joydelf.com

Barb Ellis
Lexington & Louisville, Kentucky
(606) 224-2190

Emily England
Miami & Ft. Lauderdale, Florida
(305) 385-4435
miamiseen@aol.com

Kathy Goldmark Media Escorts
San Francisco, California
(415) 664-3333

Karen Hebert
Hebert Management
Los Angeles, California
(323) 655-2010

Lucky Hill
Boston, Massachusetts
(781) 788-0566

Emily Laisy
Pro-Motion Network Inc.
Baltimore, Maryland
(410) 877-3524
Laisy coordinates a network of escorts nationwide, including many on this list. For one-stop shopping, contact her first and she can probably put you in touch with an escort in the city you're visiting.

Esther Levine
Atlanta, Georgia
(404) 252-4587

Lenore Markowitz
Dallas, Texas
(214) 361-6892

Lisa Maxson
Denver, Colorado
(303) 690-8820

Joan Mendel
Media Connections
Philadelphia, Pennsylvania
(610) 667-7843

Pierre O'Rourke
Phoenix, Arizona
(602) 946-2423

Ruth Pitts
Birmingham, Alabama
(205) 967-5369

Halle Sadle
HMS Media Services
Portland, Oregon
(503) 241-4100

Becky Stewart
Houston, Texas
(713) 465-6143

Kathy Tirschek
Cincinnati, Ohio
(513) 522-6771

David Wenger
The Wenger Agency
Washington, D.C. (202) 544-3305

Bill Young
Chicago, Illinois
(708) 848-7501

INTERNET MARKETING RESOURCES AND SERVICES

Bridge Marketing

www.bridgemarketing.com

This site offers a wealth of information about setting up a Web site, the importance of key words, and how to choose a Web site designer. Contact Karyn Zoldan through the site.

The Internet News Bureau

www.internetnewsbureau.com

Offers tips on pitching the media via the Internet as well as on writing press releases. The site includes sample press releases. The company's e-mail service includes a books-related e-mailing list.

Submit Plus

www.submit411.com

Offers free and paid search engine registration services.

www.howstuffworks.com

The Internet section offers great information about Web sites and search engines.

www.netread.com

Offers authors the ability to notify local media about their appearances and events. You can also sign up for e-mails notifying you of events in your area. This is a good way to learn about author events and venues.

www.rankwrite.com

Includes excellent free articles on key words and search engines by search engine and Internet writing specialists, Jill Whalen and Heather Lloyd-Martin.

www.searchengines.com

Here is information about registering your site including hot links to the important search engines and directories, and charts that explain the registration information required by each search engine.

www.whatsnextonline.com

A site that offers services for building and promoting Web sites, as well as tips for writing press releases and conducting PR professionally.

www.wilsonWeb.com
A site that explains Web marketing including e-newsletters and e-mail marketing. The site is geared to small businesses but still offers useful background information for authors.

LIBRARIES

www.publiclibraries.com links to libraries throughout the United States

www.nlc-bnc.ca/canlib/epublic.htm links to libraries throughout Canada

MEDIA DIRECTORIES (FREE AND PAID) AND MEDIA LINKS

All media
Bacon's
www.bacons.com

Burrelle's
www.burrelles.com
These two companies are the old warhorses of media directories. They've been around for years and provide the printed directories that most publishing houses use.

Gebbie's All-In-One Directory
www.gebbieinc.com
Paid media directories

Literary Marketplace
www.literarymarketplace.com
The site includes many free searchable databases, though some services are restricted to paid subscribers. The media directories are overall very good and include producer contacts.

MediaMap
www.mediamap.com
The Media Watch area of this site provides information about producers and reporters.

www.publist.com
A free database of 150,000 magazines, newspapers, journals, newsletters, and periodicals worldwide.

Newpapers
www.newspaperlinks.com
www.usnewspapersabout.com

Alternative weeklies and periodicals
www.newpages.com

All print media
www.publicrelations.about.com

Radio
Talkers Magazine
www.talkers.com
The trade magazine of the talk radio industry. Click onto the "Heavy 100" section of the archives to find an annotated list of the top 100 talk radio hosts, and a brief description of their shows and contact information. The site also sells a radio media directory.

www.RadioPublicity.com
Offers several radio media packages. If you can't find radio media lists for free, then these more expensive radio media databases are up-to-date and downloadable on mailing labels and as call sheets.

www.radio-locator.com
Search for stations by zip code, city, state or province, format and call letters.

www.npr.org
Links to all the National Public Radio stations nationwide, and many of the sites will give you information about the shows' producers.

Syndicated columnists
www.blueagle.com
www.headlinespot.com/opinion/columnists

Television
www.govspot.com/pulse/talkshows.htm

MEDIA TRAINERS

CMG Productions
New York, New York
www.cmgproductions.com, (212) 691-5611
A full service communications firm including media training. Its services are oriented to businesspeople, so authors of business books will be comfortable in this environment.

Harrow Communications
Oakland, California
www.prsecrets.com
Susan Harrow offers marketing consulting and media coaching to cover any interview situation. Fees are $1,000 minimum for a five-hour session. Her site also offers a newsletter and terrific publicity tips.

The Newman Group
New York, New York
www.newmangroup.com, (212) 752-3351
Has a speciality in training authors. The site has contact information and explains all the media services offered.

Parkhurst Communications
New York, New York
billparkhurst@parkhurstcom.com, (212) 675-5650
Offers speech and media training and specializes in work with authors. Contact Bill Parkhurst.

Joel Roberts
Los Angeles, California
JDRob36@aol.com, (310) 286-0631
A former radio interview host who offers media training to authors and others.

PERIODICALS AND ONLINE NEWSLETTERS

The American Journalism Review
http://216.167.28.193
As well as offering selections from the *Review*'s content, the site links to newspapers, magazines, newswires, and TV and radio sites nationwide (as well as internationally).

Authors on the Web and *Book Reporter*
www.authorsontheweb.com
Free e-mail newsletters that cover new books, and news of authors and publishing. Also offers contests and other features.

Bookselling This Week
www.bookweb.org.
The free e-mail newsletter for booksellers from the American Booksellers Association.

Columbia Journalism Review
www.cjr.com
Offers its own online content as well as links to newspapers, magazines, and TV stations around the country.

Foreword This Week
Covers news about independent publishing for booksellers and librarians.
E-mail lists@brightbridge.net and write "subscribe foreword" in the subject line.

Independent Publishers Online
www.bookpublishing.com
Sponsored by the Jenkins Group, which offers marketing services to authors and publishers, the free online newsletter includes news and opportunities in publishing and marketing. Aimed at self-published authors.

Library Journal
www.libraryjournal.com
The monthly trade magazine for the library market.

The Publicity Hound's Tips of the Week
www.PublicityHound.com
Practical publicity tips from a PR specialist.

Publishers Lunch
www.publisherslunch.com
Free daily e-mail with publishing industry news and gossip.

Publishers Weekly and *PW Daily*
www.PublishersWeekly.com
The weekly trade magazine for the book industry also offers a free daily e-mail newsletter. The site offers industry news, reviews, and interviews from back issues of *Publishers Weekly*.

Salon
www.salon.com
This alternative news and opinion site includes good ongoing coverage of the publishing business.

School Library Journal
www.slj.com
The monthly publication for the school librarian.

Writers Weekly
www.writersweekly.com
Angela Adair-Hoy, the coauthor of *How to Publish and Promote Online*, offers a useful forum and resources for writers looking for editorial and marketing ideas. Subscribe to the free weekly e-newsletter.

www.cybereditions.com/aldaily
Links to top arts and literature stories at the leading daily and weekly newspapers, magazines and journals. Includes a list of links to many of these publications.

Yahoo! News
dailynews.yahoo.com
Go to the literary news section of this site to find current publishing news stories and an eclectic though helpful list of links.

Your Publishing Poynters
www.parapublishing.com
Free weekly e-mail newsletter about publishing, aimed mostly at self-published authors, with tips on writing, marketing, and technology.

PRESS RELEASE SERVICES

www.bridgemarketing.com
This Internet marketer will review and or write press releases, among other services.

www.elance.com
Allows you to post your press release project for writers to bid on. The writer's credentials and rates and a feedback and rating system are displayed on the site.

www.xpresspress.com
Offers a press release writing service, online distribution of press releases, as well as a customized publicity campaign with a publicist calling media contacts to follow up on a press release e-mail. The site says that unlike other press release distribution sites, it does not send the releases out in batches, but one at a time to a customized list of contacts.

PUBLICISTS (FREELANCE AND AGENCIES)

As a former publicity director, I have hired some of these agencies and I also freelanced at Goldberg McDuffie Communications some years ago. Most of the agencies prefer that potential clients contact them through their Web sites because the Web sites address many frequently asked questions about their services. You can find an even more extensive list of publicity firms at www.literarymarketplace.com. (Register for free and go to the advertising and marketing link, then to the public relations services link.)

Carol Fass Publicity and Public Relations
New York, New York
(212) 691-9707 or e-mail FASSPR@aol.com.
Fass is a former director of publicity at Ballantine Books. The agency handles PR campaigns for all kinds of fiction and nonfiction books. The agency's fiction work includes a specialty in mystery novels.

FSB Associates
Basking Ridge, New Jersey
(908) 204-9340
www.fsbassociates.com
With a background in publicity and marketing at book publishers, Fauzia Burke founded FSB to bring Internet-based book and author marketing services

to the publishing community. Her agency handles the Internet campaigns for books in all topic areas.

Goldberg McDuffie Communications
New York, New York
www.goldbergmcduffie.com
Lynn Goldberg and Camille McDuffie have run this boutique agency for more than twenty years. They offer services for a general range of books in all subject areas, including literary fiction and serious nonfiction, and with a specialty in business books. They will not take on self-published books, but will work directly with authors who have a publisher. They must be hired before the bound galley stage.

The Literary
Philadelphia, Pennsylvania
(215) 878-BOOK
Vlloydsgam@aol.com
Vanesse Lloyd-Sgambati handles books in all subject areas, specializing in books by African-American and women authors.

MarketAbility
Golden Colorado
www.MarketAbility.com
Tami DePalma and Kim Dushinski are the partners of this book publicity and promotion firm that represents publishers and authors of business, lifestyle, self-development, and women's titles. Their site offers free articles about publicity, including how to work with your publicist, how to pitch the media, what your media kit should include.

Morse Partners
New York, New York
Rmorse@morse-partners.com
(212) 861-2397
(212) 517-5652
Rosemary Morse and Katy Keiffer's agency handles literary fiction, general nonfiction, high-end cookbooks and gardening books, art and photography books, thrillers, and mysteries.

Meryl L. Moss Media Relations
Westport, Connecticut
(203) 226-0199
www.mediamuscle.com
This agency conducts campaigns for books in all subject areas and offers a full
range of publicity services as well as a speaker's bureau. The agency will often
book speaking engagements as part of a publicity tour, and works directly
with authors as well as publishers.

One Potata
New York, New York
onepotata@aol.com
Headed by Diane Mancher, who has directed the publicity departments for
several publishing houses, the agency handles nonfiction of all types—whether
cookbooks, biography, health, gay/lesbian, as well as commercial fiction.
Query by e-mail and specify when your book will be published, what it is
about, and what sort of publicity you are looking for.

Patron Saint Productions
New Orleans, Louisiana
www.patronsaintpr.com
(504) 488-2114
Steve O'Keefe's company specializes in online marketing consulting for
publishers and authors. He is the author of *Publicity on the Internet* and
Complete Guide to Internet Publicity.

Phenix and Phenix Literary Publicists
Austin, Texas
info@bookpros.com
www.bookpros.com
The site offers a detailed explanation of the services offered to authors, as well
as information about how to choose a PR firm.

Planned TV Arts
New York, New York
www.ruderfinn.com/pta/index.html
The Planned TV Arts division of the PR agency Ruder Finn specializes in book
publicity. The tip sheet section of their Web site offers many useful tips about
the media.

Pubinsider.com
Tucson, Arizona
www.pubinsider.com
Jeff Bowen's agency offers publicity consulting to coach authors how to do
their own publicity, as well as full service publicity campaigns. Bowen focuses
on nonfiction titles with an emphasis on self-help, spirituality, business, and
education books.

Raab Associates
Westchester, New York
(914) 241-2117
www.raabassociates.com
This firm, headed by Susan Salzman Raab, specializes in marketing children's
and parenting books. The site has great information about publicizing
children's books.

Rowland & Associates
Toronto, Ontario, Canada
dara@rowlandfiringpr.com
(416) 916-7377
Dara Rowland's agency specializes in book publicity and handles all subject
areas.

Judy Spagnola
New Jersey
Judyspags@aol.com
Spagnola promotes romance novels and mysteries to independent booksellers.
Romance and mystery writers can query by e-mail.

Susan Ostrov Associates Public Relations
Brunswick, Maine
So48@aol.com
(207) 725-4416
Susan Ostrov has many years of experience in publishing as a publicity
director for several major houses. Her agency specializes in literary fiction,
nonfiction, politics, public affairs, and science and offers full services PR for
authors including tours, media and Internet promotion, and consulting.

Talion.com/Red Dog Publicity
Renton, Washington
www.talion.com
The agency offers a content-rich Web site with free reports about top ten publicity blunders and other publicity advice, as well as dozens of press kits and sample story ideas for a range of books. Will handle publicity campaigns for books in all subject areas and offers a range of prices to suit your budget.

Tracey George Public Relations
New Jersey
(973) 275-1055
George has worked for several major publishing houses. She has designed campaigns for children's books, adult fiction—both commercial and literary—nonfiction, biography (including celebrity bios), cookbooks, academic, and reference books. Query by phone.

Yorio-Connolly Communications
New York, New York
(212) 609-5009
www.ycfoodpr.com
caitlinconnelly@hotmail.com
The agency specializes in cookbooks and works directly for publishers, and less often directly with authors. The principals, Kim Yorio and Caitlin Connelly, will consult authors to help them formulate a publicity strategy.

PUBLISHING AND WRITERS ASSOCIATIONS, NEWS AND RESOURCES

American Booksellers Association
www.bookweb.org
Offers links to sites specializing in writers resources and other industry groups. Lists the regional book shows with contact names and numbers. Includes a bookstore search directory. Subscribe to *Bookselling This Week* here.

ASJA (American Society of Journalists and Authors)
www.asja.org
A membership group that offers guidance for freelance nonfiction writers and journalists.

The Book Report Network
www.authorsontheweb.com
www.bookreporter.com
www.kidsreads.com
www.readinggroupguides.com
www.teenreads.com
Headed by Carol Fitzgerald, the network offers a community for readers and writers, with links to authors' Web sites, recommended reading, news of the publishing industry, message boards, articles about reading and writing, and more. The site also offers services for writers such as Web site building and hosting.

Canadian Booksellers Association
www.cbabook.org
Information and news for Canadian booksellers. Also posts the dates of the annual convention.

Central Booking
www.centralbooking.com
A "by the people, for the people" kind of readers site with author interviews, bulletin boards, and a great community feeling. Includes good links to other reading and publishing sites.

Christian Booksellers Association
www.cbaonline.org
News and information about the Christian book market.

Connecticut Authors and Publishers Association
www.aboutcapa.com
A group of published and self-published authors, and publishers, with regular meetings and presentations.

Horror Writers Association
www.horror.org

Media Bistro
www.mediabistro.com
This site for media professionals has a "how to pitch" area that talks about pitching specific media. Great advice with concrete leads.

Mystery Writers of America
www.mysterywriters.org

New England Booksellers Association
www.newenglandbooks.org
Offers regional bookseller news as well as a good store locator for the region.

Northern California Independent Booksellers Association
www.nciba.com
The directories area has great links to local literary groups and libraries.

Novelists, Inc.
www.ninc.com
A resource for fiction writers that offers publishing information and writers networking. Offers advice on contracts, taxes, incorporating, and other business matters, as well as discussions about writing.

International PEN
www.pen.org
The mission of this writers' fellowship is to advance literacy, promote reading, and defend free expression. You'll find good information here about events and resources.

Poets & Writers
www.pw.org
The site for the monthly magazine, *Poets & Writers,* offers publishing advice, online services, panel discussions, and awards.

ProfNet
www.profnet.com
A service that notifies publicists of dozens of press leads twice daily by e-mail. The leads are queries from reporters who are on deadline and looking for experts to interview on all kinds of topics. The subscription is expensive for an individual but certainly affordable for a publicity department or for several departments to share in a larger publishing house.

Readerville
www.readerville.com
Offers many friendly, smart online forums about books and publishing.

Romance Writers of America
www.rwanational.org

Science Fiction and Fantasy Writers of America
www.sfwa.org

Sisters in Crime
www.sistersincrime.org

Society of Children's Book Writers and Illustrators
www.scbwi.org

Southeastern Booksellers Association
www.sebaweb.org

www.about.com
This site has a useful publishing bulletin board, as well as good publishing resources and news.

www.antion.com
A source of advice on giving speeches and presentations.

www.authorlink.com
An information site for editors, agents, writers, and readers. It offers news of the publishing industry as well as manuscript marketing service to publishers. Also includes marketing advice and information about new awards and writing contests.

www.bookbrowse.com
Offers reading recommendations and news of the publishing industry. Also offers excerpts from current popular literature, author interviews, and reading-group guides.

www.bookbrowser.com
The reading lists on this site were started by a librarian, a site for readers designed to help them browse and find books.

www.bookfinder.com
A free search service for new and used books.

www.bookspot.com
The associations section of this site offers great links to all kinds of resources and organizations for writers as well as information about awards. The site is particularly useful for its links to e-newsletters and e-zines in genre and other categories. For instance, the pages on African-American writing link to Blackwriters.org and to Black Women in Publishing.

www.bookwire.com
Offers useful links to industry services.

www.bookzonepro.com
Hundreds of articles about publishing aimed at small publishers and authors.

www.modernpostcard.com
A service that produces custom postcards for budget prices.

www.pageonelit.com
A literary site that includes news, book recommendations, essays, author interviews, tips for writers and contests.

www.prplace.com
This site offers good links to PR services, publications, and databases. It includes free listings of top newspapers and TV and radio outlets, though these do not include names of producer contacts.

www.shawguides.com/writing
A free online guide to writers' conferences around the United States.

SPEAKER'S BUREAUS (LECTURE AGENTS)

Literary Marketplace (www.literarymarketplace.com) has a good listing of lecture agents. The two agencies listed below specialize in authors and arrange speaking engagements at corporations, trade associations, colleges, religious organizations, and more.

Authors Unlimited
New York, New York
www.authorsunlimited.com

The Chelsea Forum
New York, New York
www.chelseaforum.com

WEB SITE CONSULTANTS, DESIGNERS, AND SERVICES

Anne Gerdes
Anne Gerdes Web Design
Seattle, Washington
gerdesdesign.com, (206) 364-1994

Authors on the Web
www.authorsontheweb.com
Web site development service specializing in creating and hosting author sites.

Bridge Marketing
www.bridgemarketing.com, (520) 318-1222
A Web site content, copy, and consulting company. Contact Karyn Zoldan.

Kristen Powers
Web designer
Los Angeles, California
kristenpowers@yahoo.com

Milo-18 Media Group
Asaf Shakham
Web designer
New York, New York
www.milo-18.com, milo-18@milo-18.com, (917) 514-4436

www.authorguild.net
Offers Web site templates and hosting for reasonable prices.

www.bookzone.com
Web site development service with a specialty in author sites.

www.homestead.com
Free Web site building, but you must use the service for hosting.

www.literati.net
Builds, hosts, and markets author Web sites.

www.planetnet.com
Budget Web building and Web hosting capabilities.

www.previewport.com
Web site development service with a speciality in author sites.

www.register.com
Budget Web building and Web hosting capabilities.

www.searchengines.com
Helps you submit your site to search engines.

www.submit411.com
Submit Plus helps you submit to search engines and learn how to optimize your site.

www.tophostreview.com
Reviews the top host servers. Useful if you are shopping around for a host server.

www.tripod.com
Free Web sites, but you must use the service for hosting.

www.verisign.com
Budget Web building and Web hosting capabilities.

APPENDICES

SAMPLE TIP SHEET

Title: Decorating with Flea Market Finds

Authors: Marie Proeller and the editors of *Country Living*

ISBN: 1-58816-057-2

Price: $30.00 U.S./$46.00 CAN

Pages: 176

Trim: $9 \times 10\frac{1}{2}$

Index: No; includes appendix and glossary

Photography & art: More than 200 color photos

Rights: World

Category: Decorating

Pub Month: April

Format: Hardcover

First Printing: 25,000

Positioning Statement: As the flea market craze continues to grow, so too does the concern with what to do with these finds. Here's the answer: Decorate effectively so that your purchases create highly individualized and personal room settings.

Intended Market: Anyone interested in a bargain that is a unique purchase and will enhance home décor.

Selling points:
- Huge numbers attend flea markets, looking for the perfect "find" for their homes.
- Graphically shows how to use items in decorating—often in unexpected ways.
- Photos demonstrate artful ways to display single items as well as collections.
- *Country Living* magazine devotes the entire April issue every year to flea market finds.
- Energetic, lively design includes numerous tips and sidebars, clearly demonstrating a range of decorating styles.
- An ever-growing collectors' market—witness the success of *Antiques Roadshow*.

A brief description: The thrill of the chase compels a huge number of people to attend flea markets whenever possible, hoping for a "find" that will be perfect in a room enhancing (or even creating) the décor.

Table of Contents:
- Chapter 1—The Flea Market Experience
- Chapter 2—Adapt and Reuse
- Chapter 3—The Art of Display
- Chapter 4—Flea Market Forensics
- Appendix
- Glossary

Competition:
- *Flea Market Style: Decorating with a Creative Edge,* by Emelie Tolley and Chris Mead, 1998, Clarkson Potter, ISBN: 0517701677, 7¾ × 10¼, 208 pages, $30.00, Hardcover.
- *Rachel Ashwell's Shabby Chic: Treasure Hunting and Decorating Guide,* by

Rachel Ashwell, 1998, Regan Books, ISBN: 0060392088, 8½ × 10½, 209 pages, $35.00, Hardcover.

- *Flea Market Makeovers: 25 Projects for Fabulous Home Furnishings,* by BJ Berti, 2000, Random House, ISBN: 0609604910, 9 × 11¼, 150 pages, $30.00, Hardcover.

Author's biography: Marie Proeller, former Arts & Antiques editor of *Country Living* magazine, has traveled to and written about many of the best flea markets and antiquing enclaves in North America. A graduate of New York University's master's program in American Folk Art Studies, she can often be found scouring the antiques and flea markets in her hometown, New York City.

Country Living originated and popularized the concept of "country" that has emerged as a major decorating and lifestyle trend over the past two decades. *Country Living* has the distinction of being the only magazine to rank as one of Adweek's "Ten Hottest Magazines" three years in a row.

SAMPLE TIP SHEET

Title: Married Lust
Subtitle: The 10 Secrets of Long-Lasting Desire
Authors: Pamela Lister and the Editors of *Redbook*
ISBN: 1-58816-001-7

Price: $23.00 U.S./$36.00 CAN

Pages: 224

Trim: 6⅛ × 9¼

Index: No

Photography & art: No

Rights: World

Category: Relationships/Self-Help

Pub Month: May

Format: Hardcover

First Printing: 50,000

Positioning Statement: Keeping excitement alive, night after night, year after year.

Intended Market: Married women, especially those with young children and a harried lifestyle.

Selling points:
- Open, frank approach, with real-life examples of issues and solutions.
- Ten chapters, each exploring a "secret" to enhance sexual pleasure, with explicit suggestions.
- Within each chapter, "Top Ten" lists (e.g., sexual positions, games sexy couples play, ways to get—and give—each other more time and attention).
- Lots of factoids about how *other* couples keep sex hot in their marriages.
- Sometimes surprising results of an exclusive *Redbook* reader survey: For example, just what *are* the most common fantasies for men—and for women.
- Real scenarios from couples polled who seemed quite troubled—and expert analysis for each situation.
- Book is published to coincide with May sweeps month and is sure to get major national TV coverage.
- *Redbook* will excerpt the book in the June issue.
- National publicity campaign with the author and the editor of *Redbook*.

A brief description: A red-hot how-to, with explicit advice for keeping boredom at bay in a marriage, with sex tips that keep the thrill alive.

Table of Contents:
- Introduction
- The First Secret: Enthusiasm
- The Second Secret: Variety
- The Third Secret: Adventure
- The Fourth Secret: Generosity
- The Fifth Secret: Authenticity
- The Sixth Secret: Attention
- The Seventh Secret: Courage
- The Eighth Secret: Confidence
- The Ninth Secret: Attraction
- The Tenth Secret: Absolute Delight

Competition:
- *Hot Monogamy,* Dr. Patricia Love and Jo Robinson (Plume, 1999, 320 pages, Hardcover, ISBN: 0452273668, $13.95)

- *Passionate Marriage: Love, Sex, and Intimacy in Emotionally Committed Relationships,* David Schnarch (Henry Holt, 1998, 432 pages, Paperback, ISBN: 0805058265, $16.00)
- *The Seven Principles for Making Marriage Work,* John Mordechai Gottman (Crown Pub, 1999, Hardcover, ISBN: 0609601040, $23.00)
- *10 Great Dates to Revitalize Your Marriage: The Best Tips from the Marriage Alive! Seminars,* David and Claudia Arp (Zondervan Publishing House, 1997, 208 pages, Hardcover, ISBN: 0310210917, $12.99)
- *100 Ways to Make Sex Sensational and 100% Safe: Enjoy Monogamy Without Monotony,* Rachel Copelan (Lifetime Books, 1997, 240 pages, Paperback, ISBN: 0811908631, $14.95)

Bottom Line: *Redbook* addresses the issue of great sex in marriage in every issue, usually as the lead story. *Married Lust* deals with the issue of keeping sex fresh and fun year after year, while dealing with kids, money, and all the other romance-draining aspects of life for a married couple.

Author's biography: As a senior editor at *Redbook* magazine for many years, Pamela Lister was instrumental in helping set the tone and direction for the magazine's outstanding coverage of marriage and sex trends in America. Her work has also appeared in *Good Housekeeping, Time,* the *New York Times, American Health, New Woman, Working Mother, Family Life, Self, Mirabella,* and *The Columbia Journalism Review,* among others.

This press release shows how a publisher established the news value of its book.

FOR IMMEDIATE RELEASE   CONTACT: Kaye Phillips
                               (540) 381-9077
                               Fax: (540) 381-0113
                               E-Mail: wpi@watergate-history.com

NEW BOOK, *DEEP THROAT—FACT OR FICTION*, REVEALS
IDENTITY OF WATERGATE INFORMANT

(Washington, D.C., June 14, 2002) WPI Publishing announced today the publication of a new book, entitled DEEP THROAT—FACT OR FICTION, by a former United States District Attorney in the District of Columbia, Thomas O'Malley. As the 30th anniversary of the Watergate break-in approaches, the book finally reveals the identity of one of America's greatest, yet until now anonymous, heroes—Deep Throat.

Kept secret for decades by the *Washington Post*, Deep Throat's identity has until now been the subject of speculation with most surmising that the famous source was a well-known and highly placed individual. In DEEP THROAT—FACT OR FICTION, attorney O'Malley debunks the myths and reveals the real Deep Throat: Joseph A. Lowther, administrative assistant to Watergate Judge John Sirica.

An experienced and gifted trial attorney, Deep Throat was a manic-depressive, according to the book. A veteran of the OSS (the precursor to the CIA), who enjoyed good connections to the FBI and CIA, he often drank too much and could act irrationally. Despite all his frailties, during Watergate when our country faced its greatest constitutional crisis, this one man came forward and made a difference. He took on Sirica and Watergate, not for personal acclaim or to gain notoriety, but so that he could be of service to his nation and his court. According to O'Malley, those were his sole motivations and were only a part of what he did as a lawyer.

O'Malley, a former United States District Attorney in the District of Columbia, and close friend of Lowther, makes his case in DEEP THROAT—FACT OR FICTION by citing the deathbed confession of a man, who, by Bob Woodward's own admission, was a source. Just why Woodward and the *Washington Post* continue to keep Deep Throat's identity a secret is painstakingly examined. Here is the inside story, told from the offices of the court where Watergate was tried. DEEP THROAT—FACT OR FICTION unveils the mystery—who the man was, why he became Deep Throat, how he helped bring down a president and why his identity has been kept secret for so long.

#

The electronic book is currently available for sale at www.watergate-history.com. The price is $12. The hardcover edition will be available later this year.

This is an example of an informative press release about a service-oriented book.

RETIRE IN STYLE—NEW BOOK NAMES TOP 50 AFFORDABLE TOWNS IN WHICH TO RETIRE

(Chester, NJ, July 30, 2001) Seventy-six million American "baby boomers" born between 1946 and 1964 are moving toward retirement in an era of increasing affluence and mobility, and the number of relocating retirees is expected to rise substantially above the current annual rate of 1,000,000. Award-winning geographer and professor at California State University, Warren Bland, Ph.D., has done your homework for you in this beautifully illustrated book, RETIRE IN STYLE: 50 AFFORDABLE PLACES ACROSS AMERICA (Next Decade, $22.95), scheduled for release in the fall.

Drawing on the professional research he has done during the last 20 years, Bland identified the 12 criteria most important to retirees. According to the AARP, today's retirees are living longer and more actively, and are demanding a different mix of opportunities than did earlier generations. For many, upscale retirement no longer implies country club or beach resort living, but rather an active lifestyle in a safe, friendly, community that is rich in amenities. What criteria are retirees looking for?

RETIRE IN STYLE will provide readers with the information they need to make intelligent choices among 50 outstanding upscale communities widely distributed across 10 regions and 23 states. Careful consideration was given to the final 12 criteria covered for each place (landscape, climate, quality of life, cost of living, transportation, retail services, health care, community services, cultural activities, recreational activities, work/volunteer activities, and crime). Each place discussion includes 5–6 pages of text, plus a beautifully crafted illustration page featuring a climatic table, a 12-variable rating table, and a map of the city and its surroundings.

Current books on American retirement towns are typically superficial or uneven in content, overly reliant on anecdotal information from local residents, and weak in their understanding of the physical environment of these places. RETIRE IN STYLE, written by an economic geographer and award-winning professor specializing in the regional geography of North America, takes a more objective, scientific approach to the study of retirement places and the result is a readable and informative book.

#

Contact: Barbara Kimmel
            Next Decade
            (800) 595-5440

SAMPLE PITCH LETTER

The second paragraph of this letter lists the talking points in bullet format. I prefer this style as it highlights the salient discussion points for the interviewer, although you can choose to present this information in a normally formatted paragraph. In this instance, the interview subject is not the author of this book, which is a perfectly acceptable approach if the author is not available for interviews.

July 26, 2002

Dear Producer/Interviewer:

I am writing to suggest an interview with Cookie Washington, an entrepreneur featured in TURN YOUR PASSION INTO PROFITS: START THE BUSINESS OF YOUR DREAMS, by Janet Allon. In the last recession, many people who lost their jobs started their own businesses, turning what seemed like bad news into the success of their lives. In this current economic downturn your audience will want to know:

- When to switch careers and launch a business.
- How to tell if you've got a marketable product or service.
- The five most important qualities/resources needed to launch a business.
- How to avoid the top three pitfalls in the start-up years.
- How to find seed money.

TURN YOUR PASSION INTO PROFITS features 35 successful women entrepreneurs who reveal what you need to know to start your own business. In this tenuous business climate, going it alone can be a risky venture. Cookie Washington, who markets her line of custom clothing and accessories out of her home in Charleston, S.C., can explain why she decided to take the plunge, the risks she took, and how she's beating the odds. I'll call soon to discuss having her as a guest on your show.

Sincerely,

Publicist
(xxx) xxx-xxxx
e-mail address

SAMPLE MEDIA ALERT

MEDIA ALERT   Contact: Jane Doe

INVITATION FOR COVERAGE   (212) xxx-xxxx

                               jdoe@janedoe.com

AUTHOR OF NEW BOOK ABOUT PREVENTING CAR THEFT TO DEMONSTRATE ANTITHEFT TECHNIQUES

WHAT   A demonstration of new theft-prevention techniques

WHO   Frankie Franks, car expert and mechanic and author of EVERYTHING YOU NEED TO KNOW ABOUT YOUR CAR, will reveal new low-cost methods to prevent car theft. Police sergeant Bill Myers will join him to discuss the most common types of car thefts in Daytona.

WHERE   Parking Lot of Barnes & Noble bookstore at 2655 Laramie Road

WHEN   Thursday, July 25, from 12:00 noon to 1:00 P.M.

NOTES   Over the past ten years, author Franks has been developing fail-safe techniques to prevent car theft. His advice is endorsed by the police department of Daytona and the American Automobile Association.

INTERVIEW Franks will be available for interview before and after the demonstration on July 25 and 26. To arrange an interview beforehand, contact Jane Doe at 212-xxx-xxxx.

PHOTO OP   Frankie Franks and Police sergent Bill Myers will demonstrate five simple car protection features that anyone can afford.

# # #

SAMPLE TOUR SCHEDULE

The following tour schedule shows the media portion of the itinerary only. The schedule provided by your publicist will also include information about hotels and escorts. This particular schedule shows that the author conducted interviews by phone before arriving in Columbus to help promote in advance his bookstore and university appearances.

Thursday, May 23
ADVANCE PHONE INTERVIEWS TO PROMOTE YOUR EVENTS ON MONDAY AND TUESDAY IN COLUMBUS

9:30 AM to 10:00 AM cst
Live by phone

SUBURBAN NEWS PUBLICATIONS
5257 Sinclair Rd
Columbus, OH 43229
Contact: Kathleen Radcliffe
(614) xxx-xxxx
You are to call Kathleen.
Mention your bookstore and university appearances next week.

1:30 PM to 2:00 PM cst
Live by phone

COLUMBUS MESSENGER
3378 Sullivan Avenue
Columbus, OH 43204
Contact: John Matuszck
(614) xxx-xxxx
You are to call John. His article will run prior to your events in Columbus.

Monday, June 3
COLUMBUS

8:15 AM arrival
8:30 AM to 9:15 AM
Live, in-studio

WLVQ-FM
Wags & Elliott Morning Show
Two Nationwide Plaza, 10th Floor
Columbus, OH 43215
Contact: Dan Orr (614) xxx-xxxx

10:10 AM to 10:45 AM
Live by phone

KHOW-AM
Peter Boyles Show
4695 S. Monaco
Denver, CO 80237
Host: Greg Dobbs
Contact: Bill Thorpe
(303) xxx-xxxx
Backup studio number (303) xxx-xxxx.
Peter will call you at the Columbus Hilton.
Mention your forthcoming event in Denver.

1:05 PM
Live in studio

WOSU-AM (NPR)
"Open Line"
2400 Olentangy River Road
Columbus, OH 43210-1027
Host/Contact: Fred Anderle
(614) xxx-xxxx

4:10 PM to 4:30 PM
Live, in-studio

WTVN-AM (ABC)
John Corby Show
1301 Dublin Road
Columbus, OH 43215
Host: Steve Cannon Show
Contact: Joe Bradley
(614) xxx-xxxx

6:45 PM
Taping at bookstore

WBNS-TV (CBS)
Evening News
Will come to B&N and tape an interview to run
on either 10:00 P.M. news or the next morning.
Contact: Angela Pace
(614) xxx-xxxx

7:00 PM to 8:00 PM
Discussion & signing

BARNES & NOBLE
Easton Town Center
4005 Townsfair Way
Columbus, OH 43219
Contact: Amy Mann
(614) xxx-xxxx

Tuesday, June 4
COLUMBUS

8:00 AM arrival   **ONN OHIO NEWS NETWORK**
8:15 AM   *Morning News*
Live, in-studio   770 Twin Rivers Drive
                                Columbus, OH 43216
                                Host: Mike Kallmeyer
                                Contact: Jeremy Naylor
                                (614) xxx-xxxx

9:50 AM arrival   **WSYX-TV** (ABC)
10:00 AM to 10:15 AM   *Newsmakers*
Taped, in-studio   1261 Dublin Road
                                Columbus, OH 43215-7000
                                Contact: Carol Luper
                                (614) xxx-xxxx

11:45 AM arrival   **WCMH-TV** (NBC)
12:00 PM   *Newschannel News at Noon*
Live, in-studio   3165 Olentangy River Road
                                Columbus, OH 43202-1518
                                Contact: Sean Seagroves
                                (614) xxx-xxxx

4:00 PM   **JOHN GLENN INSTITUTE FOR PUBLIC**
Book talk & signing   **SERVICE AND PUBLC POLICY**
                                THE OHIO STATE UNIVERSITY
                                400 Stillman Hall; 1947 College Road
                                Columbus, OH 43210
                                Contact: Debbie Merritt
                                (614) xxx-xxxx
                                Talk, followed by Q&A, reception, & booksigning.
                                The Film Theatre holds 300. Books to be sold by
                                campus bookstore.
                                (Parking at Ohio Union Garage)

INDEX